AFTER THE VICTORIANS

AFTER THE VICTORIANS

Private conscience and public duty in
modern Britain

Essays in memory of John Clive

*Edited by Susan Pedersen and
Peter Mandler*

London and New York

First published 1994
by Routledge
11 New Fetter Lane, London EC4P 4EE

Simultaneously published in the USA and Canada
by Routledge
29 West 35th Street, New York, NY 10001

Typeset in Palatino by Intype, London
Printed and bound in Great Britain by
T.J. Press (Padstow) Ltd, Padstow, Cornwall

British Library Cataloguing in Publication Data
A catalogue record for this book is available from the British Library

Library of Congress Cataloging in Publication Data
After the Victorians: private conscience and public duty in modern
Britain / edited by Susan Pedersen and Peter Mandler.
p. cm.
Includes bibliographical references and index.
1. Social reformers—Great Britain. 2. Social movements—Great
Britain. 3. Civic leaders—Great Britain. 4. Intellectuals—Great
Britain. 5. Duty. 6. Conscience. I. Pedersen, Susan.
II. Mandler, Peter.
HN385.A38 1994
303.4'84'0941—dc20 93–17693

ISBN 0–415–07056–2 (hbk)

Contents

CONTENTS

Contributors

Peter Clarke is Fellow of St John's College and Professor of Modern British History at Cambridge University. He is the author, most recently, of *The Keynesian Revolution in the Making, 1924–1936* (1988) and *A Question of Leadership: Gladstone to Thatcher* (1992).

Jeffrey Cox is Professor of History at the University of Iowa and author of *The English Churches in a Secular Society* (1982). He is at work on a book entitled *Protestants and Imperial Culture in Punjab, 1870–1930*.

Seth Koven is Assistant Professor of History and Women's Studies at Villanova University. He is the editor, with Sonya Michel, of *Mothers of a New World: Maternalist Politics and the Origins of Welfare States* (1993). He is currently completing a study of social welfare and the London poor, 1870–1920.

D.L. LeMahieu is the author of *The Mind of William Paley* (1976) and *A Culture for Democracy: Mass Communication and the Cultivated Mind in Britain Between the Wars* (1988).

F.M. Leventhal is Professor of History at Boston University. He has written biographies of George Howell (1971), H.N. Brailsford (1985) and Arthur Henderson (1989). He is editor-in-chief of the forthcoming *Encyclopedia of Twentieth-Century Britain*.

Peter Mandler is Senior Lecturer in Modern History at London Guildhall University. He is the author of *Aristocratic Government in the Age of Reform* (1990) and editor of *The Uses of Charity: The Poor on Relief in the Nineteenth-Century Metropolis* (1990). He is writing a book on the absorption of the English country house into the national heritage.

Standish Meacham is Professor of History at the University of Texas at Austin. He has written extensively on Victorian and Edwardian religion, society and culture. His most recent book is *Toynbee Hall and Social Reform, 1880–1914: The Search for Community* (1987).

Susan Pedersen is Associate Professor of History at Harvard University and an Associate of its Center for European Studies. She is the author of *Family, Dependence, and the Origins of the Welfare State: Britain and France, 1914–1945* (1993).

Simon Schama is the Old Dominion Foundation Professor of the Humanities at Columbia University. His books have covered topics as diverse as early modern Dutch culture, the French Revolution and the Rothschilds' Zionism. His latest is *Dead Certainties (Unwanted Speculations)* (1991).

Peter Stansky is the Frances and Charles Field Professor of History at Stanford University. He has written on the cultural and political history of modern Britain, most recently *Redesigning the World: William Morris, the 1880s, and the Arts and Crafts* (1985).

Chris Waters is Assistant Professor of History at Williams College, Williamstown, Massachusetts. Author of *British Socialists and the Politics of Popular Culture, 1884–1914* (1990), he is currently undertaking a study of working-class culture and national identity in twentieth-century Britain.

Preface

The essays that make up this volume – biographies of eminent post-Victorians – are meant to serve a dual purpose. First, they seek to contribute to a better understanding of intellectual life in our own century by employing some of the techniques and striking some of the themes already successfully developed in writing about the Victorians. They treat twentieth-century intellectuals and reformers as psychologically complicated individuals whose life stories, private as well as public, are closely bound up with their public philosophies and actions. In doing so, they portray men and women who still felt as strongly as their Victorian parents that the privileged and propertied had the responsibility to shape national life. While changes in society and economy were obviously working to limit the effectiveness of such individual interventions, nevertheless the persistence of these Victorian values is worth asserting. And we find them in an increasingly diverse range of activities: not only in high politics, religion and philanthropy, those characteristic Victorian theatres of reform, but also in town planning and architecture, social and economic policy, imperial administration and missionary work, broadcasting and publishing.

Our second purpose is to pay a tribute to an historian who contributed so signally to that full psychological as well as sociological grasp of the Victorians that we feel we have today. John Clive, for many years Professor of History at Harvard University and best known to a wider public as author of a classic biography of Thomas Babington Macaulay, was friend, mentor, teacher – or all three – to each of the contributors. Initially this volume was conceived as a tribute to John on his retirement, but we were sadly overtaken by his death early in 1990 at the age of sixty-five. We offer it instead as a memorial to a man whose life and writings bear many of the characteristics of his Victorians and our post-Victorians: a tender conscience, a gentle liberalism, a belief in the meaning and value of individual striving. The plan of the book reflects this dual purpose. In the introduction, the editors offer an overview of the situation of the cultivated elites in Britain from the end of the Victorian period to the immediate aftermath of the Second World War. There follow ten biographies drawn from roughly three generations of thinkers and writers, from Henrietta Barnett born in the year of the Great Exhibition to John Summerson born in the reign of Edward VII. Although contributors were free to choose their own protagonists – we make no claim for the selection to be fully "representative" of anything – the biographies feature common themes that we point to in the introduction and affirm the value of biography in giving deeper texture to our understanding of twentieth-century Britain. Finally, Simon Schama concludes with a parallel meditation on the life and art of John Clive, conveniently representing one further generation and bringing our book of lives nearly – but, sadly, not quite – up to the present day.

That this volume has not had the elephantine gestation of many similar collections is owing to the efforts of a team of civic-minded collaborators. We thank them first and foremost. We are also grateful to John Clive's many friends and colleagues at Harvard who encouraged us in this project, particularly Bernard Bailyn and Wallace MacCaffrey. The Center for European Studies at Harvard kindly hosted a two-day symposium on the themes of the volume; we thank Guido Goldman, Abby Collins and Brigitte Carangelo for their hospitality. Susan Kingsley Kent, Robin Kilson, Janet Oppenheim, Susan Pennybacker and Jim Cronin provided helpful commentary on versions of these essays presented at the symposium. Claire L'Enfant at Routledge offered a safe berth for the kind of book-project editors nowadays rarely smile upon, and supplied shrewd substantive suggestions at crucial stages.

The editors and publishers wish to thank the following copyright holders for permission to reproduce illustrations: First Garden City Heritage Museum, Letchworth for Plate 4; Harry Ransom Humanities Research Center, University of Texas at Austin for Plates 5 and 6; University of Liverpool for Plate 7; Private Collection for Plate 8; Mrs Trekkie Parsons for Plate 9; National Portrait Gallery for Plate 10; Mary Evans Library for Plates 11 and 12; Architectural Association for Plates 13 and 14(b) (Plate 14(b) © Arnold Whittick); Illustrated London News Picture Library for Plate 14(a); Professor Bernard Bailyn for Plates 15 and 16.

Introduction

The British intelligentsia after the Victorians

Peter Mandler and Susan Pedersen

"In or about December, 1910, human character changed." What Virginia Woolf meant by this famous dictum was, of course, that in or about 1910 her intellectual friends began to perceive human character differently. Specifically, she drew attention to a movement in literature beginning with Samuel Butler and George Bernard Shaw and culminating with her soulmate Lytton Strachey that had begun to throw off the overpowering weight of Victorian social convention and form, and to reach towards a somehow truer estimate of human feelings and relationships: how they were and how they might be.[1]

Woolf's dual formulation – first, demarcating her generation strictly from the Victorians, and second, identifying private feelings and relationships as the crucial sphere of the later generation's achievement – was echoed by much of the fiction and critical writing of her time, not least in Strachey's *Eminent Victorians*. It has, if anything, gained further credence from the torrent of introspective biographies that have poured forth as the last of Woolf's contemporaries leave the scene. It has also had a decisive influence on thinking about twentieth-century intellectual and high-cultural life, with historians falling roughly into two camps. One tendency has been to depreciate the biographical importance of such characters, to see their introspection as a necessary retreat from a public realm dominated after the First World War by different players – "masses" and "classes" – and different values – the material rather than the moral or aesthetic. A second tendency, evident in Noel Annan's recent (auto)biography of "Our Age" (his age, the children of the Victorians), has been to celebrate the turn to private life as a kind of victory over a public life dominated by hypocrisy, repression and corruption.[2]

In this introduction, and in the essays that follow, we want to question

1

both of Virginia Woolf's assumptions, and equally to challenge both of the historiographical tendencies that have followed her lead. We hope to show that the liberal intelligentsia after the 1880s by no means simply rejected the values of their Victorian forebears. Far from "retreating" into an intimate realm, the writers and reformers we examine sought to maintain not only a quintessentially "Victorian" tendency to link private behavior to public morality, but also their parents' concern to reconcile democracy with those cultural and aesthetic values that they usually described with the laden term, "civilization." True, post-Victorian intellectuals splintered, in comparison with their Victorian forebears, over where and how such values might best be maintained, and we can trace in the lives of the individuals discussed here that widening diversification of view. Individual service gave way to institution-building, and essayists became professionals – yet it is the continuity of their activism and the consistency of their analysis that is striking. To understand the roots of both, we need to return briefly to the tenets of Victorian liberalism itself.

I

Victorian liberalism, even at its birth, could be the creed of a gentleman. Thus Alexis de Tocqueville, that "most typically English French liberal,"[3] when visiting John Stuart Mill in 1835, aptly found the social position of the political and philosophical Radicals quite as significant as their reforming views. The extremism, anti-clericalism and violence of intellectuals in France were inevitable corollaries, Tocqueville feared, of their social marginality, poverty and ignorance; English radicals, by contrast, being "in easy financial circumstances," versed in history and political economy, and "recognized as 'gentlemen,'" were correspondingly firm believers in the rights of property, respectful of religious belief, and civil in method as well as profession.[4] Position and ideals were inextricable and mutually reinforcing: this is the central insight. Noel Annan's seminal essay on that cousinhood of Darwins, Huxleys, Wedgwoods, Arnolds and Frys who brought the moral rigor of the evangelicals into a secular age once again reiterates the point: Britain presents "the paradox of an intelligentsia which appears to conform rather than rebel against the rest of society."[5]

If we move forward a generation, to the heyday of Victorian liberalism between the Second and Third Reform Acts, and to the decades in which the first figures discussed in this book reached the age of majority, we find a similar linkage of social place and moral or political belief. Thus Stefan Collini, in describing the world inhabited by the intellectual heirs of Mill – the generation of Henry Fawcett, Leslie Stephen and Bernard Bosanquet – unconsciously echoes many of Tocqueville's observations. Established men of letters in the high Victorian period, writes Collini, were well-connected, well-educated and successful, yet still sought to diffuse the comforts and virtues of their position to an increasingly elusive "public." They remained part both of the educated and of the governing classes of the day, almost invariably on the right side of that "most sensitive dividing line in Victorian society . . . between those who were and those who were not recognized as 'gentlemen.' "[6] Even as professional expertise grew in importance and specialist journals came from the 1890s to supplement the great Victorian quarterlies, liberal intellectuals continued to write in an accessible language and to seek an audience beyond the restricted circles of the universities or the professions. They were seen, and saw themselves, as (in Collini's phrase) "public moralists," determinedly in the world but not irredeemably of it, exhorting their fellows "to live up to their professed ideals."[7]

But what ideals were these, exactly? Certainly social position (as Tocqueville thought) provided intellectuals with an incentive to devise an ethic reconciling social stability with individual freedom, and material progress with morality. It was John Stuart Mill, however, who most coherently linked the two key values of his class: the belief in the widest scope for individual liberty – a value dear to a class forged in the effort to establish a meritocratic ideal in the face of "old corruption" – and the equally powerful belief in a fixed moral hierarchy. Especially in *Considerations on Representative Government*, Mill made these two values interdependent. Self-government, he argued, was the "best" form of government, being conducive equally to the happiness and the growth of popular virtue; it was possible, however, only among people who had reached that level of moral and intellectual development – that "stage" of "civilization" – which would enable them to make decisions with sufficient wisdom and impartiality.[8] One could gauge the level of civilization, he quite characteristically thought, not only of individuals but of whole cultures: India, for example, he defined as being in a stage of "semi-barbarism" and (as yet) too crushed by past despotism and by custom to exercise self-rule effectively. Yet India, like the working class, could be brought to a "more advanced stage": the test of British administration there, like that of government at home, would be its capacity to help the people, both individually and collectively, to advance.[9] With this formula Mill provided liberals with a justification for their own role (both as imperial proconsuls and domestic moralists) and a basis from which to criticize any more populist politics or less "disinterested" foreign adventurism: a "civilizing" framework only effectively challenged with the rise of more pluralist ideals after the First World War.

To bring "the people" to exercise self-government (individually, collectively and – when they felt especially optimistic – in the empire and

internationally) in ways conducive to "civilization": this was the ultimate goal. But how could an intellectual elite inculcate the moral qualities that would enable people to exercise these powers virtuously? How
would they be able to foster and judge the progress of civilization?
Victorian liberals looked to three values in particular when measuring
moral progress – the values of competition, cultivation and domesticity.
Or, to put it another way, they sought to make mutually supportive the
market economy, the education of the people, and the bourgeois family.
Each part of this triad was important, and could school the citizen in
necessary virtues, but together the three could act as a kind of locomotive pulling the nation as a whole along the track of material and
moral progress. Market forces and meritocratic public services would
train the citizen in self-restraint and industry; a self-confident cultural
establishment would teach him to distinguish between the higher and
lower pleasures; while the family, that "immediate and primitive relation
which holds men together,"[10] would not only provide him with the
softening influences of love, but also spur him to renewed efforts in
the competitive world beyond the threshold. Small wonder that domestic idioms pervaded political discourse, that men of all classes pointed
to their exemplary familial behavior when arguing for political rights,
that they justified colonial rule with a rhetoric of subject men's effemi-
nacy or lasciviousness. Women, by contrast, were both central and
effaced: as Mary Poovey has argued, they anchored and defined men's
status as productive, public, even cultured by representing the presumably timeless values of the domestic, private and natural.[11]

Such was the ideal, but it was not only an ideal. The politics, writings
and everyday life of the liberal intelligentsia were all conducted in its
reflection. Gladstone as much as Mill is an emblematic figure here, both
in his unremitting efforts to lead an exemplary private life and in his
own commitment to bring "morality into politics" – which, equally
characteristically, he first thought would be achieved by the Established
Church and later thought more reliably guaranteed by a rigid adherence
to free trade, financial austerity and franchise reform. His plan in 1866 to
extend the franchise to all men liable to income tax perfectly captures
the concern to make morality and politics mutually reinforcing: to craft
a polity based on the bourgeois virtues of thrift, industry and self-
improvement, and to admit to citizenship progressively those who by
demonstrating those virtues demonstrated also their material interest in
preserving that polity.[12] Mill, conscious that these bourgeois virtues were
crucial to but not the same as the higher cultural values, would have
preferred an educational qualification, but fell back on the idea of plural
votes for businessmen, professionals and university graduates, in order
to retain the tie between cultivation and power while continuing to
court the uncultivated.[13] Democracy, in this view, offered opportunity

as well as danger – the opportunity to draw civilization and politics closer together, the danger that as they approached they might not in reality be so easily blended. The transition to democracy therefore required managers, and in their more optimistic moments Victorian intellectuals conceived themselves as the ideal agents of enlightenment and political acculturation, inducting successive sections of the population – suitably virtuous and instructed – into the liberal polity.

One of those more optimistic moments came on the eve of the election of 1880, when the success of Gladstone's barnstorming attack on the excesses of "Beaconsfieldism" – corruption at home and adventurism abroad – seemed to offer the Liberals a chance to inaugurate a new rule of virtue, meritocracy and tolerance. Viewed retrospectively, that Indian Summer of British liberalism marked the beginning of the end. For the next two or three generations of liberal intellectuals, the generations covered by this book, the challenge of keeping all three legs of the Victorian tripod on level ground simultaneously was to become more and more difficult. In the following three sections, we look at three challenges to the cohesiveness and centrality of liberal Victorianism. First we consider those political changes – the widening franchise, the rise of the Labour Party and the challenge to imperialism – that alarmed many intellectuals and led others to doubt whether democracy and their conception of civilization could ever be made mutually reinforcing. Second, we look to the successive assaults on bourgeois domestic values, and especially on the ideals of separate spheres and of sexual repression – an assault that the sons and daughters of the Victorians themselves began, but that also left them unable to point to their own familial ideals as the model for reconciling hierarchy and mutuality. With both their public authority and their private confidence wavering, the intellectual elites came to realize that their influence would increasingly depend on the ability to demonstrate expertise, especially in the realm of culture. Finally, then, we turn to those cultural spheres, where the hegemony of elites was also under threat, but where their institutional position made them more resilient. All three challenges began but by no means culminated before the Great War. In this introduction and the essays that follow we will trace them up to and just beyond the Second World War, when the allegiances and analyses of the liberal intelligentsia seemed, finally, to have so fragmented as to limit their impact on the public life of the nation.

II

How perfectly their formula for harmonizing individual cultivation and social progress suited liberal intellectuals becomes clear when in the 1880s its seeming breakdown became the source for so much political and intellectual disarray. The principal source of breakdown was, as the liberal intelligentsia saw it, that the progress of democracy, for which they themselves had worked, had outpaced the progress of civilization. In the course of the 1880s, as a result of shortsighted party bids for popular favor, an approximation of democracy had been installed: something approaching universal manhood suffrage in the Third Reform Act, an end to the weighted voting system traditionally maintained by unequal electoral districts (and favored by figures as disparate as Mill and Bagehot) in the Redistribution Act, and local government reforms that substituted elected councils for the rule of the magistracy. Yet such reforms could, many feared, merely institutionalize the demagoguery towards which the established parties had already long been tending. Instead of acting as a meritocratic filter, democratic politics were only amplifying sectional demands. Civic values were being supplanted by caucus-driven municipal socialism or populist conservatism: which was worse?

If Gladstone's Liberal Party at first appeared less infected by these viruses than Salisbury's Tories, Gladstone himself seemed determined to guarantee that his party would play no active role in the resistance to them. On the contrary, his obsession with Irish Home Rule – in his view the very climax of the historic struggle for individual expression – was perceived by many intellectuals as at best a fatal abdication of state responsibility for the making of citizens, at worst an unprincipled caving-in to the worst kind of sectionalism. Many educated dissenting professionals shared Millicent Garrett Fawcett's view that the Irish were "idle, priest-ridden and shiftless"; had Henry Fawcett lived, she assured *The Times*, he also would have opposed Home Rule.[14] Not a few accompanied her into the dead-end of Liberal Unionism – not the last time intellectuals would gravitate towards an "independent" (but peripheral) political party.[15] The high Victorians had assumed that political change would march hand-in-hand with intellectual renewal; their late-Victorian heirs, as Richard Shannon has put it, "shared this general radical assumption as to the badness of the old political order yet could find no comfort in the conditions of the new."[16]

Still, one has to be impressed by the large section of the cultivated classes that stuck by organized Liberalism, and attempted to make a New Liberalism that preserved as much of the Gladstonian formula as possible in modern conditions. The boldest and most charitable such attempt involved a recognition that the eruption of "sectionalism" and "materialism" in politics might not after all stem inevitably from the advent of democracy. There was, indeed, plenty of empirical evidence for this assumption in the 1880s and 1890s, the classic decades of the "social question." What if, the New Liberals asked, "materialism" represented merely a just rebuke to the failure of laissez-faire adequately to stimulate and reward manly enterprise and thrift? What if misfortune and poverty were not symptoms of moral failure, but rather lack of moral opportunity? If this injustice were rectified by the interposition of an active or at least an enabling state, and men's capacity for self-support restored, the Gladstonian engine would be set back on the tracks. The virtuous would better themselves, qualify as full citizens, and exercise self-government again, at which point perhaps the enabling state could be allowed to wither away.[17]

Such a strategy, for an emergency state apparatus to restore true liberal conditions, naturally had its appeal to the educated upper-middle classes whose enlightened philosophy would call the state into being and whose offspring would fill its budding bureaucracies. But by challenging the market and with it the economic base for the existing social hierarchy, gentlemanly New Liberals had always to worry that they might be abetting the gathering of class sentiment and forcing themselves to make an unappetizing choice between the proletariat or the governing classes. One way around this difficulty was to target as the enemy only the very cream of the governing classes, big landowners whose philistinism and unearned income in any case cast doubt on their virtue. Death duties and taxes on unearned income thus had the double advantage of funding state programs for the relief of poverty and applying to the rich the same moral standard – i.e., that income must reward individual effort – that liberals had always applied to the poor. In the long run, however, mobilizing public opinion against even a thin stratum of aristocrats would prove too demagogic and too statist for most liberal professionals, as the fastidious revulsion from Lloyd George and Winston Churchill in the prewar People's Budget and Land Campaigns (and *a fortiori* from Lloyd George's wartime regime) would demonstrate.[18]

For most of the liberal intelligentsia, indeed, support for the enabling state was only made possible by a continuing, gut-level confidence in the traditional governing classes. This confidence underpinned the extraordinary flowering of intellectual conclaves around the turn of the century, such as the Rainbow Circle and the Co-Efficients, in which "young" elements of all parties came together to agree on the necessary extent of state action. In its more extreme form, this governing-class solidarity manifested itself among progressive intellectuals in a sneaking envy for the "efficiency" of German authoritarianism, fascination with the biologically-determinist explanations and "eugenic" fallacies of Francis Galton and Leonard Darwin, or in an otherwise inexplicable affection for Arthur Balfour.[19] Democracy did not really come into it. By persuading themselves that sectionalism and social protest were a symptom of economic and political exclusion rather than an expression of a new type of politics, the question of their own response to that new politics could be neatly avoided. At best, they were optimistic that the action of the enabling state and the efforts of the conscientious section of the governing classes were, as Graham Wallas put it, gradually awakening "an absorbed and indifferent public to realise its own opportunities."[20]

For all its "socialism," therefore, the New Liberalism was at root a Gladstonian project, one which required only a minimal amount of casuistry or special pleading in order to keep liberal values alive and integral in twentieth-century politics. During and after the First World War, however, the New Liberalism was first disrupted and then gradually destroyed by a whole host of factors, and thereafter no single cause, flag or rallying cry can even in the loosest sense be identified with the cultivated elite as a whole. This failure of the New Liberalism has offered one of the strongest arguments for taking the Great War as a watershed, after which the intellectuals – like their party – fragmented, following no single model in their response to the problems of public life.

For the war and its aftermath not only damaged the institutional edifice of New Liberalism, they undermined its intellectual project as well. The carnage of the First World War was clearly disillusioning as much for "New" as for "Old" Liberals, leading many to doubt whether international politics could be governed by "reason" at all. A generation of junior officers and (even more) conscientious objectors came to question the political capacity and disinterestedness less of "the democracy" than of their own high-minded class. A vindictive peace did little to restore faith in the morality of Britain's foreign policy, while the pledge that, in Campbell-Bannerman's words, Britain's colonial wars and policies would not be conducted with "methods of barbarism" was all but bankrupt in the wake of the Amritsar massacre and the Black and Tans. Equally disheartening for those schooled in Gladstonian principles was the tremendous expansion of the state's expenditures and functions that took place, not only during and due to the war, but also consistently thereafter. Even the New Liberals thought that an expanded state should encourage rather than replace individual effort: by 1918, they were disconcerted to find a coalition Government led by a New Liberal acquiring new Ministries and functions with abandon, openly responding to the loud chorus of sectional demands. Worse, what looked to many like a return to old corruption was funded increasingly from income tax and thus from earned income, hitting directly at the professional's pocketbook.

And democracy, instead of biding its time until further civilized, was making more impetuous demands. The Fourth Reform Act of 1918 achieved something short of (but approaching) universal suffrage, and the new groups could not easily be incorporated into established politics or established ideas. The loyalties of Liberal women had already been sapped by a decade of Liberal Party vacillation over women's suffrage; the wartime and coalition Governments' pledges to roll back women's wartime economic gains drove some activist women to abjure the "male" parties well into the interwar period.[21] Worse, although liberals had defined themselves in terms of their sensitivity to the "social question" (even viewing women's suffrage as a distraction from this more central problem), they were sometimes discomfited by the form in which it was posed between the rise of a militant labor movement in 1917 and the collapse of the postwar boom in 1921. In 1910, the New Liberal *Nation* looked to the "artisan classes" to save Britain not only from the Tories but also from the clamorous voice of "the public house and unorganised labour."[22] In 1918, by contrast, the enthusiasm within the labor movement for measures that were frankly rights-based and redistributive rather than selective, enabling or contributory – programs like universal, tax-funded pensions for widows, orphans, the aged and even mothers with young children – showed that demands on the state could not be contained within the still-individualistic and moralizing framework of New Liberalism. Finally, Liberals in the 1920s no longer had a viable party within which to face these dilemmas. The unappetizing choice was between a small and vacuous Asquithian fragment, or a small and authoritarian Lloyd George fan club, both wings resembling "a cluster of shepherds without a flock and possibly – as the cynics said – with more crooks than sheep."[23]

Faced with this spectacle, some of the intellectual aristocracy's most distinguished political offspring – among them H.W. Massingham, Arthur Ponsonby, C.P. Trevelyan, Leonard Woolf, Josiah Wedgwood and Charles Roden Buxton – determined to entrust the Radical heritage into new hands and cast in their lot with Labour.[24] Many of them were motivated primarily by opposition to the war or disgust at the Irish and Indian policies of Grey and Lloyd George: by the 1920s, at least some of Labour's intellectuals were beginning to criticize not only the degree to which Britain fell short of its own "civilizing" ideals but also the intolerance inherent in the "civilizing" framework altogether. (George Orwell, for example, came to the conclusion that British rule in Burma rested not on superior "civilization" but on terror.)[25] Yet relatively few of the new recruits from the Liberal Party (with the notable exception of Trevelyan, Christopher Addison and William Wedgwood Benn) were drawn by Labour's social and economic agenda, and even these had few ties to the trade unions and little understanding of the importance of their consent. Most assumed that the Labour Party, like the Liberals, would be influenced by an assortment of high-minded and humanitarian lobbies – a perception that may have been true for foreign policy, but would be sharply disproved whenever Cole, Brailsford,

Trevelyan, Cripps or other of Labour's "intellectuals" tried to advise Ernest Bevin or Walter Citrine on economic policy.[26] This conflict between the intellectuals' vision of Labour as an alliance of all progressive forces, and the trade union movement's view of Labour as a party of working-class defense, latent in the 1920s, broke into the open during the years of the Second Labour Government: a divergence summed up in Sidney Webb's famous verdict that "the General Council [of the TUC] are pigs."[27]

Yet much of the intelligentsia could not make this leap – and not only because (as Keynes put it) Labour was "a class party, and the class is not my class." Many also shared his doubts "that the intellectual elements within the Labour Party will ever exercise adequate control," and continued to see the Liberal Party as "still the best instrument of future progress." Yet Keynes admitted that "the *positive* argument for being a Liberal" was in 1925 "very weak"; only by managing the transition to "a régime which deliberately aims at controlling and directing economic forces in the interests of social justice and social stability" could New Liberalism revitalize itself.[28] When put to the test, however, Keynes's colleagues failed him: although Lloyd George ransacked the economics departments of the universities to put together a sophisticated expansionist program in the run-up to the 1929 election, when confronted with the financial crisis of 1931, most Liberals showed themselves more willing to destroy their party and jettison their volatile and creative leader than ally with Labour or abandon their inherited commitment to balanced budgets and retrenchment. True, the *Manchester Guardian*, ever the conscience of the left-leaning intelligentsia, endorsed the Labour Party in 1931 – but only because it saw Labour as the last refuge of free-trade liberalism.[29] Unable to convince anyone of their domestic relevance, some of the Party's intellectuals fell back on the empire to provide one last justification of the "civilizing mission." As late as 1940, the historian Ramsay Muir, the Liberal Party's most faithful servant in the 1930s, was defending British expansion in Africa in exactly the same terms as he had in 1917 – as a means of bringing "backward peoples" out of "the unchanging barbarism in which they have mostly rested since the beginning of time," inducting them "into the ways of civilization ... and enabl[ing them] to train themselves in the difficult art of self government."[30]

The failure of Labour and fragmentation of Liberalism also encouraged some to drift to more eccentric orbits. Perfectly peaceful and thoughtful characters like Cyril Joad, the philosopher and rambler, or Harold Nicolson, the quasi-aesthete diplomat, put themselves in the hands of Oswald Mosley in 1930 in the ludicrous hope that something called the New Party would wish away their difficulties.[31] Yet adhesion to the authoritarian movements of right or left was rarely lasting: these choices, after all, entailed an embrace of the corporate state, of illiberal means that were almost more unpleasant than illiberal ends, and over the long term an opting out from real public life which not all that many children of good family were happy to make, no matter how disoriented they were by the horrors of war and the collapse of the Liberal Party. Here the traditional historiographical lens may well have been distorted by the fact that the first and strongest statements about interwar Britain were furious envois written by refuseniks, like Robert Graves from Majorca and George Dangerfield from America. We need to listen more carefully to the evidence about those who remained.

Among them we can detect a resurgent Victorianism, taking the form of a reassertion of the civilizing or moralizing mission, often still within a recognizably political framework. A democracy which consistently returned Conservative Governments, as the interwar democracy did, was very far from the enlightened, participatory citizenry of the liberal ideal, but it was also very far from the Bolshevik horde of contemporary nightmare; it seemed a pretty toothless tiger, that one might ride. While cultivated men (and, now, women) might scruple to support the National Government, there were increasing opportunities to serve along non-parliamentary channels. This could mean policy advice, not so demeaning as official civil service, if rendered on a freelance basis, as Keynes, Beveridge and Hubert Henderson discovered. Or it could mean pressure-group activity, not as sectional as Victorian faddism if offered across party lines and under the cloak of professional expertise. Conservative Governments also continued the Labour Government's policy of relying on Liberal MPs and (more often) ex-MPs to bring their signature tone of high-minded impartiality to crucial industrial and colonial inquiries. Of course, it was hard to forego the glory of parliamentary service: hence the revival of interest among disgruntled Liberals in proportional representation and the stiff competition for the few accepted non-partisan seats, such as those for the universities.[32] But realistic analysts understood that in the era of the corporate state and the dictatorship of the parties, pressure groups and experts often had more influence on policy than independent MPs or backbenchers. Best of all would be to combine a number of these roles at once, as did Eleanor Rathbone.

So it was possible to co-exist with democracy. Was it possible to co-exist with the corporate state? Many disappointed liberals undoubtedly felt that the policy guidance they offered and the pressure they exerted could only divert or reform the growth of a state that was fundamentally anti-progressive, being more about the protection or redistribution of wealth than about the creation of virtue. True, Conservative dominance in the 1930s did ironically make some mild collectivist experiments tolerable or even appealing to many who would have rejected outright

11

Labour's more thorough-going plans. Yet the causes of industrial relations or social insurance reform were taken up in the late 1930s more by the forward-looking industrialists and technocratic experts of Political and Economic Planning and the Management Research Groups than by liberal intellectuals, at least until 1939–40, when war, party truce and the fall of Chamberlain brought Beveridge and others back into the service of the state. Two-party politics and corporatism remained hard to swallow; in 1945, even leftish intellectuals were as likely to try to revive (once again) the embers of the Liberal Party, or to flirt with the participatory ideals of Richard Acland's Common Wealth Party, as they were to join a party dominated by the "massed battalions" of the TUC.[33]

Organized politics thus offered an ever chillier climate for intellectuals after 1914, for all their efforts at adaptation. Yet the late Victorian intelligentsia had always defined morality as much in terms of "right feeling" as right doing: as Collini remarks, their thought was "marked at least as much by an obsession with the role of altruism and a concern for the cultivation of feelings as it was by any commitment to the premisses of self-interest and rational calculation."[34] The turn to voluntary action, cultural politics or even private life thus need not be seen as a retreat if those arenas were also recognized as key to the definition of the good society. The children of the Victorians agreed; but they lacked their parents' confidence in the universal fixity of their own domestic norms. By the end of the century, the realm of the "private" had been opened up to experiment, discussion and political reform itself – confronting intellectuals with a second challenge, and one that evoked their most creative response.

III

The family lay at the heart of the Victorian moral economy: it was the school for the formation of character, the cradle of all social life. The affections and responsibilities of marriage and parenthood, late Victorian moralists characteristically thought, would train both men and women in the (different) virtues appropriate to their sex, driving men towards assiduity, temperance and self-control and women towards patience and unselfish love. It was the fear of stunting the development of manly independence that led social reformers from Chadwick to the Bosanquets to deplore interference in the labor market and "indiscriminate" doles; how to foster and protect the womanly virtues (seen almost as innate) was a more vexed question. Mill, of course, optimistically believed that absolute legal and political equality would only strengthen women's domestic authority, enabling them to devote themselves to familial duties without losing their independence or their dignity. The regulation of domestic relations could safely be left to opinion rather than to law.[35]

Mill's reconciliation of sexual complementarity with equal rights gave heart to a small group of feminists, who stoutly asserted that women's capacity for self-government was as great as men's, and their national services, if different, equally necessary. Yet his views were anathema to most of the Victorian liberal elite, who insisted that women's gifts were at once too precious and too fragile to withstand the seductions of the market and the public sphere. Once again, Gladstone won out over Mill, both by argument (he opposed both divorce reform and women's suffrage) and by example. Catherine Gladstone, unlike Harriet Taylor Mill, provided for her husband's comforts without questioning his judgment, and demanded that her daughters do likewise.[36] Julia Stephen offered the same unstinting support to Leslie Stephen; when she died, she left her eldest daughter (suitably trained) as the next victim of Stephen's self-absorption.[37] Love could sweeten duty, of course, but by the end of the century daughters (if not wives) were chafing under domestic tyranny. It was another of Julia Stephen's daughters, after all, who decided that art could not be founded on selflessness, and that one of the tasks of the woman writer was "killing the Angel in the House."[38]

Yet the *fin-de-siècle* crisis of the bourgeois family began not with murder but in the most indirect of ways, with the elaboration of those single-sex institutions and ties that were the inevitable complement of "separate spheres." Men had always been able to escape the society of women at the public school, university or political club; those who wanted to do without it entirely could (and did) seek refuge in the homosocial worlds of the regiment or the settlement house. In the rarified atmosphere of Cambridge, leavened by agnosticism, Idealist philosophy and homosexuality, the generation of Keynes and Lytton Strachey explored the rituals and ideas of that most famous of male Societies, the Cambridge Apostles. Their sisters were less likely to find their way into women's colleges only a decade or two old; when they did, however, their paths rarely crossed those of male undergraduates and they were soon caught up in more ephemeral and sexually-innocent versions of the Apostles. A lifestyle that would have seemed repressive to their brothers was experienced by these women as a blessed respite from the too-tight bonds of familial love. Helena Sickert (later Swanwick), who entered Girton in the 1880s, later recalled that only the acquisition of a room of her own – complete with door, to close when she wished – made her realize how deeply she had resented her mother's demands, and how determined she was to preserve her new-found freedom.[39]

And, by the 1890s, there were a variety of ways for her to do so. Even the more patriarchal mid-Victorian liberals had conceded that middle-class women had a special mission to the downtrodden and the poor: their daughters pushed this logic further, founding communities of nurses and teachers, religious orders and settlement houses, all devoted to using the feminine virtues of selflessness, purity and empathy for social ends.[40] Feminists like Emily Davies, anti-feminists like Mrs Humphry Ward, socialists like Beatrice Webb and – as Seth Koven shows in this volume – married social reformers like Henrietta Barnett all agreed that single women could exercise their "maternal" influence in the public rather than private sphere. As single-sex professions and sociability grew in interest and variety, however, they threatened to supplant rather than supplement family ties. Ostensible "new men" like George Gissing and Grant Allen discovered with consternation that Mill had been wrong; that, given a choice, "new women" might well prefer to do without home and family altogether.[41]

Bourgeois domesticity, one of the main supports of Victorianism, was thus under threat by the 1890s – and from women who preferred to preach its virtues to others than submit to its limitations and hierarchies themselves. And their choices, even if veiled in an older rhetoric of mission and duty, raised worrying questions. If women preferred hard work in public to pedestals in private, perhaps the Victorian conception of marriage was not, after all, so very "civilized." The model in which female love sustained and whetted male enterprise (or, more crassly, in which women exchanged love for material support through a marriage contract that feminists were fond of calling "legalized prostitution") seemed outdated, even mercenary, when women were also enterprising and love the aim of both spouses.[42] The tentative reexamination of sex, marriage and the economics of the family that began in scientific, free-thinking or even free-love circles (the Marx–Aveling coterie, the Men and Women's Club) had, by the turn of the century, some rather more respectable offshoots – not least the collections of students who flocked to the Fabian Summer Schools.[43] Even the Apostles began to look staid: Robert Skidelsky singles out 1909 as the year in which the aesthetic, idealist and homosexual style of Lytton Strachey was supplanted by the athletic, socialist and (sometimes) heterosexual style of Rupert Brooke.[44] By the time Dora Black (later Russell) went up to Cambridge in 1912, Wells's *Ann Veronica* (whose eponymous heroine found a truer emancipation in sex than in suffrage) was the Bible of the Girton undergraduate.[45]

For perhaps twenty years, then, between (say) Woolf's watershed of 1910 and the deepening of the slump in the early 1930s, a domestic drama that had begun with the revolt of their daughters was played out between the husbands and wives of the cultivated classes. It is easy and common to dismiss the sexual revolution of this period as simply an instinctual revolt against "repression," a rush for gratification in any form, but to do so would be to overlook the extreme self-consciousness with which many post-Victorians set out to live in a new way, the almost impossible burden of honesty they imposed on their new arrangements. True, honesty could be a substitute for responsibility: the "openness" of Bertrand Russell's serial monogamy or H.G. Wells's philandering did not necessarily lessen the pain they caused. Many women also discovered that work, liberty and love were less easily reconciled in practice than in theory, especially when children complicated the picture, and were forced into unpalatable compromises. Dorothy L. Sayers deposited her newborn (and illegitimate) son with a cousin and returned to her job writing advertising copy; Storm Jameson found it impossible after a divorce to care for her son and pursue her career, and, with much anguish, left him in care. Rebecca West, by contrast, kept Anthony (her child by Wells) at least intermittently with her, although Wells resented the boy's claim on her attention and West herself the distraction from her writing.[46] But not all efforts were so mixed. Fred Pethick-Lawrence never asked Emmeline to sacrifice her interests and career for his, and with Leonard Woolf the balance almost swung the other way: with such couples, as in the rational if unconventional living arrangements of Vera Brittain, George Catlin, Winifred Holtby (and children), we do find a real and successful replacement of the Victorian ideal with an equally close but more egalitarian model of private life.[47] Mill, unlike Gladstone, had always feared the stultifying effects of social conformity, and argued that society should tolerate and even encourage "eccentricity" in behavior and "experiments in living."[48] In an entirely unexpected way, the 1920s were Mill's decade.

And the personal became political, as Mill would have expected. "Emancipated" women, to begin with, began to propagandize about their views. Uncharacteristically writing on the "Problems of a Woman's Life," Rose Macaulay characteristically urged women simply to abandon that useless occupation – keeping house – conventionally considered their responsibility: "At the worst, a house unkept cannot be so distressing as a life unlived."[49] Vera Brittain agreed, denouncing "the present nightmare of domesticity" as a waste of women's talents and a destroyer of marital happiness.[50] Some of the new sex radicals also used their own lives didactically: thus, Bertrand and Dora Russell not only tried to raise their own children in a progressive manner; they opened a school to extend the experiment. (One of their pupils was the young Richard Pankhurst, whose mother Sylvia – in much the same spirit – had publicized her own pregnancy and birth in order to call attention to the plight of unmarried mothers.)[51] And some went further, insisting not only that couples live in new ways, and that women be admitted to full (individual) citizenship, but also that politics and state institutions be used to rework the family itself: to guarantee economic and personal independence to married women. The enthusiastic campaigns of the 1920s for the state endowment of motherhood and the public provision of birth control advice – which pitted "new feminists" against old, and divided the Labour Party within itself – perfectly express this optimism about the malleability and perfectibility of the hitherto sacrosanct sphere of "the private."[52]

But the trends of the times were not entirely welcoming. By the mid-1930s, we find the attempt of post-Victorian progressives to construct and popularize a new ethic of civilized private life succumbing to its own contradictions and to new economic and international priorities. Under the influence of psychoanalysis, sexology and a depression-era reaction against married women's work, the elevation of personal life could metamorphose into a new domesticity – a harrying of women into sexual or marital roles that it was deemed "prudish" or "abnormal" to avoid. "When I was a child," wrote Winifred Holtby in 1935:

> an unmarried woman who had compromised her reputation for strict chastity was an outcast; she was called fallen, unfortunate or wicked, according to the degree of charity in those who mentioned her. Today there is a far worse crime than promiscuity: it is chastity. On all sides the unmarried woman today is surrounded by doubts cast not only upon her attractiveness or her common sense, but upon her decency, her normality, even her sanity.[53]

In 1936, when Alison Neilans, feminist and moral reformer, looked back over fifty years of feminist campaigns for "changes in sex morality," she admitted that "the end of the double standard is in sight, but it is not ending in the way anticipated by the pioneers who fought for it."[54] In the wake of Freud, Havelock Ellis and the First World War, the concern of an earlier generation of feminists to foster a single standard of sexual morality was reinterpreted as prudery, their passionate commitment to their own sex as perversion. Small wonder Eleanor Rathbone and Elizabeth Macadam left instructions that their correspondence be burned after their deaths, thus shielding a lifetime of loving companionship from inquisitive and uncomprehending eyes.

Nor could the politics of the private survive long in the face of the economic and political crises of the 1930s. Jarrow, Fascism and the war in Spain – as well as the long campaigns over unemployment benefit and the means test – all pushed the concerns of the 1920s to the sidelines. By the late 1930s, private life was once again defined *against* politics, nowhere more brilliantly and scathingly than in Orwell's plea for a "decent" and "English" socialism ("present society with the worst abuses left out, and with interest centring round the same things as at present – family life, the pub, football, and local politics"), a socialism that would no longer be a refuge for "every fruit-juice drinker, nudist, sandal-wearer, sex-maniac, Quaker, 'Nature Cure' quack, pacifist and feminist in England."[55] When Cyril Connolly published *Enemies of Promise* in 1938, ties of affection, whether homo- or heterosexual, featured not as a subject for introspection and literary examination, but among those "parasites on genius" that distracted aspiring writers from their true creative task.[56]

Such writers of the 1930s did, to their credit, increasingly turn to and explore the ways in which the identities and intonations of class marked all aspects of British social life, thus tracing in imaginative literature the same course that Llewellyn Smith, Seebohm Rowntree and other "poverty experts" were following through social investigation.[57] But if the rediscovery of poverty offered some intellectuals a new field of action, it also disposed them to see the sexual obsessions of the 1920s as trivial or selfish. Employment and welfare policies that would abate class inequality became the priority (and to some extent the creation) of Liberals like Keynes and Beveridge, even when such policies assumed (and bolstered) a "Victorian" ideal of a male head of household and dependent wife, an ideal to which their own lives often scarcely conformed. Even socialist intellectuals in 1910 had exhorted people to throw off the imprisoning shackles of Victorian respectability; one generation later, J.B. Priestley and Richard Hoggart were as apt to try to preserve working-class "decency" and familialism as a bulwark against national and cultural decay.

By the fall of the Labour Government in 1951, sexual complementarity and domesticity were back in vogue, embedded equally in "New Look" fashions and in pronatalist and welfare policies. Few noticed the extent of the shift from the sexual-egalitarian ideals of the 1920s. The immediate postwar governments, whether Labour or Conservative, had little interest in such questions; both assumed (possibly rightly) that their policies simply mirrored the preferences of the vast majority of the population. Intellectuals may not have participated in the "new domesticity" of the 1950s – they may, as Noel Annan insists, have preserved Bloomsbury's emphasis on civility in private life – but they ceased to posit their own affective choices as political acts. What was radical in the Edwardian era or the 1920s seemed hedonistic or even retrograde in the 1950s. "The pleasures of human intercourse and the enjoyment of beautiful objects," as Moore so famously put it, remained core values for the "cultivated elites," but they offered only restricted scope for public action. Barricaded from party politics, increasingly reluctant to advertise their own lifestyles, they fell back on their most comfortable activity: the defense of cultural and aesthetic standards.

IV

Yet even in this realm the cultivated classes confronted the specter of dispossession. The forces propelling mass culture forwards were also more alarming because less easily explicable than the revolutionary impulse that intellectuals had been analyzing at least since Burke. Technological change, in contrast, was almost inhuman in its impact. Steam and electric power rapidly narrowed cultural as well as geographical gaps, making the production and distribution of printed matter unthinkably cheap – and, said critics, making its content unthinkably cheap, too. It has been argued that the advent of commercial telegraphy was already having the effect in the late nineteenth century that is usually attributed to the broadcast media of the twentieth century, degrading the processing of information by speeding up its flow.[58] Telegraphy was combined with photography, new printing techniques and modern graphic design to produce before the First World War racier, sleeker, more popular newspapers which were also inevitably written in a racier, sleeker, more popular style: the New Journalism.[59] Even before the gramophone record, the mass marketing of pianos and sheet music was having a similar effect on the production of music. And of course technology had in store entirely new forms of cultural product, of which the motion picture was the first and most immediately successful: 400 million tickets were sold in Britain in 1914, including more than a few to schoolboy-elitists like Evelyn Waugh.[60] Sustained economic growth from mid-century, the disproportionate expansion of the better-educated white-collar sector, and indeed virtually universal primary education from 1870 ensured that there would also be a growing market for these products at all levels.

It might be thought that the popularization and mass marketing of old forms, as well as the invention of new forms, should have widened the earning opportunities of traditional cultural producers and needn't have appeared to them as a threat. But change on this scale was difficult to assimilate. The explosion of popular cultural goods seemed liable to swamp, rather than to augment, the supply of elite goods. Thus George Gissing bemoaned in *New Grub Street* (1891) the fate of writers scraping a living from the underpaid mass market, while perhaps not appreciating the positive implications of the heavy demand he noted on seats in the British Museum Reading Room. The coincidence of this burst of cultural democracy with rapid political change, and with a deterioration of the value of unearned incomes, made it appear all the more likely to be subversive of elites' position and culture alike.

One reaction among the cultivated elite to the onslaught of popular culture was a fastidious distaste, and if anything a stiffening of the barriers between – indeed, perhaps the invention of the distinction between – high and low culture. Lawrence Levine has drawn a connection between assertions of cultural hierarchy in Europe and America at the end of the nineteenth century across a wide range of media and institutions: from the performance of Shakespeare to the institutionalization of the modern symphony orchestra to the arrangement of museums to the policing of public parks.[61] Yet the revulsion from popular culture that was part of the aestheticism of the 1890s was neither very intense nor longlasting in Britain – although there was no enthusiastic about-face either, no counterpart to the continental avant-garde's celebration of the more "authentic" values of the *quartier* or cabaret.[62] Here again the cultivated elite's close connections to the governing classes ensured a moderate response. An intelligentsia that had accepted and profited from the commercialization of so many profane spheres was unlikely to recoil too forcefully from the commercialization of culture. John Galsworthy's token Forsyte aesthete in *The Man of Property* (1906) was grimly realistic about the degree of independence his Bohemian friends could expect – or desire – from the Upper Ten Thousand:

> It's their wealth and security that makes everything possible – that makes your art possible, makes literature, science, even religion possible. Without Forsytes, who believe in none of these things, but turn them all to use, where should we be?[63]

These connections between the cultivated and governing elites were not severed by the death of Liberal England. The standard acculturating mechanisms of that order – public schools and ancient universities – were still functioning long after the Liberal Party effectively died its death. The horrific experiences of the Great War did not displace appreciably the Officer Training Corps from its relatively new position at the center of public school life. Nor did the schools stop functioning as feeders for the standard professions – home, and especially colonial, civil service (the latter enjoying an Indian Summer in the 1920s and 1930s), the law, politics, even the Church. Despite the great anti-public school revolt that "Our Age" is supposed to have fomented, most of the revolutionaries continued to bear the stamp of their schools throughout their life, to retain close ties with their non-revolutionary school friends, and indeed to send their children to the same schools. Similarly, if Oxford in the 1920s was riven by the well-publicized arty versus hearty divide, one must remember that even the arties were careful as a rule to distance themselves from the epicene 1890s. To the contrary, among Oxford aesthetes of the 1920s Victorianism was back in vogue, often in its more muscular, self-assertive and self-advertising forms.

What did happen in the interwar period was a kind of fragmentation, a search for new arenas for action, and new media for the message. A decade of world war and sex war had made the task of communication and understanding ever more urgent, but the forms and tone of such communication were newly in question – all taste for high-minded sermonizing having succumbed to four years of official propaganda and a censored press. In cultural as well as party and sexual politics, then, the 1920s were a decade of experimentation and innovation, a decade in which Baldwin's Home Secretary Sir William Joynson-Hicks and the *Daily Mail* fought a losing battle against night-clubs, the Sitwells, *The Well of Loneliness*, and the distressing idea that pluralism, irony and detachment might be more civilized values than repression, purity and patriotism.[64] Perhaps self-interest also spurred the search for new styles and markets, since interwar intellectuals were also professionals who lived by writing journalism, reviews and even advertising copy. A sizable slice of such writing continued to be done for the political weeklies, of course, but D.L. LeMahieu has written recently of the wide-ranging efforts in the 1920s and especially in the 1930s to send highbrow messages through the mass media as well, from obvious instances like Reith's BBC – taken up again in his essay in this volume – to the less familiar crusade by Compton Mackenzie to raise the status of the gramophone record or Sir Stephen Tallents' experiments in film at the Empire Marketing Board.[65]

Yet just as the successive crises of 1899–1902 revived the fortunes of liberalism, so too the crises of 1929–31 seem to have played a crucial role in turning the cultivated elites away from personal politics. The sense that politicians had failed in their traditional duties, that the nation needed gluing back together by other means, caused many intellectuals who had flirted with a more alienated stance to return to the cause of crafting a national culture. Martin Green and Patrick Wright have pointed to a "country turn" in the early 1930s, when 1920s experiments with a more pointedly modernist, international style yielded to traditionalism and a deliberate appeal to a common national history. One explicit appeal was Noel Coward's *Cavalcade*, serialized in the *Daily Mail* in October 1931; another, subtler sign was the shift from the harshly satirical Evelyn Waugh of *Decline and Fall* (1928) or *Vile Bodies* (1930) to the more countrified Waugh of *A Handful of Dust* (1934) and, of course, the frankly elegiac *Brideshead Revisited* (1945).[66] The resonance of the "country turn" can be seen in the posthumous popularity of Mary Webb's lush and fantastical rural romances or equally in Winifred Holtby's moving chronicle of the passing of the old order, *South Riding* (1936). But some intellectuals also rediscovered in the 1930s an *urban* culture that was colorful, popular and almost Dickensian, rather than alienated, elite and "modern." "Come to Paddington!," wrote the "large-limbed, high-coloured Victorian" Robert Byron to the unrepentantly Italian Harold Acton. "Paddington is the symbol of all that Bloomsbury

20

ed., *The Victorian Revolution: Government and Society in Victoria's Britain*, New York, New Viewpoints, 1973, pp. 323–53.

16 Richard Shannon, *The Crisis of Imperialism 1865–1915*, London, Hart-Davis MacGibbon, 1974, p. 276.

17 These assumptions underlie one consistent formulation of the New Liberal project: L.T. Hobhouse, *Liberalism*, 1911; rpt, Westport, Conn., Greenwood Press, 1980.

18 Peter Clarke's treatment in *Liberals and Social Democrats* (Cambridge, Cambridge University Press, 1978) skips from the details of the 1910 budget, which the New Liberal *Nation* supported as a matter of policy, to the outbreak of war in 1914; but the change of tone in politics in the intervening years, even if exaggerated by Dangerfield, can't be disregarded altogether. Note, for instance, Charles Masterman's appalled reaction to the egoism and activism of Winston Churchill as early as 1908, as recounted by Robert Rhodes James, *Churchill: A Study in Failure 1900–1939*, London, Weidenfeld and Nicolson, 1970, p. 34.

19 On the Co-Efficients, see Bernard Semmel, *Imperialism and Social Reform: English Social-Imperial Thought, 1895–1914*, London, George Allen & Unwin, 1960, pp. 72–82; on the Rainbow Group, Michael Freeden, *The New Liberalism*, Oxford, Clarendon Press, 1978, pp. 256–7; on eugenics and "national efficiency," see especially G.R. Searle, *The Quest for National Efficiency: A Study in British Politics and Political Thought, 1899–1914*, Oxford, Blackwell, 1971; and see the bizarre encomium on Balfour ("Mr Evesham") in H.G. Wells, *The New Machiavelli*, London, Collins, 1911.

20 From Graham Wallas's "Credo" of 1903. For this and an excellent discussion of New Liberal thinking on democracy in general, see Clarke, *Liberals and Social Democrats*, pp. 134–45.

21 Claire Hirshfield, "Fractured Faith: Liberal Party Women and the Suffrage Issue in Britain, 1892–1914," *Gender and History*, vol. 2, Summer 1990, pp. 173–9.

22 The first quotation is from the *Nation*, the second from J.A. Hobson, but the juxtaposition is Clarke's, *Liberals and Social Democrats*, p. 135.

23 Ivor Brown, "C.P. Scott," in W.R. Inge, ed., *The Post-Victorians*, London, Ivor Nicholson & Watson, 1933, p. 560.

24 On the Liberal defections to Labour, see Martin Pugh, *The Making of Modern British Politics*, Oxford, Basil Blackwell, 1982, pp. 216–20.

25 George Orwell, *Burmese Days*, New York, Harper Brothers, 1934.

26 Bevin's disgust at the machinations of the Labour Party's "intellectuals" is well known. See Alan Bullock, *The Life and Times of Ernest Bevin*, vol. 1, *Trade Union Leader*, London, Heinemann, 1960, pp. 255–7, 348–50, 512–16, 530–3.

27 *The Diary of Beatrice Webb*, ed. Norman and Jeanne MacKenzie, vol. 4, *1924–1943: "The Wheel of Life,"* London, Virago, 1985, p. 252.

28 John Maynard Keynes, "Am I a Liberal?" (1925) in his *Essays in Persuasion*, London, Macmillan, 1931, pp. 324–6, 335.

29 Andrew Thorpe, *The British General Election of 1931*, London, Clarendon, 1991, p. 208.

30 The first passage is from Ramsay Muir, *The Character of the British Empire*, London, Constable, 1917, p. 28; the second from Muir, *Civilization and Liberty*, London, Jonathan Cape, 1940, p. 187. Muir directed the Liberal Summer School in the 1920s and became Chairman and then President of the National Liberal Federation in the 1930s.

31 Nicolson at various points in his life considered parliamentary candidacies

for all three main parties, sat in the House of Commons as a "National Labour" member, edited the New Party newspaper, and ended his life in the 1960s as a member of the Labour party describing himself as a "Liberal Socialist" and declaring Asquith as his greatest hero. See James Lees-Milne, *Harold Nicolson*, 2 vols, London, Chatto and Windus, 1980–1.

32 Ramsay Muir, for example, become increasingly concerned with the need to reform parliamentary machinery, while Gilbert Murray responded to the virtual extinction of the Liberal Party in 1931 by arguing that only proportional representation could fend off extreme or revolutionary politics and increase the number of "the more thoughtful elements" (read, Liberals) in politics. See *Ramsay Muir: An Autobiography and Some Essays*, ed., Stuart Hodgson, London, Lund Humphries and Co., 1943, p. 151; Gilbert Murray, "The Reform of Parliamentary Government in Great Britain," *Contemporary Review*, March 1932.

33 See, Arthur Marwick, "Middle Opinion in the Thirties: Planning, Progress and Political 'Agreement,'" *English Historical Review*, vol. 79, April 1964, pp. 285–98; Paul Addison, *The Road to 1945*, London, Jonathan Cape, 1975, *passim*.

34 Collini, *Public Moralists*, p. 62.

35 John Stuart Mill, "The Subjection of Women" (1869), in John Stuart Mill and Harriet Taylor Mill, *Essays on Sex Equality*, ed. Alice S. Rossi, Chicago, University of Chicago Press, 1970, pp. 178–80; and for a good exposition of the gender ideals of Victorian women social reformers (and especially Bosanquet), see Jane Lewis, *Women and Social Action in Victorian and Edwardian England*, Stanford, Stanford University Press, 1991.

36 Patricia Jalland, "Mr Gladstone's Daughters," in Bruce Kinzer, ed., *The Gladstonian Turn of Mind*, Toronto, University of Toronto Press, 1985, pp. 97–122.

37 Noel Annan, *Leslie Stephen: The Godless Victorian*, Chicago, University of Chicago Press, 1984, p. 116.

38 Virginia Woolf, quoted in Rosenbaum, *Victorian Bloomsbury*, p. 82.

39 Cited in Carol Dyhouse, *Feminism and the Family in England, 1880–1939*, Oxford, Basil Blackwell, 1989, p. 29.

40 Martha Vicinus, *Independent Women: Work and Community for Single Women, 1850–1920*, Chicago, University of Chicago Press, 1985.

41 Grant Allen, in "Plain Words on the Woman Question," (*Fortnightly Review*, vol. 46, Oct. 1889, pp. 448–58) insisted that feminism had blinded women to the "fact" that maternity was women's natural function and social duty. His *The Woman Who Did* (London, John Lane, 1895) tells the story of one woman's principled choice of unmarried motherhood, but its dire ending (the daughter reverts to type while the mother commits suicide) may only have convinced readers to follow the lead of Gissing's Rhoda Nunn (*The Odd Women*, London, Lawrence and Bullen, 1893) in preferring work to free love.

42 See especially, Cicely Hamilton, *Marriage as a Trade*, 1909, rpt London, The Women's Press, 1981; Lucy Bland, "Marriage Laid Bare: Middle-Class Women and Marital Sex, *c.* 1880–1914," in Jane Lewis, ed., *Labour and Love: Women's Experience of Home and Family, 1850–1940*, Oxford, Basil Blackwell, 1986, pp. 122–46; Susan Kingsley Kent, *Sex and Suffrage in Britain, 1860–1914*, Princeton, Princeton University Press, 1987.

43 The literature on such groups is extensive. For a summary, see Jeffrey Weeks, *Sex, Politics and Society: The Regulation of Sexuality since 1800*, London, Longman, 1981, chs 8 and 9; also, Judith Walkowitz, "Science, Feminism, and

Romance: The Men and Women's Club, 1885–1889," *History Workshop Journal*, no. 21, Spring 1986, pp. 37–59.

44 Robert Skidelsky, *John Maynard Keynes. Vol. 1: Hopes Betrayed*, New York, Viking, 1986, pp. 239–41.

45 Dora Russell, *The Tamarisk Tree. Vol. 1: My Quest for Liberty and Love*, London, Virago, 1977, pp. 40–1.

46 James Brabazon, *Dorothy L. Sayers: A Biography*, 1981, rpt London, Gollancz, 1988, pp. 96–107; Storm Jameson, *Journey from the North*, vol. 1, London, Virago, 1984, pp. 133–7; Victoria Glendinning, *Rebecca West: A Life*, London, Weidenfeld and Nicolson, 1987, pp. 56–61, 103–4.

47 On the Pethick-Lawrences, see Brian Harrison, *Prudent Revolutionaries: Portraits of British Feminists Between the Wars*, Oxford, Oxford University Press, 1987, pp. 243–72; on Brittain, Catlin and Holtby, see the introduction to Paul Berry and Alan Bishop, eds, *Testament of a Generation: The Journalism of Vera Brittain and Winifred Holtby*, London, Virago, 1985.

48 John Stuart Mill, *On Liberty*, 1859, rpt Harmondsworth, Penguin, 1974.

49 Rose Macaulay, *A Casual Commentary*, London, Methuen, 1925, p. 82.

50 Berry and Bishop, *Testament of a Generation*, p. 142.

51 Russell, *The Tamarisk Tree*, pp. 191, 199; Patricia Romero, *E. Sylvia Pankhurst: Portrait of a Radical*, New Haven, Yale University Press, 1987, pp. 168–71.

52 See especially, Pat Thane, "The Women of the British Labour Party and Feminism, 1906–1945," in Harold Smith, ed., *British Feminism in the Twentieth Century*, Amherst, University of Massachusetts Press, 1990, pp. 124–43; Susan Pedersen, "The Failure of Feminism in the Making of the British Welfare State," *Radical History Review*, vol. 43, Winter 1989, pp. 86–110.

53 Berry and Bishop, *Testament of a Generation*, p. 91.

54 In Ray Strachey, ed., *Our Freedom and Its Results*, London, Hogarth Press, 1936, p. 222.

55 George Orwell, *The Road to Wigan Pier*, 1937, rpt New York, Harcourt, Brace, 1958, pp. 176–7, 174.

56 Cyril Connolly, *Enemies of Promise*, 1938; rev. edn, London, Andre Deutsch, 1988.

57 For a summary of their findings, see John Stevenson and Chris Cook, *The Slump: Society and Politics during the Depression*, London, Quartet, 1979, pp. 74–93.

58 Neil Postman, *Amusing Ourselves to Death: Public Discourse in the Age of Show Business*, London, Methuen, 1986, ch. 5.

59 D.L. LeMahieu, *A Culture for Democracy: Mass Communication and the Cultivated Mind in Britain Between the Wars*, Oxford, Clarendon Press, 1988.

60 See Michael Davie, ed., *The Diaries of Evelyn Waugh*, London, Weidenfeld and Nicolson, 1976, for Waugh's youthful taste not only for films but also for commercial music hall.

61 Lawrence W. Levine, *Highbrow/Lowbrow: The Emergence of Cultural Hierarchy in America*, Cambridge, Mass., Harvard University Press, 1988.

62 On the limits to high cultural identification with popular culture, see John Stokes, *In the Nineties*, Hemel Hempstead, Harvester Wheatsheaf, 1989, esp. chs 1, 3.

63 John Galsworthy, *The Man of Property*, 1918, rpt New York, Charles Scribner's Sons, 1969, p. 189.

64 See especially, Ronald Blythe, "The Salutary Tale of Jix," in his *The Age of Illusion: Glimpses of Britain between the Wars, 1919–1940*, 1963, rpt Oxford, Oxford University Press, 1983, pp. 15–42.

65 LeMahieu, *Culture for Democracy, passim.* Cf. John Carey, *The Intellectuals and the Masses*, London, Faber and Faber, 1992, which, while employing LeMahieu's research where it seems serviceable, entirely ignores the thrust of his argument about cross-class cultural proselytism by the cultivated elites.

66 Both Martin Green and Humphrey Carpenter see the abandonment of cosmopolitanism and modernism for the comforts of religion and history as the central theme of Brideshead. Martin Green, *Children of the Sun: A Narrative of Decadence in England after 1918*, New York, Basic Books, 1976, p. 210; Humphrey Carpenter, *The Brideshead Generation: Evelyn Waugh and His Friends*, London, Weidenfeld and Nicolson, 1989, pp. 358–70.

67 Harold Acton, *Memoirs of An Aesthete*, London, Methuen, 1948, pp. 119, 155.

68 Quoted by Green, *Children*, pp. 68–9.

69 Even John Gross, charting the relentless fall of the "man of letters" from some great Victorian height, acknowledges the degree to which MacCarthy filled Gosse's shoes in the 1920s and 1930s. *The Rise and Fall of the Man of Letters*, London, Weidenfeld and Nicolson, 1969, pp. 240–5.

70 For instance, in Tallents' *The Projection of England*, London, Faber and Faber, 1932, and in Keynes' "Art and the State," for which see below.

71 The Rowntree and Leverhulme trusts functioned similarly and crucially, as in this period (like our own) the Treasury would only offer subsidy to projects proved worthy by prior private investment.

72 J.M. Keynes, "Art and the State," *The Listener*, 26 August 1937, rpt in Clough Williams-Ellis, ed., *Britain and the Beast*, London, J.M. Dent, 1937, pp. 1–7.

73 C.E.M. Joad, "The People's Claim," in ibid., pp. 64–85.

74 Mark Amory, ed., *The Letters of Evelyn Waugh*, London, Weidenfeld and Nicolson, 1980, p. 210.

75 Quoted in Mervyn Jones, *A Radical Life: The Biography of Megan Lloyd George*, London, Hutchinson, 1991, p. 223.

76 Michael Frayn, "Festival," in Michael Sissons and Philip French, eds, *The Age of Austerity*, London, Hodder and Stoughton, 1963, p. 320.

77 John Summerson, "South Bank Postscript," *New Statesman*, 6 October 1951, pp. 363–4.

78 Francis West, *Gilbert Murray: A Life*, London, Croom Helm, 1984, pp. 236, 239, 242, 244.

79 Bertrand Russell, "A Fifty-Six Year Friendship," in *Gilbert Murray: An Unfinished Autobiography*, London, George Allen and Unwin, 1960, p. 209.

80 Michael Oakeshott, "Political Education," in Peter Laslett, ed., *Philosophy, Politics and Society*, Oxford, Basil Blackwell, 1956, esp. pp. 1, 17–18.

81 Raymond Williams, *Culture and Society, 1780–1950*, London, Chatto and Windus, 1958.

1 Henrietta Barnett around the time of her marriage

1

Henrietta Barnett 1851–1936
The (auto)biography of a late Victorian marriage

Seth Koven

On 4 February 1872, the "pretty, witty and well-to-do"[1] Henrietta Octavia Rowland received a letter that "surprised [her] very much."[2] It was a marriage proposal from a singularly unattractive older clergyman named Samuel Barnett. He conspicuously lacked those qualities that a fashionable young woman was taught to cherish in her suitors: wealth, social standing and personal ambition. It was not, however, the unsuitability of this particular match that shocked Miss Rowland. She was troubled by different matters. She had heretofore interpreted his interest in her as entirely dependent on their common work to improve the lives of the London poor in Marylebone. What place could there be for private passion and sexual desire among men and women joined together in the "passionless"[3] comradeship of social reform? Was matrimony compatible with female independence of thought and action?

Henrietta Rowland Barnett's life, and the way in which she chose to depict it in her monumental two-volume biography of her husband, *Canon Barnett, His Life, Work and Friends* (hereafter referred to as the *Life*), offer one set of answers to these questions and form the subject of this essay. Born in the year of the Great Exhibition of 1851, she died a much honored (CBE, 1917; DBE, 1924) and still "wonderful old lady"[4] in 1936. By dint of sheer longevity alone, her life forms an unbroken bridge between the moral certitudes and convictions of the late Victorian urban gentry and the growing intellectual, political and cultural doubts that engulfed this class on the eve of the Second World War.

Henrietta's public activities were wide ranging and influential. She was a respected architect of state policies for Poor Law children; her husband's partner in the development of the famous university settlement in Whitechapel, Toynbee Hall; an early advocate of women's suffrage and a life-long critic of war; initiator and organizer of the Hampstead Garden Suburb, a suburban housing development committed to cross-class communitarian ideals; and founder, honorary secretary and president of many organizations and institutions to improve the lives of working-class girls and women. *The City and East London Observer* declared in 1932 that she occupied a "place all to herself" among "those notable women of the first quarter of the twentieth century" "who rendered most distinguished public and social service."[5]

In a brief essay, it is difficult to do justice to a career in public service that spanned more than sixty years. And this task is even more difficult because not a single scholarly essay – much less a full-scale biography – treating Henrietta's ideas and accomplishments has ever been written, despite considerable academic interest in her husband and in Toynbee Hall.[6] I have long been puzzled by this gap in scholarship, especially since women's historians for the past three decades have examined the lives and ideas of many of her less influential peers.[7]

In attempting to explain why posterity has ignored Henrietta, I found myself returning to her own ideas about singleness and marriage, to her partnership with Samuel Barnett, and to her biography of him. Despite the fact that she wrote or edited eight books and numerous pamphlets and articles, only the biography is read today. The *Life* remains the most important source of information about both its ostensible subject, Samuel Barnett, and its author, Henrietta Barnett. It is an autobiography *manqué*. Any attempt to write a biographical essay about Henrietta Barnett must reckon with her strategies as biographer, as well as with how posterity has interpreted her deliberate blurring of autobiography and biography in the *Life*. This essay thus examines how Henrietta Barnett sought to construct for herself a life of social action first as a spinster and then as a married woman, while paying close attention to how she chose to represent spinsterdom and marriage in the *Life*.

HENRIETTA ROWLAND: SPINSTERDOM AS VOCATION

It is easy to forget that men and women who later married were not necessarily destined for matrimony, or bachelors and spinsters for an unmarried life. It seems inconceivable to us, for example, that the spinster "heroine of [Henrietta's] life," Octavia Hill, hoped to become Mrs Edward Bond as she approached the mature age of forty.[8] Similarly, in light of the fact that Henrietta Rowland married at twenty-one, there initially seems to be something faintly absurd about calling her a spinster at the time she met Samuel Barnett. Nonetheless, despite her youth, beauty and social position, Henrietta Rowland saw herself as committed to spinsterdom as a social vocation during the short interval between leaving her home in 1869 and her marriage to Samuel Barnett in 1873. Many factors, some political, others personal, contributed to Henrietta Rowland's identity as a spinster in 1872.

Single women were better positioned than their married counterparts in the 1860s and 1870s to take advantage of expanding work, educational and political opportunities for women.[9] In the years that Rowland came into young womanhood – the late 1860s and early 1870s – the disabilities of married women were widely discussed in middle-class circles. Groups like the extra-parliamentary lobby, the Married Women's Property Committee, sought to establish a measure of legal equality within marriage, but with only limited success. Only single women retained unambiguous control over their purses and their persons, and, with the passage of the Municipal Corporations Act of 1869, some spinsters and widows gained a local franchise as well. As historians have recently recognized, local government was the linchpin of the Victorian state and the key arena for the design and provision of social welfare. Possessing the right to vote and hold local office gave single women rate payers access to precisely the political venues that were most vital to the education and welfare of the poor.[10] Henrietta Rowland was well aware of spinsters' legal and electoral privileges in local government. In 1870, she canvassed on behalf of the pioneering medical woman, Elizabeth Garrett (later Anderson), who was elected to the first London School Board.[11]

A broadening of political opportunities for single women was accompanied by the construction of a new voice. The archly polemical but playful writings of Frances Power Cobbe in particular revealed unmarried women as happy and useful members of society for whom singleness was a choice, not an unfortunate accident.[12] To be sure, many spinsters' lives were dogged by financial insecurity and social isolation, but Henrietta Rowland, like Cobbe, had ample money to support herself in comfort. Orphaned by the death of her indulgent father in 1869, she was free to make choices about her future unfettered by financial worries or parental social ambitions. For Henrietta Rowland, spinsterdom offered freedoms that most marriages could not.

While the wider political climate made the single life especially attractive for women seeking independent and useful lives, Henrietta's conventional upbringing seems scarcely to have prepared this high-spirited young girl for a life of social action. No bluestocking intellectual, she was raised by her father and a maiden aunt – her mother died giving birth to her – who "did not agree with girls being educated." While the battles to establish the first women's colleges were waged in Cambridge in the late 1860s, her formal education consisted of only "three glorious terms" at a boarding school at Dover kept by three ladies, the Haddon sisters.[13] Why she decided to leave the pampered luxury of her pet dogs and horses to embark on a single life devoted to helping the poor remains something of a mystery. The only clue Henrietta offered about her social awakening consisted of a short vignette from her school days with the Haddons. A school visit to the boy inmates from the Dover

Workhouse stimulated her "ignorant mind" to revolt "against the social injustices made evident by boys, odorous of institutionalism, dulled to inanity."[14]

As is so often the case, Henrietta's omissions are at least as revealing as her statements. Henrietta must have been aware of the extremely close ties of marriage and intellectual discipleship binding her beloved teachers to James Hinton, the controversial moral and social philosopher and aural surgeon. Hinton had been married to Margaret Haddon and, after his death, Caroline Haddon edited and elucidated his writings. Henrietta must have been exposed to Hinton's radical views about women and his passionate belief that personal service to humanity was necessarily linked to pleasure, not asceticism. Hinton anticipated Henrietta's own path: he longed to live among the poor of Whitechapel and loaned his collection of fine art for exhibition there in 1870. Perhaps scandalous rumors about Hinton's private life which circulated in the 1880s after his death explain Henrietta's distancing silence.[15] We cannot know this for certain.

Grieving but perhaps also liberated by her father's death, and under the influence of the Haddons, she sought to give purpose to her life by joining ranks with that selfless paragon of spinsterly civic duty, Octavia Hill. Henrietta believed that her short apprenticeship with Hill marked a formative epoch in her life and that her later achievements could not be properly understood apart from it. Hill and her band of mostly female and unmarried workers were in the vanguard of the experiments in housing and charitable relief in London associated with the newly established, mixed-sex voluntary organization, the Charity Organisation Society (COS). The COS aimed to promote thrift and self-help through scientific investigation of the circumstances of each applicant for relief. The work of visiting the poor was, in Hill's eyes, preeminently though not exclusively suited to women. The more strictly the COS applied its parsimonious principles, Hill explained, "the more tenderly gentle, the more patiently watchful should be the messenger and interpreters of those decisions."[16] Samuel Barnett was a founding member of the COS, and it was through Octavia Hill that he and Henrietta met in 1870.

These were the political and personal circumstances surrounding Henrietta's receipt of Barnett's unanticipated marriage proposal. In her biography of her husband, she offered her own account of her feelings about the proposal. It is a noteworthy passage, not the least because it recaptures her ambivalence toward Samuel and the uncertainty of the outcome of his suit.

He [Samuel Barnett] dressed very badly, generally obtaining his clothes by employing out-of-work tailors in the district. He always

34

wore a tall silk hat which, as he had purchased by post, never fitted, and so was usually tilted over his forehead or rammed on at the back of his head. His umbrella was a byword, and he always bought his black cotton gloves two or three sizes too large ... he was often at the same time both shy and aggressive, defects which he covered by a frequent nervous laugh. ... Insignificant as were these externals, they happened to be peculiarly unattractive to a girl who had been reared in a luxurious home, accustomed to lavish living and entertaining, who revelled in hunting and gardening and outdoor life. ... He was entirely different from any of the men I had known, and in the plans I had formed for spending my life in Bethnal Green [in the East London slums] I could see no place for marriage with its obedience and its ties. My inclination was to give a decisive 'No' to his beautiful letter, but I knew that, if I did so, either he or I would have to give up Miss Octavia's work; and to injure her schemes at that juncture was an impossible conception, worth the demand of any sacrifice on the part of either of us. I therefore wrote to tell him that my feeling for him was only that of respect, and suggested that we should go on with our work for six months and not refer to the matter during that period.[17]

The courtship narrative frames the entire *Life* and explicitly connects questions about spinsterdom, marriage and social action with strategies of (auto)biographical representation. It highlights Henrietta's role as the vehicle by which Samuel's manliness and powers can be realized. It sets up Samuel's wife, who also happens to be the author of the biography, as the central figure in the courtship and its representation. It thus raises the question of who is the actual subject of the biography, Samuel or Henrietta. As the reviewer for the *Morning Post* approvingly observed in 1918, the book was a "commingling of biography and autobiography."[18]

The passage also performs the vital task of establishing Henrietta's credibility as biographer. It anticipates and deflects readers' doubts about her ability, as the grieving widow and (auto)biographer, to present us with a truthful portrait. By so often finding imperfections in her husband, Henrietta precludes the need for her readers to do so. Contemporary reviewers consistently noticed and applauded the unbiased candor of her criticisms of her husband and the veracity of the biography.[19] The trappings of biographical objectivity and critical distance coexist with autobiographical subjectivity and intimacy in the text.

Finally, Henrietta Barnett's desire in 1918 (the year she completed the *Life*) to represent Henrietta Rowland in 1872 as an independent spinster allowed her to develop a central but unstated thesis of the *Life* about marriage. Henrietta Barnett believed that marriage could be a partnership of equal-but-different beings *because* she believed so strongly that it was possible to live a purposeful and happy life as a spinster. Thus, Henrietta Rowland's independence before marriage is a precondition for the unfolding of Henrietta Barnett's interdependent marital relationship with Samuel. Similarly, Samuel's lack of distinction as a bachelor curate sets the stage for his growth to greatness as her husband. The intertwined trajectories of their lives illustrate the ways in which each perfected his or her individuality within a partnership that made it virtually impossible to distinguish the impulse and activity of the one from the other.

The generic elision of biography and autobiography is thus not only a literary conceit, but also an expression of Henrietta's true subject in the *Life*: the expansive possibilities of marriage for women and men. She assures her readers that it has cost her dearly to share the intimate and private story of the love letters she has published. But share she must, for the story of their marriage is at once private and political, a matter rooted in the particularities of their lives and a tale of love and duty to guide readers in the social and sexual confusion of the postwar world.

MRS SAMUEL BARNETT: MARRIAGE AND SOCIAL REFORM

Overburdened with cares for her voluntary work and anxious to distance herself from her ardent and persistent suitor, Henrietta Rowland escaped to Germany in the spring of 1872. But her studies there were cut short when Alice, her beloved older sister, beckoned her home to attend her hastily arranged wedding to Ernest Hart, a philanthropic doctor and agnostic Jew. Alice, with whom she had shared a flat in Bayswater since 1869, suggested that she resume residence with their spinster aunt – an arrangement that must not have pleased her. With virtually no explanation, Henrietta tells her readers that she returned home and the very next day "plighted" Samuel her troth. In a passage remarkable mostly for what it does not say, she concluded that "the gift of his love was too holy to refuse."[20]

Most Victorians, even those polemicists like Mona Caird and Annie Besant who were its harshest critics, acknowledged that marriage ought to be the sacred foundation of the family, and most concurred with Samuel that "family is and must be the unit of society."[21] In the months of their engagement, Samuel and Henrietta exchanged views on the proper roles of men and women within marriage and in society. Samuel compensated for his lack of physical and social charms by his unusual appreciation of women's independent powers and abilities. He deplored the ways in which the record of women's achievements was hidden from history. "Have you ever noticed how much women's influence has been wanting in history?" he asked Henrietta in April 1872. "It is hard to mark the mighty work it doubtless has done because it works secretly."[22] In one particularly revealing letter, he assured her that he had no intention of displaying her like a pretty doll or ornament. "We will talk the books over together," he continued, "and in Queen's Gardens marvel among King's Treasuries."[23]

Of course, Samuel was alluding to the chapter titles of the immensely popular book, *Sesame and Lilies*, by the art critic, John Ruskin. Although often interpreted today as a paradigmatic expression of the separate spheres ideology that legitimated women's subordination, many readers at the time, including Henrietta and Samuel, found in *Sesame and Lilies* quite a different vision of marriage. Ruskin wrote *Sesame and Lilies* as part of his radical assault on capitalism and the value system that it generated in private and public life. For Ruskin, women's control over consumption (which he believed was more important than production in determining economic life), reproduction and social values placed them in the vanguard of his crusade to remake society. Women's moral sensibilities and powers were greater than those of men, he insisted. It was therefore incumbent upon them to bring their exquisite moral force to bear not only upon their husbands and children, but upon their wider communities. Female disciples, including Octavia Hill, had followed Ruskin's lead and combined a commitment to improving society with his aesthetic ideals.[24]

Ruskin's exposition of sexual difference as the foundation of complementarity between men and women and his vision of women's moral imperative to help others appealed deeply to Henrietta and to many other Victorian women committed to both social action and the emancipation of their sex. In her 1885 book, *The Making of the Home, A Reading-Book of Domestic Economy for School and Home Use*, Henrietta offered an extended commentary on *Sesame and Lilies*. She asked her readers to heed Ruskin and "take all the duties which fall to our queenly lot." "A woman's mission is a high one. On her, to a large extent, depends the good and the happiness of the family, and through the family, of the nation.... Women's duty, though it begins in the home ... does not end there."[25] Yet Henrietta followed Ruskin to conclusions far different from those of the master himself. Her admiration for women sometimes pushed her beyond notions of complementarity to espouse the position that women were innately superior to men. She once candidly admitted that "I like the female nature far better than the male nature, and think women much more influential in the world than men."[26] And, in marked contrast to Ruskin, she was an enthusiastic and early supporter of women's suffrage. Like so many other Victorian suffragists, her justification echoed Ruskin's faith in what she called women's "keener sense of morality."[27]

While we will never know what conclusions they drew from their discussion of *Sesame and Lilies*, Henrietta clearly believed that marriage to Samuel Barnett would give each wider scope and authority in public life. Her marriage, unlike Beatrice Potter's two decades later,[28] reinforced rather than ruptured her ties with the female world of charity and social welfare. It had been extraordinary for a wealthy and vivacious young woman like Henrietta Rowland, barely out of her teens, to spend most of her time visiting the poor; by contrast, it seemed quite natural for Mrs Samuel Barnett, the wife of the new vicar of St Jude's, Whitechapel, one of the poorest parishes in the metropolis, to assist her husband and undertake parochial responsibilities for women and children. She quickly established herself as the leader of a band of devoted, mostly single, women workers. Together they conducted mothers' meetings, and introduced COS principles, friendly visiting and rent collecting to dismayed female parishioners accustomed to less discriminating and more generous female charity. After almost fifteen years of marriage, she still resented as a "blasphemy" the "common opinion that a woman is a nonentity unless joined to a man."[29]

Henrietta's involvement with the community of single women social workers was a notable continuity between her public and private lives before and after marriage. Her chief helper in all her work was Marion Paterson, who joined the Barnetts in 1876, never married, and remained inseparable from Henrietta. Marion seems to have combined several different roles in Henrietta's life: friend, confidante, secretary and nurse. It is difficult to say precisely when Marion ceased to be merely one of many talented single women in Henrietta's orbit and became "Dear Childie" (Henrietta's term of endearment for her) and a member of her household. Marion certainly accompanied Samuel and Henrietta on most of their extensive travels around the world beginning in the 1880s and was an integral member of their family from the 1890s onwards. In the *Life*, Henrietta specified the circumstances of their first meeting and, in marked contrast to her description of Samuel's unattractiveness, she remembered Marion as a "girl of nineteen, whose childish face and violet eyes spoke of innocency."[30] In the decades after Samuel's death, Marion even more visibly shared the cares and duties (though little of the glory, or so it seems) of Henrietta's public and private life.

While marriage did not interrupt her close relationships with single women, it did facilitate her entry into a new arena: a crusade against sexual impurity among working-class girls and women. "Impurity" loomed large in her imagination as "the main factor in debasing women from a status of independence to one of physical dependence."[31] As a married woman, she had much greater freedom than she would have had as an innocent, young, and single woman to undertake social work that assumed familiarity with the facts of human sexuality. The projection of a womanly and motherly persona was crucial for those few women who dared to speak in public about sexuality in the 1870s. For example, Josephine Butler, Henrietta's senior by twenty-three years, was always careful to represent herself as a Christian wife and mother as she led the successful campaign to repeal the Contagious Diseases Acts.[32] Annie Besant's failure to do this, compounded by her well-publicized separation from her husband, her loss of legal custody over her children and her ties to Charles Bradlaugh, severely compromised her effectiveness as an advocate of marriage reform and birth control.[33]

Marriage also gave Henrietta a quasi-official role in the lives of female parishioners as the vicar's wife. With its scores of doss houses and open traffic in prostitution, St Jude's was an ideal place for Henrietta to inaugurate her "purity" work. "If the girls left the [Poor Law Lock Ward of the Whitechapel] infirmary and flung themselves back into their ungodly lives," she remembered, "I went after them, to woo them to take the hard self-restraining path which leads to righteousness."[34] Like so many other Victorians, she was simultaneously drawn to and repelled by the figure of the fallen woman. Having "arrived at woman's estate in a condition of almost incredible innocence," she explicitly acknowledged that she was "absorbingly interested" in but physically sickened by the depravity she encountered in the East End sexual underworld.[35] Despite her intimate knowledge of the personal circumstances that led women to prostitution, she insisted on viewing prostitution as a moral and not an economic issue. She appears to have played no part in Butler's crusade to repeal the Contagious Diseases Acts, nor did she challenge the prevailing sexual double standard that condoned male vice. Her readiness to blame women for impurity may well have stemmed from her higher expectations about women's morality. A parishioner in St Jude's apparently once overheard her "declaring her conviction that men were what women made them."[36]

As the Barnetts' first wedding anniversary approached, Octavia Hill wrote approvingly to Henrietta that,

> it does me good thus to follow you in your work now and again when I can. . . . How changed for you is all since this time last year, surely you are more, have learned much, and done much. I daresay what solemn wonderful thoughts are gathering around your Christmas and New Year. God bless you both very heartily.[37]

While the tone of Hill's letter is still very much that of a mentor writing to an apprentice, only three years later the balance of power between the women imperceptibly began to shift in favor of her married former student. In 1876, Hill hesitated to accept an invitation to address

Henrietta's workers in Whitechapel. "My own feeling," she explained, "was that as the people will be those who gather round you it would be your thoughts about them, their work, and their relations to one another that they ought to be hearing."[38]

In the next few years, Henrietta enjoyed the security and status of marriage, as well as her increased visibility as a creative, independent social reformer. She was the first nominated woman guardian and manager of the Forest Gate District Schools, where she developed that intimate knowledge of the deplorable conditions of Poor Law children that led the Prime Minister, H.H. Asquith, to call her the "unofficial custodian of the children of the state."[39] She launched an experimental scheme to send London children into the country for summer holidays that later became the immensely successful and long-lived Children's Country Holiday Fund. Finally, she helped create MABYS, the Metropolitan Association for Befriending Young Servants, a society of lady visitors who advised Poor Law girls as they entered domestic service.

Biological motherhood was the one element conspicuously absent from her life during these expansive first years of marriage. Why the Barnetts had no children of their own, and what the impact of childlessness on Henrietta's life was must remain matters for speculation. Samuel and Henrietta were entirely reticent about this subject.[40] Samuel's disapproval of birth control[41] raises the question of whether infertility or some combination of abstinence and sexual incompetence accounts for their childlessness. The weight of fragmentary evidence suggests the former. Despite her initial physical revulsion toward Samuel, Henrietta later described him pointedly to Jane Addams as "the man, my lover, the humble Christ follower."[42] She exalted motherhood and motherliness as the essential and defining qualities of true womanhood.[43] "It is a privilege to be allowed to be a mother," she declared, and the gift of bearing a child was "the most valuable thing in the world" that "God the All-Father" had granted women.[44] In light of these views, it seems unlikely that, having chosen marriage, she would then have voluntarily forsaken motherhood.

Despite (or perhaps because of) her childlessness, Henrietta worked hard to promote the welfare of children. One commentator observed that "if Canon Barnett was called to 'the ministry,' Mrs Barnett was called just as certainly, and equipped also, for the ministry of 'mothering.' "[45] The image of her as a social mother caring for all the strays and waifs who crossed her path is a recurring one – and one that she encouraged.[46] The composition and organization of her own private household with Samuel reinforced this image. She arrived at their first home, the small vicarage of St Jude's, accompanied by her nurse Mary Moore and her brain-damaged, child-like older sister, Fanny. Fanny, "sweet tempered" and "generous" but "deformed in body, frail, incapable of thought, and unable to learn,"[47] lived with Henrietta for fifty-eight years until her death. Henrietta also regularly offered sanctuary to rough and wayward Whitechapel girls and eventually outfitted a succession of homes for them and for aged poor women within or near the Barnetts' Hampstead residence. She became the legal guardian of Dorothy Noel Woods, the sickly, orphaned daughter of a co-worker, whom the Barnetts treated as if she were their own child.[48]

Henrietta's marriage with Samuel Barnett, far from constraining the life of social action she first had imagined for herself as a spinster, opened up new and more explicitly maternal roles for her while allowing her to maintain close ties to the community of independent women. But did Henrietta's ostensible embrace of Victorian notions of complementarity and her social maternalism mean that in practice the Barnetts' married lives conformed to traditional expectations about men's and women's roles?

SAMUEL AND HENRIETTA BARNETT: SUBVERSIVE COMPLEMENTARITY IN MARRIAGE

We so often associate marriage with the shibboleths of high Victorianism that we all too often overlook its possibilities and usefulness, not as a site of female oppression, but as a site for reworking social and sexual conventions. When we examine contemporaries' recollections of the Barnetts as well as Henrietta's own account, we see that for her, marriage, even more than spinsterdom, made it easier to challenge Victorian gender roles and hierarchies. Published and unpublished descriptions of Henrietta and Samuel suggest an untraditional but complementary distribution of masculine and feminine traits between them. C.R. Ashbee, an early resident at Toynbee Hall, struggling to understand his own homosexual identity, both admired and disliked the gender ambiguity he observed in the Barnetts. At first he revered Samuel, but soon he grew disillusioned and described Samuel as a "moral eunuch." If Samuel struck Ashbee as sexless and indecisive, Henrietta seemed refreshingly to combine masculine and feminine traits. Ashbee wrote in his diary that "Mrs Barnett is . . . the Prior and Prioress of this place – the worthy head. A fine, noble, bright-eyed, vigorous woman she appears; and one that will have her own way and not be sparing of her own opinion."[49] Ashbee had no way to resolve his feelings about the Barnetts since he was seeking male (not female) role models, someone like the homosexual apostle of the simple life, Edward Carpenter.

Beatrice Webb also detected something disconcerting about the Barnetts' sexuality. Samuel, she felt, possessed the moral insights of a woman while Henrietta's directness and sense of humor struck her as distinctly "masculine." Webb, however, felt compelled to reassure herself and her readers that while Henrietta was "the direct antithesis of her husband ... exactly on that account, she served as complement to him, as he did to her."[50]

G.P. Gooch's description of the Barnetts reiterated some of Ashbee's and Webb's impressions.

Identity of thought and aim was combined with a striking diversity of temperament. Though there was nothing the least flabby or sentimental about him, the Canon [Samuel] was almost feminine in his gentleness and tenderness, whereas the inflexible will of his wife is almost suggestive of the stronger sex. The one seemed born to persuade, the other to command.... I occasionally heard rumour of ruffled feathers when Dame Henrietta had been on the war-path. Despite their differing natures, it was a perfect partnership.[51]

Gooch attempted to resolve the potential gender dissonance of their roles by viewing them within a "perfect partnership." Their disturbing individual sexual identities almost (but never quite do) disappear into the larger, harmonious and productive social institution of marriage. Gooch also rehabilitated Samuel's sexuality by distinguishing between acceptable ("gentleness" and "tenderness") and undesirable ("flabby" and "sentimental") "feminine" qualities.

When we return to the *Life*, we find that Henrietta also deliberately destabilized accepted gender categories – albeit less obviously and for a somewhat different purpose. She often presented her husband as feminine: he was a "docile" son who accepted criticisms with "patient meekness" and openly acknowledged their mutual "dependence" on one another.[52] Even when she described him as occupying an ostensibly patriarchal position within the female world of their private home, she hints that he was as much a member of his harem of "Canon's ladies" as its male dominator.[53] He had, she informs us, an extraordinary gift for friendship with women whom he treated as his equals.

Likewise, Henrietta's self-portrayal in the *Life* corroborates descriptions of her as "masculine." She presented herself as a "bold," "audacious," decisive and independent-minded person.[54] As the reviewer for the *New Statesman* noticed, "the wife acted as a lightning-conductor to hostile criticism." Without challenging notions of complementarity between men and women, Henrietta's depiction of this aspect of her relationship with Samuel reverses Ruskin's expectations of male and female roles. She was the public warrior who battled their detractors thereby allowing him to remain in the feminine position, "in the background as conciliator and peacemaker."[55]

What are we to make of the representation of the Barnetts' ambiguous sexual identities in the *Life* and by contemporaries? And what does this tell us about marriage and social reform in late Victorian Britain? Let me take up these interrelated issues in turn.

At first glance, Henrietta's representation of their fluid gender roles in marriage seems incompatible with her essentialist vision of male and female difference. However, with great literary ability, she extends her representation of the indeterminability of their gender roles so as to force the reader to ask who should be credited for their most important public achievements. In narrating the stories of many of their key accomplishments (the founding of Toynbee Hall, the Children's Country Holiday Fund, the Whitechapel Art Exhibitions and, later, the Gallery, among others), she recreates "verbatim" conversations with Samuel. She does this in order to create the illusion that her readers are eavesdropping on the actual moment of inception of a great idea. As "witnesses" to events, we should be able to make a clear assessment about which of them should be given credit as the prime mover. But Henrietta constructs her dialogues so ingeniously as to make such a judgment impossible. Ideas begin with one but are then taken up and given form by the other. In the end, we must accept her view that the achievement was neither his nor hers, but their joint work. These episodes in the *Life* are juxtaposed with others that retell their separate work. For example, Henrietta devotes an entire chapter to her own independent work for barrack school children and she felt so unfamiliar with Samuel's influence on university reform that she asked one of his protégés, R.H. Tawney, to write the chapter. The total effect reinforces Henrietta's view that marriage respects and encourages individuality even as it creates harmonious and productive solidarity among unlike types of people.

This conception of marriage mirrored and perhaps helped to shape her vision of social relations as a whole. Her ideas about the benefits of gender difference in marriage elided into her views on class difference in society. She believed that differences between the sexes were innate and salutary, but her own persona, her partnership with Samuel, and her public work contradicted the simple bipolarities of male and female. So, too, she (and Samuel) accepted class difference as an inalterable and potentially enriching fact of modern life. Her (and Samuel's) "practicable socialism" never hinted at a more Utopian longing for a classless society; and she was, compared to Samuel, less democratic and more intolerant of others. Her disparaging attitudes towards her Jewish neighbors in Whitechapel and Blacks in the United States contrasted markedly with her faith in the essential goodness of the English working class.[56] But in their work, they both decried the segregation and alienation of classes from one another and struggled to forge a common culture that would bind all sorts and conditions of people together.

The Barnetts never doubted for a moment that elites, men and women like themselves, were the rightful arbiters of the content of this unifying culture, what Matthew Arnold had called the "best that had been thought and said." However, Henrietta, perhaps more fully than Samuel, also argued that the values she associated with the working class were indispensable to the moral health of society. Loyalty, generosity to others in need, mutual aid and communal solidarity were the special gifts that the working class (even the most demoralized prostitutes) had to offer elite men and women blinded by their pursuit of wealth and status. The creation and supervision of the Hampstead Garden Suburb, which preoccupied the decades of her widowhood, celebrated the ways in which differences among people – differences in class, occupation, sex, marital status, age and even physical capacities – could be knit together to create a vibrant society. Henrietta insisted that the Garden Suburb set aside affordable housing for spinsters, the elderly, disabled veterans, rich and poor alike.[57]

The Barnetts' marriage partnership also illuminates the relationship between men's and women's philanthropic and social welfare activities. The practice of charity, like so much else in Victorian society, was endowed with gender-specific attributes. Men like Samuel Barnett expressed their discomfort with a hardened, disengaged bourgeois manliness by their attraction to certain features of Victorian culture that were coded "feminine."[58] Perceptions of Samuel's feminine nature cannot be dissociated from his championship of a "feminine" style of philanthropy, one that gave greater weight to "right" feeling than to doing. Both Samuel and Henrietta stressed the centrality of personal ties, friendship, and neighborhood as bulwarks against the impersonal forces of the market, bureaucratization and urbanization. If Toynbee Hall resembled an Oxbridge college transplanted into the heart of Whitechapel, it was also self-consciously a domestic space whose occupants were encouraged to see themselves as members of an extended, albeit unnatural, family. The artificiality of Toynbee Hall's domestic arrangements – it was a transitory and all-male household – in part inspired Henrietta to build the Hampstead Garden Suburb. The suburb, with its carefully planned mingling of different kinds of people and dwellings, expressed in bricks and mortar Henrietta's belief that the architecture of private life was essential to the production of the public good. Toynbee Hall, and even more insistently, the Suburb, expressed the Barnetts' view of the ways in which domestic arrangements and relationships ought to influence public welfare and social life.

The ease with which Henrietta and Samuel moved between largely single-sex charitable networks calls attention to the distinct but also interlocking character of men's and women's charity in late Victorian England.[59] Samuel's all-male world of Toynbee Hall functioned alongside the (virtually) all-female work of mothers' meetings, rent-collecting and parish visiting superintended by Henrietta. "My wife and I had a great deal to do with starting Toynbee Hall, my wife quite as much as myself," he insisted. "That always has to be remembered. In such a work the woman element, which is sometimes forgotten, is often, after all, the most potent."[60]

The Barnetts' marriage and their ideas about social reform outline a quintessentially Victorian pattern of transgression but also recuperation of public and private gender and class roles. Let me examine this pattern first in relation to their views of gender roles and then turn to class relations. By representing their marriage within the traditional framework of complementarity, the Barnetts and their contemporaries mimimized the disruptive possibilities of their ambiguous sexual personas. Henrietta's social motherhood on behalf of working-class children and youths not only conformed to larger patterns of female philanthropy in the nineteenth century, but also appeared to rectify the most glaring irregularity in her private life: her failure to be a "real" mother and produce offspring.

At a time when Edwardian feminists like Cicely Hamilton linked marriage to women's involuntary servitude,[61] Henrietta saw her marriage not as a site of oppression but as one of liberation, self-expression and achievement. Her partnership with Samuel emphatically affirmed the Victorian ideal of the compatibility of marriage and morals. As Henrietta Rowland's sacrificial acceptance of Samuel's marriage proposal was meant to illustrate, private duty was the wellspring of public life – and, in this case, of personal fulfillment and happiness as well.

We find a similar pattern of transgression and recuperation in their ideas about class roles in society. The Barnetts' jeremiads, individually and as a couple, against the callous indifference of the wealthy toward the needs of the poor appeared to threaten but ultimately reaffirmed the worth and status of their class and its culture. After all, it was men and women like the Barnetts who presumed to define what culture was, and what it was not. And Henrietta never questioned her right to instruct and superintend the lives of the domestic servants and fallen girls whom she wooed and exhorted to live righteously.

Henrietta and Samuel felt free to challenge so many of the accepted conventions and ideals of their time about relations between men and women and between social classes not in spite of, but because of their profound faith in the high Victorian values and aspirations they embodied. Marriage lay at the very heart of those values and aspirations. Not surprisingly, it was their fictive children – the children of the high Victorians – who could imagine no more fitting stage than the institution of marriage on which to perform their first acts of adult rebellion. In retrospect, we might surmise that it was this younger generation, and not their parents, who paid the higher price for their rebellion.

SETH KOVEN

HENRIETTA BARNETT'S DISAPPEARANCE FROM HISTORY

Henrietta wrote her *Life* to ensure her husband's place in history and her own as well. In July 1913, she unburdened herself to Jane Addams that "what now I feel chiefly is *torture of memory* of his long illness and all he suffered, and almost a terror in case it remains foremost and that the dear bright loving spirit shld be hidden by it." The act of writing was how Henrietta strove to "revivify his spirit." She wondered whether she was equal to the task of writing "his life" and quite explicitly acknowledged that writing "his life" was a means of helping her recapture her own life with him. She lamented that "the newspapers are too full of his doings, too little of his being wh. is what I shld try to write if I am worthy." She concluded that "we have so interwoven in our work that I feel *uncertain* of what I can do without him."[62]

Writing the *Life* was the first major task she undertook "without him." Its composition was a long, painful but therapeutic process for her and almost forms a subplot within the *Life*. She frequently interrupts the narrative to specify the time and circumstances under which she has written any given chapter.[63] At one point, she unfolds a bundle of letters about long forgotten, unhappy controversies and decides, seemingly at the very moment we read the passage, that the letters "will now be burnt."[64] These interjections not only amplify her and our active presence within the *Life* but redouble the nature of her authority over the representation of their lives. She asserts her irrevocable control not only over the actual documents which she has used to compose their lives, but their interpretation as well. If every marriage consists of two distinct marriages – and marriage stories as well – Henrietta ensured that only her authorized version would be available to posterity.

The peculiar and self-conscious *doppelgänger* form of the *Life* – the insistent presence of Henrietta's autobiographical narrative clothing Samuel's biography – must not be dismissed as merely a literary anomaly. It is also a revealing piece of historical evidence about her. The renowned child welfare reformer, Margaret McMillan, adopted a similar strategy of self-revelation and self-concealment when she inscribed her life story within her biography of her sister, *The Life of Rachel McMillan* (1927). Carolyn Steedman has recently argued that McMillan's choice of narrative form reflected her deeply rooted insecurity about herself, her social position and her self-worth. McMillan literally erased herself from old photographs so that she could depict Rachel standing alone.[65] Henrietta, by contrast, included as many photographs of herself as she did of Samuel, and several of the two of them together. Her choice of narrative form reflected no lack of self-esteem, but rather her immense

46

self-confidence that Samuel's story could not be understood apart from her contributions.

"My friends often ask me to write my reminiscences," Henrietta explained in 1930, "but I do not do so for many reasons." "For forty years, 1873–1913, I spent my life with Canon Barnett, and in writing his biography, I had perforce to chronicle much in which I was concerned." After listing over twenty-five significant initiatives with which she was intimately associated with Samuel as either "playwright" or "actor," she concluded,

> I have all my life felt honoured by the close co-operation between my husband and myself, and have no wish to disentangle it now, and as I had to tell of these activities in his "Life," it is neither possible nor desirable for me to write my biography or deal with them again.[66]

For Henrietta, autobiography threatened to negate, to violate, the guiding principle of her life and its representation in her *Life*: her vision of marriage as a union of unlike but "interdependent" and complementary equals.

Posterity, however, did not scruple to represent the Canon without Henrietta. The many historians who have mined Henrietta's *Life* for information about class relations and social reform in Victorian and Edwardian Britain are in effect accessories to Henrietta's disappearance from history. By contradicting Henrietta's own vision of her equal partnership with Samuel, they have imposed precisely those hierarchical assumptions about women and men that the Barnetts worked so hard to undermine.

Henrietta Barnett's removal from history has its own history which can be poignantly illustrated by two short vignettes. The first illustrates a seemingly willful misrepresentation of Henrietta, the second, an extraordinary imaginative act of erasure. William Beveridge, the father of the postwar welfare state, paid fulsome homage to Canon Barnett's influence over his life in his autobiography. At the end of his chapter, almost as an afterthought, he included a short paragraph about Henrietta.

> The Canon had with him another creature of equal force. As curate of a fashionable church in Kensington he had been offered the vicarage of St Jude's at the moment when he and Henrietta Rowland, devoted to country pursuits and pleasures, were coming together. So he took Henrietta to look at Whitechapel and she decided then and there both that she would marry him and that he must accept the offer. It is a heartening story of young courage. We young people of the Canon's House often spoke irreverently of Henrietta, but our irreverence was a cloak for profound respect.[67]

2 Henrietta and Samuel Barnett, portrait by Hubert von Herkomer (1908)

Beveridge seems to have intentionally overlooked Henrietta's prior social action and her central role in the Barnetts' joint work.[68]

Even more striking, however, is the posthumous divorce of Henrietta and Samuel enacted by another former Toynbee Hall man, the journalist Henry Nevinson. Like Beveridge, Nevinson devoted a chapter of his autobiography to his Whitechapel experiences and to Samuel Barnett's influence on him. To help his readers visualize Samuel, Nevinson described two portraits of the Canon. He contrasted G.F. Watts's portrait, which captured Samuel's "impatient expression" with Hubert von Herkomer's. Herkomer, he explained, "caught the interested and almost benign, though half-satiric, smile with which he [Samuel] listened to something humourous or outrageously paradoxical."[69]

What Nevinson did not tell us is that Herkomer's canvas, like Henrietta's *Life*, is a double portrait of Samuel and Henrietta Barnett. Just as Nevinson never mentioned Henrietta in his autobiography, so too he chose to ignore her presence in the Herkomer portrait – an exclusion reproduced in historical writing.[70]

Yet Henrietta, at least as much as Samuel, is the active focus of Herkomer's picture. Samuel stands behind his seated wife and gazes gently at and beyond the viewer to the unseen spiritual world. Henrietta, by contrast, strikes an attitude that combines thought and action. In a characteristic gesture,[71] her right hand touches her face suggesting a moment of inspiration. Her left hand draws the eye to papers dealing with the realization of an ambitious idea, the creation of the Hampstead Garden Suburb. When the Prime Minister, H.H. Asquith, came to Toynbee Hall to unveil the portrait, he told the audience that "it was a happy thought that has united Mr and Mrs Barnett's portraits in one picture, for united they always have been in their ideals, in their work for this parish, for London and for England; happily united in their love of, and confidence in, one another."[72] Herkomer's portrait and Asquith's speech perfectly captured Henrietta's fondest vision of her marriage and social reform. The day of its unveiling must have deeply gladdened her. It is a portrait that we need to look at once again; critically, to be sure, but also with new eyes.

NOTES

My thanks to the Spencer Foundation for supporting me at the time I researched and wrote this essay and the Osrins for housing me. Susan Pedersen provided very effective editing, and comments by Nancy Hensler, Adele Lindenmeyr, Lucy McDiarmid, Sonya Michel, Janet Oppenheim, Chris Waters and Judith Walkowitz in various ways helped me clarify my thoughts.

1 This is how Beatrice [Potter] Webb began her brilliant portrait of Henrietta Barnett in *My Apprenticeship*, London, Longman, 1926, p. 204.

2 Henrietta Barnett, *Canon Barnett, His Life, Work and Friends*, cheap American edition in one volume, New York, Putnam, 1921, p. 37. Hereafter, this work is cited as *Life*.

3 See "Passionless Reformers," *Fortnightly Review*, August 1882, reprinted in *Practicable Socialism*, London, Longman, 1888. On the private and public dynamics of romance, social and sexual reform in the 1880s, see Judy Walkowitz, "Science, Feminism and Romance: the Men and Women's Club, 1885–1889," *History Workshop Journal*, no. 21, Spring 1986, pp. 37–59. For a richly contextualized analysis of women's public and private roles within marriage, see M. Jeanne Peterson, *Family, Love and Work in the Lives of Victorian Gentlewomen*, Bloomington, Indiana, Indiana University Press, 1989.

4 This is how she described herself in a letter to her American tour promoters. Henrietta Barnett to Mr Adams and Mr Buckley, 1 March 1920, Jane Addams Memorial Collection, University of Illinois, Chicago Circle.

5 "Dame Henrietta Barnett's 81st Birthday", in *City and East London Observer*, 7 May 1932.

6 She has received some attention for her work as founder of the Hampstead Garden Suburb. For two helpful works written by women associated with the suburb, see Katherine Slack, *Henrietta's Dream, A Chronicle of the Hampstead Garden Suburb 1905–1982*, London, K.M. Slack, 1982; and Brigid Grafton Green, *Hampstead Garden Suburb 1907–1977*, London, Hampstead Garden Residents' Association, 1977.

7 Her omission from Olive Banks' *The Biographical Dictionary of British Feminists*, vol. I, *1800–1930*, Brighton, Wheatsheaf, 1985, is noteworthy since she satisfies fully Banks' extremely loose and expansive definition of feminism.

8 Hill's family destroyed the letters that detailed her broken engagement with Edward Bond. See Gillian Darley, *Octavia Hill. A Life*, London, Constable, 1990.

9 There is an excellent literature on single women in Britain, including Sheila Jeffreys, *The Spinster and Her Enemies: Feminism and Sexuality, 1880–1930*, London, Pandora, 1985; and Martha Vicinus, *Independent Women: Work and Community for Single Women 1850–1920*, London, Virago, 1985.

10 See Patricia Hollis, *Ladies Elect: Women in English Local Government 1865–1914*, Oxford, Clarendon Press, 1987.

11 Henrietta Barnett, "Education by the Press," A radio talk between Dame Henrietta Barnett and the Right Hon. Viscount Burnham, 27 July 1926, transcript reprinted in Henrietta Barnett, *Matters that Matter*, London, John Murray, 1930, p. 258.

12 Frances Power Cobbe, "What Shall We Do With Our Old Maids?", *Fraser's Magazine*, November, 1862, reprinted in Frances Power Cobbe, *Essays on the Pursuits of Women*, London, Emily Faithfull, 1863.

13 "Note by Henrietta Barnett," October 1929, in Henrietta Barnett, *Matters*, p. 150. In the *Life* she claims to have spent "four short terms" at the school; p. 116.

14 In the *Life*, she attributes her first philanthropic initiatives to the Haddon sisters who ran her school; p. 116.

15 On Hinton, see Ellice Hopkins, *Life and Letters of James Hinton*, London, Kegan and Paul, 1878, esp. pp. 290–6 on Whitechapel. On Caroline Haddon's relationship with Hinton, see Caroline Haddon, *The Larger Life: Studies in Hinton's Ethics*, London, Kegan and Paul, 1886; *A Law of Development. An Essay*, London, J. Haddon, 1883; and *James Hinton, Philosophy and Religion*, ed. Caroline Haddon, London, Kegan and Paul, 1881.

16 Octavia Hill to Rev. W.H. Fremantle, 1 November 1874, Hill Papers, British Library of Political and Economic Science (BLPES).

17 H. Barnett, *Life*, pp. 37–8.

18 *Morning Post*, 6 December 1918.

19 One reviewer, James Douglas, commented that "as a rule, the widow-biographer is a tiresome hypocrite who whitewashes all the human nature in her victim. Mrs Barnett has broken all the traditions of widowhood. She has taken her readers into her confidence and shown them her husband and herself as they really were during their marvellous life of service." *The Star*, 24 January 1919.

20 H. Barnett, *Life*, p. 53.

21 Ibid., p. 65.

22 Ibid., p. 43.

23 Ibid., p. 59.

24 On her work with Ruskin and his influence on her, see C.E. Maurice, ed., *The Life of Octavia Hill*, London, Macmillan, 1914.

25 Mrs Samuel A. Barnett, *The Making of the Home, A Reading-Book of Domestic Economy for School and Home Use*, London, Cassell, 1885, pp. 1–5.

26 Henrietta Barnett, "The Place of Women in the Established Church," *Westminster Gazette*, 23 March 1921, reprinted in *Matters*, p. 343.

27 *Opinions of Various Women on Women's Suffrage*, London, National Society for Women's Suffrage, 1879, pp. 11–12.

28 The contrast between Henrietta's response to marriage and Beatrice Potter's two decades later is instructive. For Potter, marriage to Sidney Webb completed her move away from the community of the "working sisterhood" of spinster social reformers in East London and signalled her entrance into the masculine world of social scientific research. See Deborah Nord, *The Apprenticeship of Beatrice Webb*, Amherst, University of Massachusetts Press, 1985, chapter 5; and Jane Lewis, *Women and Social Action in Victorian and Edwardian England*, Aldershot, Edward Elgar, 1991, ch. 2.

29 Norman and Jeanne MacKenzie, eds, *The Diary of Beatrice Webb*, vol. 1, *1873–1982*, London, Virago, 1982, entry for August 1887, p. 214.

30 H. Barnett, *Life*, p. 104.

31 *Diary of Beatrice Webb*, vol. 1, p. 214.

32 Butler made her Anglican minister husband, George, a central figure in her account of the moment she launched her Crusade for Repeal. It is his words, "Go! and God be with you," that tacitly give her permission. See Millicent Garrett Fawcett and E.M. Turner, *Josephine Butler*, London, Association for Moral and Social Hygiene, 1927, p. 46. See also George W. Johnson and Lucy Johnson, eds, *Josephine Butler, An Autobiographical Memoir*, Bristol, J.W. Arrowsmith, 1915, pp. 78–9.

33 Besant's husband, like Butler's, plays a key role in her own account of her social awakening. Her own ignorance of sex and her distaste for her husband was the "terrible shock" that contributed to her disastrous marriage. See Constance Rover, *Love, Morals and the Feminists*, London, Routledge and Kegan Paul, 1970, p. 111.

34 H. Barnett, *Life*, p. 211.

35 Ibid., p. 209.

36 Ibid., p. 102.

37 Octavia Hill to Henrietta Barnett, 26 December 1873, Coll. Misc. 512, BLPES.

38 Hill to Henrietta Barnett, 29 March 1876, Coll. Misc. 512, BLPES.

39 H. Barnett, *Life*, p. 757.

40 This silence is not surprising especially since Henrietta wrote a detailed physiology text, *The Making of the Body, A Children's Book on Physiology and Anatomy*, London, Longman, 1894, that makes no mention of the genital or excretory organs.

41 On liberal principles, Samuel supported Bradlaugh and Besant's right of free publication even though he deplored their ideas on birth control. He held "all methods wrong except self-control." H. Barnett, *Life*, p. 195.

42 Henrietta Barnett to Jane Addams, 10 July 1913, Jane Addams Papers, Swarthmore College Peace Collection.

43 Henrietta called women "the mother sex" in "Women as Philanthropists" in Theodore Stanton, ed., *The Woman Question in Europe*, New York, G.P. Putnam's Sons, 1884, p. 109.

44 Mrs Samuel A. Barnett, *How to Mind the Baby*, London, 1887, pp. 12–13.

45 John Northcote, "Introductory, Dame Henrietta Octavia Barnett, D.B.E." in H. Barnett, *Matters*, p. 2.

46 See Harold Spender, "Barnett the Sower," *Contemporary Review*, January, 1919, p. 33.

47 This was how Henrietta described Fanny in a short printed notice at the time of Fanny's death. Archives of the Hampstead Garden Suburb, Folder of printed miscellany.

48 When Dorothy died in late adolescence, Henrietta movingly recalled "the desolate pain of sorrowing parents." H. Barnett, *Life*, pp. 533–7.

49 C.R. Ashbee, Journals, 28 June 1886, King's College, Cambridge.

50 Beatrice Webb, *My Apprenticeship*, p. 205.

51 George Peabody Gooch, *Under Six Reigns*, London, Longmans Green, 1958, p. 63.

52 H. Barnett, *Life*, pp. 11, 25, 56.

53 Ibid., p. 107.

54 On her audacity, see ibid., pp. 305, 510. On her independent judgment and disagreements with Samuel, see pp. 194, 198, 202.

55 *New Statesman*, 18 January 1919.

56 Henrietta's attitudes towards Jews and Blacks were complex and disturbing. She saw both groups as complicating and perhaps even compromising any national identity across class lines. While she adored her Jewish brother-in-law, Ernest Hart, she used racist categories and language in describing both Jews and Blacks. She lamented the density of Jews in Whitechapel, writing Jane Addams that she "loved them not" because of their selfishness. Henrietta Barnett to Jane Addams, 13 September 1924, Jane Addams Papers, Swarthmore College. Proximity seems to have hardened her prejudices. The Warden of Toynbee Hall in 1917 reported that, "With regard to the Jews, Mrs Barnett has suggested some frigid scheme of demarcation by which they should use the place within certain stated hours. This is absolutely impracticable." E.F. Hitchcock to Lord Milner, 19 October 1917, A/Toy/6, Toynbee Hall Papers, Greater London Record Office. See also, "The Toynbee Halls of America," *Cornhill Magazine*, March 1921, where she discusses the problems of making racially and ethnically different peoples into Americans.

57 Consistent with the pattern of overlooking Henrietta's contributions is Delores Hayden's treatment of the "spinsters' quadrangle" at the Hampstead Garden Suburb, Waterlow Court. See *The Grand Domestic Revolution*, Cambridge, MIT Press, 1982, p. 237. Hayden mentions the architect, M.H. Baillie Scott, but not Henrietta, although the buildings reflected her longstanding commitment to single women.

58 My thanks to Judy Walkowitz for comments on this point. See Frank Prochaska on the distribution of philanthropic tasks by sex in *Women and Philanthropy in Nineteenth Century England*, Oxford, Clarendon Press, 1980. On the feminine character of Samuel's charitable ideal, see Emily Klein Abel, "Toynbee Hall, 1884–1914," *Social Service Review*, 53, 1979, pp. 609–10.

59 Their social reform work therefore does not support the recent description of men and women's charity in the nineteenth century as delineating "parallel power structures." See Kathleen McCarthy, "Parallel Power Structures: Women and the Voluntary Sphere," in McCarthy, ed., *Lady Bountiful Revisited*, New Brunswick, Rutgers University Press, 1990.

60 H. Barnett, *Matters*, p. 2.

61 Cicely Hamilton, *Marriage as a Trade*, 1909, rpt London, The Women's Press, 1987.

62 Henrietta Barnett to Jane Addams, 10 July 1913, Swarthmore College Peace Collection, Jane Addams Papers.

63 For examples, see H. Barnett, *Life*, pp. 100, 283, 714.

64 Ibid., p. 267.

65 For a brilliant analysis of autobiography in general and McMillan's in particular, see Carolyn Steedman, "Biographical Questions, Fictions of the Self," Part Three, in *Childhood, Culture and Class in Britain: Margaret McMillan, 1860–1931*, New Brunswick, Rutgers University Press, 1990; also Deborah Nord, *The Apprenticeship of Beatrice Webb*, ch. 3.

66 "Foreword," in H. Barnett, *Matters*, pp. vi–vii.

67 Lord Beveridge, *Power and Influence*, London, Hodder and Stoughton, 1953, p. 38.

68 Beveridge's treatment of Henrietta in *Power and Influence* is particularly odd in light of his much more balanced assessment several years earlier in his *Voluntary Action*, London, Allen and Unwin, 1948, pp. 179–80.

69 Henry Wood Nevinson, *Changes and Chances*, London, Nisbet, 1923, pp. 87–8.

70 Historians have all too willingly followed Beveridge's and Nevinson's lead. A recent six-hundred page Harvard doctoral dissertation on the settlement movement, of which perhaps a third is devoted to issues of gender, never seriously evaluates Henrietta's ideas or contribution to the movement. See Seth Koven, "Culture and Poverty," Ph.D., Harvard, 1987; also, Standish Meacham, *Toynbee Hall and Social Reform 1880–1914: The Search for Community*, New Haven, Yale University Press, 1987. Asa Briggs and Anne Macartney give a slightly fuller sense of Henrietta's role in *Toynbee Hall, The First Hundred Years*, London, Routledge and Kegan Paul, 1984. Martha Vicinus mentions Henrietta's role in the origins of the Women's University Settlement but implicitly credits Samuel with the ideas and management of Toynbee Hall. See *Independent Women*, ch. 6. Even A.M. McBriar's study of marriage partnerships and social politics, *An Edwardian Mixed Doubles: The Bosanquets versus the Webbs*, Oxford, Clarendon, 1987, pays remarkably little attention to the Barnetts and subordinates Henrietta to Samuel.

71 Henrietta was often photographed in later life with one hand positioned thoughtfully on her cheek or chin and the other resting on some kind of book or document. For examples, see the photographs attached to two long feature articles about her: Marjorie Shuler, "Half Hours with Interesting Women, Canon Barnett's Wife Tells of the Hampstead Housing Plan," *The Woman Citizen, A Weekly Chronicle of Progress*, 1 January 1921; Florence Low, "The Home of the Woman Who Built a Garden City," *Queen*, 23 December 1931.

72 Barnett, *Life*, pp. 756–7.

3 G.A. Lefroy

2

George Alfred Lefroy 1854–1919
A bishop in search of a church
Jeffrey Cox

After George Alfred Lefroy's death in Calcutta on New Year's Day in 1919, the obituaries and memorial sermons spoke of him as an influential man. It might be said that his entire life had been intended to produce that description, for the idea of influence dominated to an extraordinary degree the rhetoric of Lefroy and of the movements and institutions that he represented. The *Delhi Mission News* described him as "one of those Christian lads from our great English public schools of whom Archbishop Benson once said: 'The army of heaven which follows the Son of Man on white horses has no more fair, more beautiful recruits.' "[1] After leaving Cambridge for Delhi in 1879, he ascended the ecclesiastical hierarchy in India, from Head of the Cambridge Mission to Delhi, to Bishop of Lahore, finally becoming Bishop of Calcutta and Metropolitan of India, first among equals of the Bishops of the Anglican Ecclesiastical Establishment.

Although disestablished in Ireland and Wales, the Anglican church remained an established church in India, performing important ritual and rhetorical functions for the government in return for considerable subsidy. The *Tribune* of Lahore, a nationalist newspaper that had followed Lefroy's career, mourned "the passing away of so true-hearted an Englishman," and quoted Lord Morley's comments on Lefroy in a letter to the Viceroy of 1908: "Yesterday the Bishop of Lahore called, one of the most attractive men I ever met. In the midst of a rather heavy day, he not only interested but excited me and carried me for a while into the upper ether. Why did you not recommend him to be Lieutenant Governor of the Punjab? There is an experiment for you. His ideas delighted me."[2]

The Times of London attributed to him influence extending beyond the high circles of government to the religious elites of India: "The Mahomedans held the late Metropolitan in especial esteem, and he was one of the few Europeans who have been invited by the Maulvies to

55

visit the mosques and discuss religious questions with them. His rare linguistic gifts and wide knowledge of the religions of India gave him great influence among all classes."[3] According to *The Mission Field*, "he seemed to have the gift of thinking like an oriental."[4] The journal of the Society for the Propagation of the Gospel, *East and West*, stressed Lefroy's devotion to India, citing as evidence of self-sacrifice the fact that he had not only lived there but, like many other Bishops of Calcutta, died there.[5] (Lefroy had at least avoided the fate of one of his predecessors, Bishop Cotton, who slipped on the gangway to a boat and drowned in the holy waters of the Ganges.)

The pious conventions of eulogy make obituaries an unlikely source for critical judgments on the significance of a person's influence, but there is considerable continuity between judgments made about Lefroy before and after his death. Late Victorian clergymen possessed a sturdy sense of self-confidence about their ability to influence those around them. The sheer physical presence of a clergyman in a poor parish was believed by nineteenth-century Anglican partisans to have a beneficial moral effect. The moral improvement, they felt, would be even greater in parts of the world lacking several centuries of exposure to Christian influence. Early in Lefroy's career, a former headmaster of Rugby predicted success from Lefroy's residence in Delhi, for it was impossible to think that "men of such high quality, so devout, so earnest, so disinterested, so intelligent, should live years there without making a deep and durable impression."[6]

By the time of Lefroy's death, however, such sweeping claims for Christian influence were becoming increasingly unpersuasive outside of missionary and government circles. As the smoke settled from the Amritsar massacre in the spring of 1919, it would have been difficult to think of an institution farther from the minds of most Indians than the Anglican church in India, or a person more remote than the Metropolitan of India. The entire missionary enterprise, then at its peak strength, had been judged and found marginal by educated Indians and excluded from the rhetoric of India's national movement in any role except as notably presumptuous agents of imperial arrogance. This judgment has found its way into the writing of Indian nationalist and post-nationalist history, where missionaries only appear in lists of "dominant foreign groups" such as "British officials of the colonial state and foreign industrialists, merchants, financiers, planters, landlords and missionaries."[7] There is no recognized scholarly rhetoric for the history of imperialism in a post-imperial age that does not either run the risk of sounding neo-imperial, thereby losing almost any conceivable audience, or treat the cultural legacy of colonialism as an undifferentiated "other," or reduce all aspects of western culture in an imperial context to one of several "masks of conquest."[8]

The dismissive judgments of educated Indians were spreading even among missionaries during Lefroy's last years in India. Lefroy had been one of the key figures in an ambitious late Victorian attempt to extend the influence of the Church of England to India: the Cambridge Mission to Delhi, affiliated with the Society for the Propagation of the Gospel (SPG). Writing in the SPG's journal *East and West*, a veteran missionary summarized the predicament of the missionary movement in 1920: "We are asked to accept the sweeping dictum that the West, because it has been the West, has failed, and must fail, in the interpretation and manifestation of Christ to the East, that the Christ shown forth by the Englishman is, almost necessarily, a strangely disfigured and weirdly Anglo-Saxon representation of our Lord which no Eastern nation, with its finer spiritual intuitions, and its firmer religious grasp, could possibly expect to receive."[9] This he blamed on "those in Britain who complain that the whole relationship of Great Britain with India now ... is one miserable failure," and portray eastern culture "in such glowing terms that no one would possibly want to be a foreign missionary."[10] Even before Lefroy's death one of the Cambridge Mission's most talented recruits, C.F. Andrews, had resigned. In an eloquent and moving parting sermon in Lahore Cathedral in 1914, he condemned the mission for its complicity with imperial rule, and asked whether "the modern, aggressive wealthy nations of the world, armed to the teeth against each other, trafficking in the souls of men for gain, can be for long the dwelling place of the meek and lowly Christ."[11] God's work in India, Andrews argued, lay with the nationalist movement, not the missionary movement, with Tagore and Gandhi rather than Lefroy.[12]

In England many educated men and women had also concluded by 1920 that religion had little influence in the modern world, but for different reasons. Very few people regarded the institutional decline of the Protestant churches in England as in any way puzzling or exceptional or in need of explanation. The rapid decline in church attendance was explained by the deeply rooted Eurocentric conviction that the decline of religion is a natural part of the historical development of every society in the modern world, a consequence of the secularization of thought or the progress of scientific and utilitarian assumptions about social organization. The churches were part of the colorful or menacing or hypocritical apparatus of Victorianism, perhaps, but they belonged to the past century. Serious inquiry into the nature and causes of religious change became the victim of secular habits of thought, which marginalized all religion in the twentieth century and with it the missionary movement.

In India it was difficult to argue, with any plausibility, that religion in general was unimportant or likely to become unimportant soon. That India was "caste-ridden" was an axiom of almost all western thought about India, and of much progressive nationalist thought in India as well. Furthermore, Hindu–Muslim tension over politics kept religious issues prominent in public debate. The failure of Christianity in India was thus seen not as the inevitable corollary of a wider secularization, but rather as the failure of the missionary movement to influence decisively the history of India. This failure was in part a question of conversions, or the lack of them. The Christian community in India had been growing more rapidly than any other religion since the 1880s, but missionaries were the victims of their own optimism. The slogan of the Anglo-American Student Christian Movement, "The conversion of the world in this generation," had created expectations which made even mass conversions appear insignificant. Furthermore, in India a large number of people may form a small percentage of the population.

The Cambridge Mission had an extraordinarily dismal record of failure at converting Indians, taking four years to baptize even one adult convert after the arrival of the first missionaries. Delhi was the only major north Indian city with a declining Indian Christian population in the 1880s. Yet the important question was one of influence rather than numbers: the Cambridge missionaries, although hoping for converts, principally sought to affect the course of national life through their association with an Indian social and educational elite. As this elite repudiated the imperialism with which the church was also associated, however, the Anglican missionaries' influence became difficult to discern. Lefroy himself admitted in 1906, in his Third Triennial Charge to the Diocese of Lahore, that the British in India and educated Indians have "come to a parting of ways."[13] In 1914 a senior student at St Stephen's College, which Lefroy had helped to found in the 1880s, commented that "the period of decline in the progress of Christianity among educated Indians is, curiously enough, contemporaneous with the birth and growth of a national consciousness in India."[14] C.F. Andrews was only responding to broader public opinion with his verdict that educated Indians had consigned the missionary movement to the imperial establishment and ultimately to the dustbin of history. Just as serious inquiry into religion has been obscured by the secularization of thought in Europe, so has serious inquiry into the importance of the missionary enterprise in India been hampered by its association with imperialism, a discredited cause.

Lefroy's attempt to export late Victorian clerical and academic culture to India through the Cambridge Mission to Delhi appears to have been one of history's blind alleys. But if his career was a failure, perhaps it was an instructive failure. Lefroy's behavior in India throws into sharp relief some aspects of the mind of the educated late Victorian elite. He and his colleagues were playing out an Indian imperial-clerical drama that reached its peak of influence at precisely the time when imperialism became discredited in India, and at a time when both imperialism and unembarrassed elitism became much more difficult to defend in Britain. The schools and hospitals that he and his colleagues created became important institutions in a very different India from the one that Lefroy had imagined. But the sheer durability of some missionary institutions, even in independent India, raises the possibility that Lefroy had a long-term influence of a kind anticipated by no one, and therefore difficult to recognize.

I

Lefroy was born in 1854 in Ireland, where his family was prominent in an institution described by Macaulay as "the most absurd ecclesiastical establishment that the world has ever seen,"[15] the Church of Ireland. He was sent to Marlborough and then went up to Trinity College, Cambridge, where he fell in with the religious set, frequenting meetings of the Cambridge University Church Society and the Cambridge Graduates Mission Aid Society, and teaching in one of the most important missionary recruiting grounds of late Victorian England, the Jesus Lane Sunday School. In this atmosphere, orientalist scholarship and missionary idealism blended to produce a vision of a special mission from Cambridge to the Orient, a vision which would produce a new reinterpretation of Christianity based on oriental insights, but valuable for Europeans as well. Presiding over this enterprise was the Regius Professor of Divinity, B.F. Westcott, who believed that "the Universities are providentially fitted to train men who shall interpret the Faith of the West to the East and bring back to us new illustrations of the one infinite and eternal Gospel."[16]

Westcott's influence extended into many worlds other than his special field of biblical scholarship. He promoted Anglican social Christianity, advocated an active role for the church in social reform at home, and used the insights of his biblical scholarship to outline a missionary-oriented ecclesiastical orientalism. In his missionary lectures, he encouraged idealistic undergraduates to think in terms of recreating the achievements of the Alexandrian School of the second and third centuries. The Alexandrian theologians Clement and Origen had, in his view, used Greek thought to reinterpret the Christian message in a way intelligible to educated citizens of the Roman Empire. Westcott urged Cambridge undergraduates to travel to the banks of the Ganges or the Indus and use the wisdom of the East to convey the same message to educated Hindus and Muslims. The Greeks and Jews of the Classical World had been in some sense, he argued, orientals, and Cambridge missionaries were to exploit the oriental dimensions of Christianity in an appeal to the oriental mind.[17]

Six Cambridge men responded to proposals to establish a moderately high church, celibate brotherhood for missionary and literary work in India. They inaugurated the Cambridge Mission to Delhi with a breakfast at Pembroke College in 1877; two years later the same six met in Delhi "for breakfast and a truly 'common' life."[18] Lefroy and his friend, S.S. Allnutt, became the effective leaders of the Delhi mission during its formative years. Both served in India for another forty years, dying within a year of each other. Lefroy plunged into Delhi with great self-confidence and conviction, bringing with him a mixture of imperial providentialism, Anglican clerical assumptions about the relationship between clergyman and parishioner, and Westcottian orientalist liberalism.

Westcott's ideas have much to commend them even from a late twentieth-century liberal point of view. His theories were part of a larger attempt in the nineteenth century to disentangle Christianity from western culture, not only for missionary purposes, but to allow a newly formulated Christianity to survive and even thrive in a pluralistic, secular society. Westcott encouraged insular Cambridge undergraduates to listen to other cultures instead of merely addressing them. He held out the prospect of a universal gospel unbounded by western civilization, a gospel which could only be discovered by extricating Christianity from western culture. Four of his sons served as missionaries in India. His calm approach to the modern world, whether it appeared in the form of German biblical scholarship or Durham trade unionism, helped to prevent the Church of England from lapsing into pure Tory reaction. In the iconography of late Victorian England, detractors of Westcott are difficult to find.[19]

However, one of the things that Edward Said has taught us is to cast a skeptical eye on western scholars who claim to be special friends of, or have special knowledge of, the non-western world. In some ways the more the Victorians learned about other religions, the less they understood, and Westcott understood hardly anything about Hinduism and even less about Indian society. He not only treated Indians as if they were Hellenistic Greeks, he avoided altogether questions of gender and caste which provided immediate dilemmas for Lefroy in Delhi. His male, clericalist imperial drama generated multiple levels of exclusion in the Cambridge Mission to Delhi, both in its rhetoric and in the allocation of power within institutions. That gender must have been an issue of overriding importance for Lefroy in his early years is not at all obvious from either the standard histories or the archival records of the Delhi mission, which are organized around records of men's work even though women missionaries outnumbered men by a factor of at least three to one.[20]

If the woman's voice has been excluded from missionary histories and even from the missionary archives, even more so has the Indian Christian voice, male and female. (It is also largely missing from nationalist and post-nationalist histories of India, a victim of its association with missionaries.) Yet Indian Christians were a presence, even if neither the classicist/orientalist view of Indians nor the traditions of Anglican parochial care and missionary practice provided any guidance for Lefroy's encounter with their community. In Delhi it is possible to see how Westcott's social Christianity took a more virulent form in an imperial setting, and also to see with great clarity the consequences of Victorian clerical professionalism, which has left the Church of England one of the most helpless and ineffective institutions in modern Europe. Lefroy never expected to find a community of Clements and Origens in Delhi, but as Westcott's disciple he hoped to find a community of potential Clements and Origens, and the Delhi Christian community could hardly have provided a more striking disappointment.

II

In the 1880s Lefroy found himself with parochial responsibility for several hundred Anglican Christians drawn from the outcaste leather-worker community, the Chamars. They had become Christians in the 1860s and 1870s as a result of work by an SPG missionary, R.R. Winter. As Lefroy's predecessor, Winter had adopted a relatively relaxed and tolerant set of requirements for Christian Chamars who were actively incorporating some elements of Christianity into their communal life. Winter had set up chapels in the Chamar Christian community scattered around Delhi, and had hired leaders designated as "catechists" who carried out minor parochial functions, acted as conduits for small amounts of missionary patronage, and endured a certain amount of anti-clericalism from Chamar Christians, who repeated proverbs about the easy lives of their catechists.[21] They were also facilitators for worship, and co-authors and composers with the missionaries of the Christian hymns, or bhajans. Missionaries were as bored with the details of Chamar hymnody as they were with Chamar social structure, leaving us with little information about bhajans, but it is clear that song was from the first the main attraction of Chamar worship services and the primary focus of Chamar Christian piety.[22]

Lefroy's first accounts of Chamar Christians show a mixture of Anglican clerical attitudes to poor parishioners exacerbated by stereotypes about the Indian national character. In June of 1880 he attended a Chamar worship service in Daryaganj, where the largest Christian community lived. "Of the melody," Lefroy wrote, "I shall not easily forget the impression they made on me the first night I heard them. . . . I am compelled to hope that the people won't get really excited over them as they sometimes do."[23] Suspicious from the first about the motives of the Chamars, he encountered an inquirer after the service and called him into his presence: "We had better have a word with him if only to make sure that the catechist or reader has been regularly to see him during the week, and to find out what progress he has made – he knew about half the Lord's Prayer when I saw him last. 'Come here, Lai Singh, and say me the Lord's Prayer. That's better.' There is a good deal to be done still before he can be ready for baptism, but there is some progress."[24]

Soon Lefroy became convinced that Winter had gotten things off on the wrong track, and that the mission's association with the Chamars was "one more and most formidable obstacle to be added to all those which make our work in this country seem to be almost humanly hopeless."[25] When confronting Indian social distinctions, Lefroy thought naturally in terms of English social class. Anglican clergymen for the most part believed that Christian influence trickled down from the top of society. Consequently, the Indian culture that interested them could only be found among the Indian elite. They had never accustomed themselves to the new rules governing religion in a competitive market-place, where influence depends in part upon popular persuasion. When visiting a rural village with a small Chamar Christian community, Lefroy first tried to talk to the caste Hindu farmers, but they "told me most bluntly that they did not want me, I had better go to my friends the Chamars. And how much such rudeness means out here – how far more than it would in England – one sees when one remembers how naturally polite even to servility all the Hindoos are to any superior."[26]

Stung by this lack of deference, Lefroy plunged into a reorganization of the Chamar Christian community. In 1884 he published a graphic account of his dealings with the Chamars, a pamphlet entitled *The Leatherworkers of Daryaganj*,[27] which begins with an extensive apology for adopting this work with untouchables. He attributes the existence of a community of 800 Chamar Christians in Delhi to bribery by his predecessor during the famine of 1877–8. This was at least in part untrue, since Chamars began adopting Christianity in the 1860s – although the fact that many converted during the famine exposed their motives to suspicion both inside and outside the Christian and mission-ary community. The prevalent psychology of religious conversion in the nineteenth century was primitive and one-dimensional, allowing Lefroy and others to oversimplify the Christian Chamars' motives, which were as mixed and complex as those of the Cambridge Brothers.

Why then deal with them at all? Because, Lefroy reminds his readers, they are "in name Christians, and as such representing to the people of Delhi, high and low, rich and poor, the Church of Christ in this great city."[28] Like most nineteenth-century Protestant missionaries, Lefroy believed that the test of the truth of Christianity was its ability to transform society. The case for Christianity was not intellectual so much as moral, and the test of morality was its ability to improve both individual and social behavior. When he looked at the Chamars, however, he saw only degradation. If Christianity could succeed with the Chamars, it would "remove a stumbling block and a scandal which could not but most grievously affect any efforts which might hereafter be made."[29]

His extraordinary lack of curiosity about the Chamars was not shared by other British functionaries in India, who were in the process of trying to define their ideas of caste in ways that would facilitate a census of British India, redefine and recreate identities to suit orientalist social geography, and depict communal relationships in ways compatible with British rule.[30] In their accounts, the Chamars were a sprawling community that constituted both an occupational designation and a caste label. 1891 census-takers identified 1,156 Chamar sub-castes, and admitted that the category could hardly fit in with any conception of rigid or fixed caste divisions.

The large majority of Chamars were agricultural laborers in Punjab and Uttar Pradesh. Associated with leatherworking, some Chamars worked with leather, others with only certain kinds of leather, some with none at all. Some Chamars would tan but refuse to do other leatherwork; some made but refused to mend shoes; some ate carrion or beef or kept pigs, others did not. Some Chamar women worked as midwives, others would not. In Punjab the category of Mochi embraced all shoemakers, Chamar or not, and in some places meant Muslim Chamar. The Julahas, on the other hand, were defined by some as Chamars who weave, eat no carrion, touch no carcasses, and separate themselves entirely from the other sections of the Chamars. Most Julahas were Muslims, although some were Kabir-Panths, devotees of a sixteenth-century Hindi poet who had taught a Quaker-like resistance to all religious institutions.[31]

What these descriptions depict is an extraordinarily complex community that can hardly be reduced either to caste or occupation, and within which variously defined sub-groups struggled for comparative advantage through self-definition and redefinition. Furthermore, Lefroy's own account shows, however inadvertently, that Chamar Christianity was far more complicated than he claimed. The adoption of Christianity was not merely a question of missionary stimulus and Chamar response, but encompassed a genuine interest in theological egalitarianism that became part of a struggle for status by various groups within the Chamar community. How a Christian Chamar was to be defined in Daryaganj was a matter still to be determined when Lefroy arrived on the scene. What is clear is that the Christian Chamars of Daryaganj were defining Christianity in their own way, and had incorporated missionary patrons into their own social relationships (just as they had incorporated English hymn lyrics into their hymnody).

Lefroy found himself in charge of betrothals for the Christian Chamars, and complained that this took considerable time, although his condescending account of his activities betrays a certain relish for the job. Chamars who remained non-Christian continued some of their communal ties with baptized Chamars, who reciprocated by continuing to tolerate inter-marriage between non-Christian women and Christian men. Lefroy wanted to insure that Christian Chamars only married other Christians, and so began to keep a registry of the names of daughters aged between two and twelve of Christian families. He then tried to match each of them with a Christian boy who, in his account, had living parents or guardians, was lighter or at least no darker than the prospective partner, and was unconnected by either blood ties or friendship.

His fame as a matchmaker spread after he arranged a betrothal between a boy aged eight, and a girl aged six, perfect in all respects except for objections of the boy's father to Christian rites. Lefroy went to the village near Delhi to meet the entire adult male population, and in a two-hour meeting "urged my case so vigorously that in a couple of hours time a successful issue was reached, and the engagement there and then (in the absence it is true of the girl, but of what consequence was that?) formally completed."[32] Chamar Christian women had become objects of exchange in negotiations between Lefroy and Chamar Christian men.

In these activities Lefroy treated Indian Christians in a way that he might behave toward parishioners at home, with an ironic sense of affection for their shortcomings which is displayed in his account of his demise as a matchmaker: "This piece of successful diplomacy brought my fame as a matchmaker ... up to a fever heat, and applications for engagements flowed in apace. Unfortunately amid this press of business an accident, such as may occur in even the best managed institution, happened, which, for the moment at least, caused a complete reaction, for, by the slightest clerical error in the entry of the names in my book, I almost succeeded in bringing together in the important betrothal rite two young persons admirably matched in almost every other respect but both, by an amusing coincidence, of the male sex. For a time this unfortunate incident, causing, as it somehow seemed to do, a most unfavourable impression, completely stopped the run on my office."[33]

If Lefroy had retained his relatively relaxed attitude toward nominal Christianity, there is every reason to believe that the Chamar Christians would have settled into a routine position as one variety of Chamar in Daryaganj and, who knows, perhaps even seen further accessions. But another aspect of Lefroy's professional attitude toward parishioners came to the fore very quickly in his dealings with this stumbling-block. Only a small minority of the Christian Chamars were, he charged, "in any real way affected by their Christianity, the rest remaining in full fellowship with their caste, sharing in its feasts, idolatrous and otherwise, adhering to the old ceremonies of birth, marriage, death, wholly ignoring Sunday, etc. Christians in nothing but name."[34]

With some small effort of the imagination, that description could easily be applied to a Protestant parish in England, alcohol-soaked, snobbish to an idolatrous degree, and nominally Christian by anyone's definition. The Episcopal churches of the British Isles had a well-known record of attempting to drive away the poor, working people and other unfashionable groups with pew-rents and elitism. On the other hand, English Protestant parishioners doggedly made use of certain parochial services, including both rites of passage which were widely used by working people and public worship which was for the more prosperous, and had for centuries struggled to build up elaborate systems of defense against the authoritarian tendencies of their own clergymen. Clergymen had in turn developed as a matter of necessity a kind of ironic tolerance for nominal Christianity. In the Indian imperial setting, those defenses and restraints were gone, and so was the tolerance. Lefroy considered himself free to define who was and who was not a Christian, and expel from the community those who failed his own tests, i.e. to treat Indians in ways that he would no doubt have liked to treat parishioners at home.

Lefroy had originally rejected the practice of separate living quarters for Christian Chamars, arguing that the "mission compound" produced a "more or less exotic life" and dependence on the mission. Later he changed his mind, responding, he claimed, to the requests of the "best Christians" who begged us to "give them a place to themselves." The mission bought eight houses in Daryaganj, creating a Christian *basti* (neighborhood) and giving Lefroy control over religious and social practices as the price for admission to this housing. Consequently Lefroy was able to set the standards defining a Christian Chamar, which were: 1. observe Sunday as a day of rest; 2. use exclusively Christian rites for birth, marriage and death; 3. abstain from smoking intoxicating drugs.[35]

The natural outcome of this was, in his words, "a constant bickering between the different families as to what was and what was not consistent with their new and more distinctly Christian attitudes, each member being inclined to be very liberal in the concessions which he made to himself ... but very much the reverse where his neighbor was concerned."[36] Furthermore, the assumption of the role of landlord by the mission led to chronic landlord–tenant conflict, which Lefroy interpreted in the imperial terms natural to one with extensive knowledge of

Ireland. Some of the newly devout Chamar Christians proposed calling a caste meeting to renounce all ties defined as heathen. Lefroy portrayed this sentiment as spontaneous, or rather as the work of the Holy Spirit when he was out of town, but his own account makes it clear that he engineered the situation if not the circumstances. Many of the Christian Chamars were bitterly opposed to any division of the community along religious lines. Furthermore, non-Christian Chamars were for the most part perfectly content to live on good terms with baptized Chamars. They were resisting Lefroy's attempt to impose clear definitions of "caste" and "community" on them, but were swept along by the polarization caused by Lefroy's allies.

The showdown over communal definition occurred at an overnight meeting of the *panchayat* (council) of the three main Chamar divisions centered in Daryaganj, constituting according to Lefroy 10,000–12,000 males. Several hundred representatives convened at midnight in the Christian *basti*. Christian Chamars were apparently all in one of the divisions. After sweet drinks were served at 1 a.m., a group of Christians announced that in the future they would have nothing to do with the Chamar brotherhood as such. This provocative behavior by the more severe Christians elicited a strong response from non-Christian Chamar leaders who, after an hour or so of discussion, finally announced that there would be a sifting of Christians with a pot of Ganges water, which was procured with extraordinary speed. All Christians were requested to come forward and raise it to their foreheads. Those refusing would be ejected from the caste.

Lefroy and the other missionaries present, although pleased at the prospect of a parting of ways within the Chamar community, refused to take on the job of identifying the Christians, perhaps out of ignorance, but Chamar leaders had a clear enough sense of who was and was not a Christian to begin calling a list of names, summoning alleged Christians to raise the water or refuse. By 7:30 a.m. the process was complete, and only eight families of Christians remained to repair to the chapel for worship, with the status of eight or nine more still in doubt. Even after this process, the Chamar leaders did not press the question of immediate exclusion, and Lefroy grumbled that they had not been severe enough: "even in the case of those who definitely broke the bond, it turns out far more difficult than we had previously expected to say what they have given up and how they now stand."[37] In 1887 Lefroy complained that the nominal Christians outside the Christian *basti* (i.e. the mission property) were "a dead weight around our necks."[38] Another movement to purge the community was initiated, another *panchayat* of 500–600 held, another parting of the ways resulted, and only 50–60 Christian Chamars remained. "With a great sweep of the work of years," he wrote, "we start again anew with this remnant."[39]

It is difficult to avoid seeing in these events clear evidence of the severe competitive disadvantage that the Anglican churches have labored under in the modern marketplace of ideas and institutions as a result of the attitudes and assumptions of their clergy. Of the nine major British and American missionary societies at work in Punjab in the late nineteenth and early twentieth centuries, the Cambridge Mission to Delhi was the most committed to a sensitive approach to Indian culture.[40] Yet their understanding of Indian culture, like their understanding of British culture, was deeply elitist. Hence, the result of putting their program into effect was the expulsion from the church of those Indian Christians who failed to conform to their classically inspired image of a synthesis of East and West. In contrast, the theologically conservative American evangelical denominations, especially the United Presbyterians, worried very little about sensitivity to Indian culture. But they responded to the untouchable sweepers of central Punjab who wished to become Christians by compromising with them in the development of new forms of Christianity, and fostering the development of indigenous Punjabi Christian hymnody based on the Urdu Psalms.[41] The United Presbyterians encountered a different set of problems based on the unequal power of missionaries and Indian Christians, but they at least did not try to excommunicate Indian Christians wholesale.

By reducing the Chamar Christian community in Daryaganj to a handful of families directly dependent on the mission, Lefroy had ensured the irrelevance of his own mission to the large, oppressed Chamar community of Delhi. The Chamars were obviously not merely free and happy consumers in the marketplace of British imperialisms. But the religious policies of the British Raj were so immobilized by contradictions that something approaching a competitive marketplace in religion existed for many untouchable Indians, who clearly regarded conversion to Christianity as the least unattractive alternative under the circumstances. The Chamars were by far the largest untouchable community in Delhi, and in the entire Delhi district the second largest of the census caste groupings, constituting 10 per cent of the total population and exceeded in numbers only by the Jats.[42] Their untouchable status undoubtedly made them receptive to movements of religious reform, whether that took the form of allegiance to the Chamar Hindu saint Ravidas or to the Kabir-Panth or, in the twentieth century, to the leadership of Dr Ambedkar or the influence of neo-Buddhism.[43] In rural Uttar Pradesh there were mass conversions to Methodism and other forms of Christianity after 1900.[44] But in urban Delhi, for better or for worse, religious reform was not to be Christian, largely because Lefroy's attitudes made it impossible.

III

Although not interested in dealing with Chamars who were attracted to Christianity, Lefroy was interested in promoting missionary influence with those Indians who were not interested in becoming Christians. This behavior makes sense only in the light of the Anglican view of influence which determined the Cambridge Mission's attitude to caste in Delhi. Having dealt with the embarrassing presence of Chamar Christians, Lefroy turned his attention to a truly worthy opponent, a great world religion, Islam. Noted for the excellence of his Urdu, he conducted disputations with Muslim leaders before crowds of as many as 1,000 at the principal mosques in Old Delhi, encounters noted primarily for interminable wrangling about the relative corruption or purity of the Koran versus the New Testament.[45] Christians were at a considerable competitive disadvantage in that particular argument, given the obvious contrast in the unity and coherence of the texts. After several years of colorful controversy, and the successful conversion of one of his leading opponents and no one else, Lefroy noted how little progress of any kind could be derived from these confrontations, which the Muslim press routinely declared to be disasters for Christianity. He was more hopeful about his position on the Delhi Municipal Committee, where he waited for "the contact into which it would bring me with some of the leading men of the city, to whom our mission is especially supposed to address itself."[46]

More important were Lefroy's schemes to promote Christian influence among the non-Christian elite by creating Christian institutions to serve them. Since the Church of England served elites at home without inquiring too closely into their piety, building important institutions to serve the non-Christian elites of Delhi seemed natural and normal. The Government of Punjab initiated a request to the mission to create a new college in Delhi, and by 1882 Lefroy and S.S. Allnutt were deep into plans for a Christian college for non-Christian students. By 1885 the Punjab Government was providing 80 per cent of St Stephen's College's budget, and the Delhi Municipal Government another 10 per cent; the students included forty-eight Hindus, four Muslims, three Christians and one Parsi.[47] In 1889 the provincial government granted a block of land near Kashmir Gate for new college buildings along with a donation of 10,000 rupees toward the buildings and the prospect of more.[48] Except for a temporary setback around the turn of the century, the result of competition from non-Christian colleges (also government funded), the number of students grew steadily, but the college remained Hindu with small Muslim and Christian minorities.[49]

With the expulsion of most of the Chamar Christian community and the creation of prestigious and influential institutions for non-Christians, including not only St Stephen's College but also St Stephen's Hospital for Women, Lefroy set Christian work in Delhi into an institutional mold which persists today. The institutions created by the Cambridge Mission to Delhi remain among the most prestigious and important educational and medical institutions in North India. The institutional strategy came under recurrent criticism from within the missionary movement, but Lefroy defended St Stephen's tenaciously. Lefroy was convinced that any attempt at broad persuasion would require first the creation of an institutional setting to foster a Christian moral ethos. In a letter to the Secretary of the SPG on the progress of St Stephen's College, he observed that, "The more one comes to realize the extraordinary degree to which, in many respects, the people of India have become demoralized and have lost their hold on many of the essential principles of right and wrong, the more one sees how essential it is not only to preach the truths of Christ but to recreate as far as possible the entire character and mental standpoint." This dark and pessimistic view of Indian morality helped to justify St Stephen's College, where the goal was not outright conversion so much as the creation of a moral atmosphere which would, over several generations, "recreate some kind of moral faculty" among the Indian elite.[50]

Similar comments about moral depravity in the slums of darkest England can be found in the writings of the more censorious clergymen at home. In some ways Lefroy's comments on Hinduism merely reflect the scholarly consensus in Europe, where enthusiasts for Hinduism were few and far between. The best known English expert on Hinduism, Friedrich Max Müller, approached Sanskrit texts, in his own words, "as the physician studies the twaddle of idiots."[51] But Lefroy should have known better than to indulge in vitriolic anti-Hindu polemic. If his mission was unapologetic about its ties with the colonizing enterprise and its members unembarrassed about leaving a trail of self-incriminating pro-imperial comments, Lefroy was also part of an international missionary movement that had broader goals than the cultural conquest of India for Great Britain. Furthermore, he came from a tradition that was specifically committed to learning from Indian culture, and that recognized explicitly that Christianity is one thing and western civilization another. Other missionaries in his own mission, notably C.F. Andrews, took the Westcottian tradition in a very different direction, and it was not necessary to embrace Hinduism in order to be courteous about a society where he was, as he knew, an intruder. Moral censoriousness and anti-Hindu piety were being expressed in an imperial context in which Lefroy was associated with imperial power, a fact that he was perfectly well aware of and indeed took ineffective steps to compensate for by publicly praising Indian culture in other contexts.[52]

Lefroy's generous remarks, however, are overshadowed by his observations on the defects of Indian moral character, which were in some cases so extreme that they make one wonder how any Indian could associate with him. If Indian morality were as bad as Lefroy thought, an "atmosphere of suspicion and mistrust on the one hand, with their invariable correlations of deceit, falsehood, and untrustworthiness,"[53] it would explain why his partner, Allnutt, suffered from recurrent nightmares about being murdered, and could not sleep on the roof in the hot weather because of the danger that he would awaken screaming and rush toward the parapet.[54] (Allnutt's scream no doubt bore little resemblance to the scream described by Kipling in *Kim*, the "terrible, bubbling, meaningless yell of the Asiatic roused by nightmare.")[55]

Lefroy experienced private doubts himself about failure, lamenting early in his career that "our position as the ruling power puts a dead weight on the missionary enterprise which nothing but the direct Grace of God can possibly enable us to lift."[56] He confessed to the SPG Secretary in 1894 that the work proceeded "so slowly that at times one's heart almost fails, and one is ready to cry 'How long, Oh Lord, how long?'"[57] In order to get closer to the people, Lefroy took a room on Chandni Chowk, the main thoroughfare of Old Delhi: "I go there pretty often in the mornings and sit most of the day ... I hope that some may realize my accessibility ... and drop in for a talk and inquiry ... it seems to bring me closer to them, even if only in my own thought, for I confess I have not so far been encumbered by the rush of visitors, inquirers, or the like. Still, they may come."[58]

The hoped-for rush of inquirers became even less likely after Lefroy became Bishop of Lahore in 1899. Punjab was the scene of aggressive nationalist agitation while Lefroy was Bishop, a position which required not only the ecclesiastical supervision of Indian Christians but also the provision of religious services for the extensive military establishment, larger in the Diocese of Punjab than in any other diocese in the empire except for Winchester. He continued to promote the Westcottian vision of a Christian synthesis of East and West, encouraging St Stephen's College students to choose the best of each culture. Expressing qualified support for the national movement in principle, he denounced the attitude of the British in India, the "grim refusal of anything even approaching to a brotherly and sympathetic bearing."[59]

Such protestations of commitment to India rang hollow from someone with such obvious imperial associations. Lefroy made things worse by his opposition to the appointment of the first Indian Head of St Stephen's College. His well-intentioned attempts to promote Indian church self-government through the appointment of an Indian Archdeacon of Delhi ran into the racist objections that an Indian would have pastoral supervision over English parishioners, and Lefroy had to improvise with a non-territorial archdiaconate. Hoping to promote indigenous forms of piety, he promulgated a new semi-monastic order called the Brotherhood of the Imitation of Christ centered on the Christian Sadhu (holy man), Sadhu Sundar Singh. According to C.F. Andrews, Lefroy "looked upon the founding of this new Order as the greatest event that had happened to the church in the Punjab during his episcopate. He laid his hands upon them at a solemn and beautiful service in Lahore Cathedral and thus sent them forth to their work with the blessings of God." But conflict developed over clerical celibacy and the order fell apart amidst accusations of racism.[60] By the time of Lefroy's elevation to the See of Calcutta in 1913, it was clear to just about everyone in India that the hopes of this mission had never been fulfilled in any straightforward way.

IV

Faced with a consensus of authoritative judgments that the missionary enterprise has been marginal to the history of India, it is perhaps time to reconsider the views of Lefroy's small band of admirers. In ways that no one precisely anticipated, Lefroy influenced modern India through St Stephen's College and other institutions like it. One need only walk around St Stephen's College to soak up some of the atmosphere of academic elitism that the Cambridge Brothers bequeathed to Indian academia. Graduates of mission colleges in India, when asked if it made any difference at all that their schools had been mission schools, will almost always answer "no," but it is possible that they are looking for missionary influence in the form of identifiable, explicit religious teaching rather than in the broader curriculum promoted by Lefroy. The handful of BA students at St Stephen's in 1883 were taught Kingsley's *Hypatia*, Macaulay's *Essays on Chatham and Pitt*, Shakespeare's *Hamlet*, Milton's *L'Allegro* and *Il Penseroso*, and Tennyson's *Passing of Arthur*. On Prize Day Lefroy had the students wear what he called "Urdu dress" as a safeguard against westernization, which gives you an idea of Lefroy's concept of a synthesis of East and West: English literature in Urdu dress.[61] Lefroy believed that intellectual assent to the doctrine of Christianity was not enough; an atmosphere of moral rectitude had to be created to foster such assent, and the canon of English literature, especially the Romantic Poets and Shakespeare, were essential elements of the proper moral atmosphere.

St Stephen's teachers complained that the routine grammatical and rote nature of the Indian education system had left Indian students without the speculative faculties necessary to understand Wordsworth. Yet the Cambridge Mission's Annual Report for 1887 reported on the success of the mission in this area by quoting a letter from a non-

Christian graduate, Shiv Narayan, now Extra Assistant Commissioner, the "highest post open to Indians in uncovenanted civil service":

> Often on a cloudy morning when I go for field inspection it is pleasant to see all around a spectacle of verdure and fertility. The rural scenery is sometimes very picturesque, where a man of Wordsworthian mood would like to be in a state of "wise passiveness" and "silent meditation."

According to the Report, this citation was meant to "enable you to judge a little of the extent to which Christian teaching has influenced his character" and "indicates quite a new departure in its incipient appreciation of scenery to which the Indian student is as a rule quite a stranger."[62]

A definition of missionary success as an ability to judge nature from a Wordsworthian point of view would have struck most contributors to the British missionary movement as a peculiar one. However much the missionary enterprise became implicated in the colonial enterprise, it nonetheless had independent origins in the domestic expansion of Christian activity in the eighteenth and nineteenth centuries. The missionary movement thus could play a part in the redefinition of religion as a voluntary enterprise suited to a pluralistic society, but only by maintaining the distinction between Christianity and western culture – a distinction that the Cambridge Brothers tended to blur in practice. In 1913 Lefroy spoke frankly of "the very large amount of material ... being prepared for the spread of higher moral and religious standards and principles of life" in India. "This is to a large extent due to the influence of Christian missionaries and educationalists. But nothing has contributed so much to bring about the present welcome change as the spread of English education has done."[63]

By reducing the missionary enterprise to the promotion of English education, Lefroy left his mark on modern India, but his influence was far removed in both intention and conception from the universalism of the nineteenth-century missionary movement or the fruitful synthesis of East and West discussed at Cambridge in the 1870s. Lefroy's own version of Christianity was rooted in Anglican parochial and academic traditions, which assumed that an educated elite committed to raising the level of civilization would gradually bring society under the influence of the most important of all civilizing institutions, the Church. These traditions have been obstacles to popular recruitment both in India and England, and Lefroy's role in this particular civilizing mission was tainted by religious bigotry and corrupted by moral insensitivity. But a single-minded devotion to institution-building produced, in this case, durable institutions. Furthermore, the curriculum that outlived

Lefroy was, by his own definition of the relationship between religion and culture, one that promoted religious as well as secular values.

How to talk about the consequences of this form of cultural interaction is a discussion that is only now beginning. Government as well as mission schools were promoting the study of English literature, for their own purposes, as a substitute for the moral training provided by religious education in England but regarded as unsuitable for India. The formal study of English literature, as Gauri Viswanathan has shown, developed earlier in India than in Great Britain as part of an explicit strategy of colonial rule.[64] It is one thing, however, to issue official government minutes promulgating a particular curriculum, and another to promote a canon of literature with missionary zeal. Lefroy was not merely an elitist, but a specialist in the construction of elite educational institutions. The sheer tenacity of Lefroy's elitism made possible a convergence of interests with certain sections of the Indian elite, who had their own reasons to make use of imperial institutions. Like other missionary schools, and in contrast to at least some government schools,[65] St Stephen's promoted what was in effect a Romantic canon with a tenacious moralizing fervor, and became one of the most prestigious schools in twentieth-century India. For better or for worse, Lefroy's eulogists might have been correct in declaring him an influential man, even though his influence has been obscured by the rhetorical conventions of public discourse about religion, secularist in modern Britain, nationalist in modern India.

NOTES

I would like to thank Geeta Patel, Susan K. Kent, Deborah Valenze, Susan Pedersen, Peter Mandler and Daud Ali for helpful comments, and John Searle for research assistance.

1 *Delhi Mission News*, April 1919, p. 30.
2 *Tribune* (Lahore), 4 January 1919. The Viceroy at the time was Lord Minto; Morley was the Secretary of State for India.
3 *The Times* (London), 17 January 1919.
4 *The Mission Field*, March 1919, clipping in Bishop's College (Calcutta) Archive, Lahore, Box 3, Personal.
5 See M.E. Gibbs, *The Anglican Church in India, 1600–1970*, Delhi, ISPCK, 1972, pp. 79, 234.
6 Quoted in Cambridge Mission to Delhi's *Annual Report* for 1888.
7 Ranajit Guha, "On Some Aspects of the Historiography of Colonial India," in Guha, ed., *Subaltern Studies I. Writings on South Asian History and Society*, vol. I, Delhi, Oxford University Press, 1982, p. 8.
8 The phrase is from Gauri Viswanathan's important book, *Masks of Conquest. Literary Study and British Rule in India*, New York, Columbia University Press, 1989.
9 H.F. Lechmere Taylor, "Some Current Criticisms of Indian Missions," *East*

and West. A Quarterly Review for the Study of Missions, vol. 18, April 1920, p. 139.

10 Ibid., pp. 146–7.

11 *Tribune* (Lahore), 6 May 1914.

12 See Daniel O'Connor, *Gospel, Raj and Swaraj. The Missionary Years of C.F. Andrews 1904–14*, Frankfurt, Lang, 1990; Jeffrey Cox, "C.F. Andrews and the Failure of the Modern Missionary Movement," in Stuart Mews, ed., *Religious Rebels: Essays in Honour of John Kent*, London, Epworth Press, 1993.

13 "The Attitude of the British Race in India Towards Educated Indians," *Third Triennial Charge to his Diocese*, November 1906, cited in H.H. Montgomery, *The Life and Letters of George Alfred Lefroy, D.D., Bishop of Calcutta and Metropolitan*, London, Longmans Green, 1920, p. 170.

14 Satish C. Chatterji, "Indian Christians and National Ideals," *East and West*, vol. 12, April 1914, p. 209.

15 T.B. Macaulay, *The History of England from the Accession of James II*, vol. 2, Chicago, Belford, Clarke & Co., 1889, p. 127. Lefroy was well-connected in non-ecclesiastical ways as well. His grandfather was Chief Justice of the Queen's Bench, Ireland; his grandmother a niece of the Prime Minister, Spencer Perceval.

16 Cited in Montgomery, *Life and Letters*, p. 10.

17 See B.F. Westcott, *On Some Points in the Religious Office of the Universities*, London, Macmillan, 1873.

18 Ibid., p. 11. A mission to Cambridge was first proposed in papers read to the Cambridge Church Society by Edward Bickersteth and T.V. French; Lefroy asked for membership in consequence of a sermon preached by Dr Lightfoot in Great St Mary's.

19 His son once conceded that "unsound" or "shadowy" or "mystical" were terms often applied to him, but the broader verdict was more recently endorsed by Geoffrey Best: "I do not believe that even the most hardened debunker could, once he had begun to get into the subject, carry through to the finish a hostile study. The armour of Westcott's saintliness is Impregnable." Arthur Westcott, *Life and Letters of Brooke Foss Westcott*, 2 vols, London, Macmillan, 1903, p. ix; Geoffrey Best, *Bishop Westcott and the Miners*, Bishop Westcott Memorial Lecture for 1966, Cambridge University Press, 1967, p. 2.

20 On this see Jeffrey Cox, "Independent English Women in Delhi and Lahore," in R.W. Davis and R.J. Helmstadter, eds, *Religion and Irreligion in Victorian Society: Essays in Honor of R.K. Webb*, London, Routledge, 1992. The microfilm version of the SPG archives, marketed as the *complete* archives, does not include the records of the SPG's Committee on Women's Work. It is perhaps testimony to the value of quantitative methods that I only realized how thoroughly this mission was women's work, not while reading an article advocating the centrality of gender even when it appears to be absent, but when I took the trouble to count the number of SPG men and women missionaries in Delhi and Lahore, and discovered 300 women and only 50 men.

21 "Catechist ka kam, bohut aram," i.e. "the catechist's life is an easy one" or, literally, "the catechist's work is easy."

22 Bhajans were inserted into an order of service which included the following sequence in Urdu: bhajan, confession, absolution, Lord's Prayer, magnificat, creed, chapters, sermons, then bhajan, prayers, dispersal. The missionaries apparently wrote simple lyrics, or adapted the more popular Christian

hymns which the catechists set to music. See "Busti Work in Daryagange," Cambridge Mission to Delhi, *Annual Report* for 1881, 12 June 1880.

23 Cambridge Mission to Delhi, *Annual Report* for 1880, p. 100. A different account of this event appeared in two successive yearly reports.

24 Cambridge Mission to Delhi, *Annual Report* for 1881.

25 Letter from Mehrouli, New Year's Eve, 1881, cited in Montgomery, *Life and Letters*, p. 32.

26 Ibid.

27 *The Leatherworkers of Daryaganj*, Cambridge Mission to Delhi Occasional Paper, Delhi, 1884.

28 Ibid., p. 5.

29 Ibid.

30 See the summary of work by British scholars and civil servants to date in George W. Briggs, *The Chamars*, Calcutta, Association Press (YMCA), 1920.

31 Ibid., p. 33; for a more recent social geography, see A.B. Mukerji, *The Chamars of Uttar Pradesh. A Study in Social Geography*, Delhi, Inter-India Publications, 1980.

32 Lefroy, *Leatherworkers*, p. 6.

33 Ibid.

34 Ibid., p. 1.

35 Ibid., p. 11.

36 Ibid.

37 Ibid.

38 Montgomery, *Life and Letters*, p. 38.

39 Ibid.

40 The Society for the Propagation of the Gospel (including the Cambridge Mission to Delhi), the Church Missionary Society, the Church of England Zenana Missionary Society, the Church of Scotland, the Presbyterian Church in the USA, the United Presbyterian Church, the American Methodist Episcopal Church (North), the Salvation Army and the Zenana Bible and Medical Mission.

41 See James Massey, "Christianity and Culture: Their Relationship in the 19th and 20th Centuries in Punjab," *Religion and Society*, vol. 36, December 1989, pp. 18–33.

42 *Gazetteer of the Delhi District, 1883–84*, 2nd edn, Delhi, Vintage Books, 1988, p. 91, appendix p. vii; cf. Mukerji, *Chamars*, maps on pp. 122ff.

43 See R.S. Khare, *The Untouchable as Himself: Ideology, Identity, and Pragmatism Among the Lucknow Chamars*, Cambridge, Cambridge University Press, 1984, especially ch. 6.

44 See James P. Alter, *In the Doab and Rohilkhand: North Indian Christianity, 1815–1915*, Delhi, I.S.P.C.K., 1986.

45 See Montgomery, *Life and Letters*, pp. 69–74.

46 Ibid., p. 106.

47 SPG and Cambridge Mission to Delhi, *Annual Report* for 1885; Cambridge Mission to Delhi, *Annual Report* for 1886 (these are two distinct sets of annual reports).

48 H.C. Carlyon to Tucker, Delhi, 24 July 1889 (ms letter), SPG Missionary Reports, Series E.

49 82 students in 1893, 140 in 1908, 221 in 1914. From the Cambridge Mission to Delhi, *Annual Report* for 1893; SPG and Cambridge Missions to Delhi, *Annual Reports* for 1908 and 1914.

50 Lefroy to Tucker, Delhi, 12 November 1890 (ms letter), SPG Mission Reports, Series E.
51 Friedrich Max Müller, *A History of Ancient Sanskrit Literature*, Allahabad, B.D. Basu, 1926, p. 204.
52 The *Tribune* was overstating the case when it asserted that "Bishop Lefroy's observations on the attitude of Indians towards Christianity show a genuine note of sympathy for the people of India which always characterises His Lordship's utterances," but there is enough in Lefroy's public rhetoric to make this comment intelligible. *Tribune* (Lahore), 11 January 1913.
53 G.A. Lefroy, "The Moral Tone of India," *East and West*, vol. 1, 1903, p. 123.
54 Rev. W.S. Kelly was suddenly ". . . aroused by a terrible scream from Allnutt, and sat up to see him bursting through his mosquito curtains and making straight for the low parapet of the flat roof." Montgomery, *Life and Letters*, p. 47.
55 Rudyard Kipling, *Kim*, New York, Dell, 1959, p. 139.
56 Montgomery, *Life and Letters*, p. 20.
57 Letter of Mr Lefroy dated 14 February 1894, Cambridge Mission to Delhi, *Annual Report* for 1893.
58 Montgomery, *Life and Letters*, p. 111.
59 "The Attitude of the British Race in India Towards Educated Indians," *Third Triennial Charge to his Diocese*, November 1906, in Montgomery, *Life and Letters*, p. 170.
60 Charles Freer Andrews, *What I Owe to Christ*, New York, Abingdon, 1932, p. 170.
61 Cambridge Mission to Delhi, *Annual Report* for 1883, pp. 10ff.
62 Cambridge Mission to Delhi, *Annual Report* for 1887.
63 *Tribune* (Lahore), 11 January 1913.
64 See Viswanathan, *Masks*. Viswanathan locates missionary influence in the early nineteenth century but fails to notice its importance in the twentieth century.
65 See ibid., pp. 54–5 on the contrasting literary canons of government and mission schools.

4 The Unwin and Parker families at Buxton, 1898. Raymond Unwin is standing on the far left; Barry Parker on the far right. Ethel Parker Unwin, Raymond's wife, is seated front right.

3

Raymond Unwin 1863–1940
Designing for democracy in Edwardian England
Standish Meacham

George Orwell claimed to have been born into "the lower upper middle class," insisting that without knowledge of that fact, no one could comprehend the map of his life or the shape of his mind.[1] Raymond Unwin, the architect and town planner, would, if pressed, have acknowledged that he too sprang from that same particular social subdivision, though he would have argued that the matter was of little importance. Yet for the historian the matter is important. It provides the avenue to an understanding of the difficulty Unwin experienced as he attempted to marry the ideal of democracy to a conception of community, while designing houses and streetscapes, towns and suburbs in early twentieth-century Britain.

Like Orwell, Unwin was a socialist. Like Orwell, he hoped that the advance of social democracy would obliterate class distinctions. Unlike Orwell, however, he seldom addressed the issue of class directly. He appears to have been caught up in the dilemma that vexed many other late Victorian upper-middle-class professionals who played a central role in the reshaping of society at the end of the nineteenth century. These men and women accepted that Britain was fast becoming a democracy. Some, like Unwin, welcomed that fact. Others could do no more than face it – and not without a considerable degree of trepidation. Yet almost all of them feared the consequences of a democracy whose political will was driven by class antagonism. And so they did their best to minimize the existence of class consciousness when forecasting democracy's future.

They did this in one of two ways: either they thought of democracy as the expression of countless individual wills, rather than as the collective wills of classes in opposition; or, acknowledging the need for some form of collectivity, they spoke of "community," understanding that concept – sometimes consciously, often unconsciously – as it had been traditionally understood, in rural, local and hierarchical terms that recalled a pre-industrial and therefore pre-class conscious society. Unwin made it his business to improve the quality of life for English men, women and children – particularly for working-class men, women and children. He appreciated the fact that those people needed to understand their lives in terms of some sort of social aggregation beyond their individual selves and their immediate families. Yet he appeared unable to work comfortably with the reality of class consciousness. He saw it as his mission to design houses suitable for a democracy of individual selves. And he welcomed the chance to plan communities that he believed would bring those individuals into harmony with each other. Unwin's plans, however, tended to brush aside the immediate, implacable social reality of class. In that respect we should perhaps understand them as Utopian. Certainly we should see them as an expression of Unwin's own class consciousness.

I

Unwin's father Edward, about whom little is known, lived a maverick life. As a young man he worked in the Yorkshire cloth trade, and, despite the eventual collapse of the family business, was apparently successful enough to hold on to property in Sheffield, upon which he later depended for income. Raymond, born in 1863 in the West Riding village of Whiston, began his schooling at Rotherham. Soon thereafter, the family moved to Oxford. Edward took up a Fellowship at Balliol College, where he had received his degree some years earlier. Family legend has it that he was befriended by Arnold Toynbee, the economic historian, and T.H. Green, the idealist philosopher.[2] If so, association with the latter may explain the fact that Edward resigned his fellowship for reasons of religious conscience, remaining in Oxford, however, as an academic coach. Raymond attended Magdalen College School and then began training as an engineer. In 1885, he accepted a position as draftsman-fitter in a Manchester cotton mill.

Raymond Unwin's daughter maintained that at about this time her father spoke with Samuel Barnett, a family friend, who, as rector of St Jude's in Whitechapel, was laboring to create community in the slums of East London. "Raymond," he is supposed to have asked, "are you more interested in making people good or making them happy?"[3] The question implies that Unwin was contemplating a career as a clergyman. The answer, presumably, was given in favor of the latter option. And general happiness, Unwin soon concluded, depended on the realization of a socialist society in Britain. Yet in fact Unwin's particular brand of socialism, reflecting the high-mindedness characteristic of so many late Victorian social reformers, promised to make its beneficiaries both good *and* happy. Certainly that was the implicit – often explicit – purpose of the housing Unwin was to design and the communities he was to plan.

During his years in Manchester, Unwin played a prominent role in the establishment of a socialist presence within the city. He met William Morris and Ford Madox Brown, who had come there to supervise the painting of the town hall murals. That acquaintanceship encouraged Unwin to join Morris's Socialist League; in 1886 he was serving as first secretary of the League's Manchester branch. When he was 24, in 1887, Unwin left Manchester for Chesterfield, where he went to work as chief draftsman for the Staveley Coal and Iron Works. There he designed his first houses – employees' cottages – threatening to resign if prevented from including bathrooms in the plans. He joined the Sheffield Socialist Society and wrote for Morris's *Commonweal*. He began to speak regularly at outdoor meetings, most of them staged to increase local union membership. At Clay Cross, in the summer of 1887, Unwin reported in his journal that at the end of his prepared speech, "I . . . just went on speaking about [the] union and trying to make things better and said if they did not live to see it they would still be able to die feeling they had left the world better for their children."[4]

Unwin was conscious at this time of a need "to make things better." He understood evil and misery "as an injunction for us to mend our lives in some way, or the general conditions of life."[5] His high-minded socialist's sense of the way things might be drove him to disparage the banality of the way things were. A constant striver toward what he believed to be the best, he wanted others striving alongside him. He had heard John Ruskin lecture at least once at Oxford and, as a young man, continued to read and ponder what he wrote. In his inaugural address as president of the Royal Institute of British Architects in 1931, he declared that he did not feel the least need to apologize for urging the importance of harmony and beauty at a time of severe national hardship. "If you feel that I have stressed this aspect too much, I may perhaps recall that my early days were influenced by the musical voice of John Ruskin, vainly trying to stem the flood of materialism which seemed to him to be overwhelming the arts, and much else; and later by the more robust and constructive personality of William Morris and his crusade for the restoration of beauty to daily life. Those were times when it was very interesting to be alive."[6]

More than merely interesting: Unwin appears to have leapt at the challenge that Ruskin and Morris flung at the feet of their materially-minded fellow countrymen and women. In the same address, he quoted Morris: "Beauty, which is what we mean by art . . . is no mere accident of human life which people can take or leave as they like, but a positive necessity of life, if we are to live as nature meant us to – that is, unless we are content to be less than men."[7] Morris's insistence that beauty was not only to be found but to be vigorously cultivated in all aspects of daily life encouraged the young Unwin to look everywhere for what was beautiful, just as it inspired him, as he matured, to design beyond single buildings to entire landscapes. Walking through the Staveley factory in 1887, he noticed a man at work making girders, and saw the beauty – "the higher morality" – in that labor because of the way in which it was being done. "He took great notice of a bit of praise, and although he is working piece work he tries to do everything the very best way even when it was longer."[8]

The relationship between beauty – whether in art, architecture or daily work – and morality was one that Unwin tried hard to express through his own life. His continual attempt to do so as a young man was aided not only by the writings of Ruskin and Morris, but also by his admiration for Edward Carpenter, the man who more than any other helped Unwin discern the socialist vision that best accorded with his intentions for himself and his hopes for his fellow men and women. "From about the year 1881, Edward Carpenter became a great influence in my life," he wrote in 1931. The two had met following a lecture Carpenter delivered in Chesterfield, and Unwin cultivated the friendship at the Commonwealth Café in Sheffield, founded by Carpenter, and at his nearby Millthorpe farm. Years later, in an essay in praise of Carpenter's life and spirit, Unwin recalled "the sense of escape from an intolerable sheath of unreality and social superstition" he had experienced on his first reading of Carpenter's lengthy prose poem, *Towards Democracy*.[9] Carpenter's socialism, like Morris's, celebrated the sturdy individual farmer or artisan: "Who is this, ... easy with open shirt and brown neck and face ... through the city garden swinging? ... There was a time when the sympathy and the ideals of men gathered round other figures; ... but now before the easy homely garb and appearance of this man as he swings past in the evening, all these others fade and grow dim.... And this is one of the slowly unfolding meanings of Democracy."[10]

For Unwin, it became the quintessential meaning of democracy. He wrote critically of a *Commonweal* article by Belfort Bax, complaining that Bax's scientific determinism placed him in that "depressing" camp of socialists who had no "faith in man."[11] Carpenter's thought derived from Walt Whitman, and from an American insistence upon a direct, nurturing relationship between individual men and women and their natural world. In his tribute to Carpenter, Unwin quoted a passage from *Towards Democracy* that had inspired him, linking the beneficiaries of a socialist democracy with the land that was theirs by right: "I see a great land poised as in a dream.... I hear the bells pealing, and the crash of hammers, and see beautiful parks spread – as in a toy show. I see a great land waiting for its own people to come and take possession of it."[12]

They were to possess that great land as individuals. Beyond individuals there must, of course, be community. Yet both Carpenter and Unwin found it difficult to give the term specific definition. "The only society which would ever really satisfy [man]," Carpenter wrote, "would be one in which he was perfectly free, and yet bound by ties of deepest trust to the other members."[13] But what was to provide the binding? Unwin never addressed the issue clearly. He had observed the way in which class bound men and women to each other, and remained disheartened by what he saw. Class was the pathological enemy of a healthy society: "no people can be happy who are divided one against another by strong class interests. . . . " Nor could he perceive the benefits that class consciousness might bring to workers who, linked together by factory and neighborhood, derived security from the mutuality of their experience. The curse of capitalism was its insistence that the individual remain "bound to the actions of his neighbours."[14] Cooperation there had to be. But it was to be the cooperation of individual men and women above class – the strong with the weak. "Our aim is . . . to develop a society in which the good things in life shall be shared – handed round, as it were, to all – not scrambled for, and in which if there need be any extra burden carried at times, it shall not be thrust upon the weakest as it is today, but the strong shall take it."[15]

II

Unwin's apparently paradoxical grounding of his socialism in individualism directly influenced the way in which he understood his mission as architect and planner. He was drawn to a career in architecture by his desire to design houses in which individual families – from whatever class – might experience the marriage of beauty and right-living. He and his first cousin and fellow-socialist Barry Parker established a practice in Buxton in 1896, Unwin having married Parker's sister Ethel three years earlier. Parker had apprenticed with the Lancashire architect G.F. Armitage, following attendance at art schools in Derby and London. He spent several years learning the various crafts that together comprised the construction, decoration and furnishing of houses, convinced, as a disciple of Morris, that there was no proper way to subdivide the process of house design. Parker and Unwin had been close friends for years. "Before I left school," Parker later wrote, "we had quite decided that we would go into partnership someday."[16] Both apparently felt the need for apprenticeship elsewhere within the world that they were determined to change. Both shared a vision of the way that change could be made to occur.

In their early designs for houses commissioned by middle-class clients, and in a book, *The Art of Building a Home*, published in 1901, the partners demonstrated the way they intended to put socialist principles into practice. The results resembled the work of other architects that historians have since loosely confederated together as "arts and crafts" practitioners. Edgar Wood, M.H. Baillie Scott, W.R. Lethaby, C.F.A. Voysey, C.R. Ashbee and a score of less distinguished but equally dedicated designers, all subscribed to tenets absorbed from observation of Morris's example: most important, the injunction that form follow function. "The essence and life of design lies in finding that form for anything which will, with the maximum of convenience and beauty, fit it for the particular function it has to perform, and adapt it to the special circumstances in which it must be placed."[17] That declaration, published in the introduction to Parker and Unwin's *The Art of Building a Home*, remained the credo of their collaboration. The house, the streetscape, the town, must express directly through their architecture and planning the purpose of the individual lives lived within them.

Who was to determine those purposes? Unwin believed that responsibility rested ultimately with architects. Their task, as they built for the citizenry of England's emerging democracy, was to encourage the cultivation of "higher natures" and "better selves" as they – the architects – defined these terms.

> Architecture is rightly called a profession only when the architect advises his client what is best, and brings the whole weight of his knowledge and experience to persuade him from anything foolish or in bad taste.... We have just such power of influencing our clients by helping them towards a more natural life as the doctor has in such matters as diet.[18]

As teachers, architects were to play a role in the improvement of the lives of their clients not unlike that of the young university-educated gentlemen who went to live in East London settlement houses such as Toynbee Hall at the close of the century. Unlike almost all these young men, Parker and Unwin were socialists. They nevertheless understood themselves as part of a socially responsive, public professoriat, above the economic interests of the upper-middle commercial class from which they were descended, whose task it was to encourage the following of a more high-minded and hence a "better" way of life among their fellow-citizens. At Toynbee Hall, Samuel Barnett, its founder, spoke unequivocally of this mission: "The one thing necessary is that the attempt be made by those ... who having learnt through feeling what are the needs of their neighbours, are able to put into language unuttered thoughts, and who ... are trusted where they are not understood."[19]

Parker and Unwin were not, perhaps, as forthright, yet their intention was similar. They believed that they understood the needs of their clients – better perhaps, than did their clients themselves; and they saw it as their duty to respond to those needs as creatively as they could in the designs they produced. True, the architect's compulsion to tell clients what is good for them is by no means peculiar to Parker and Unwin or to the period during which they flourished as young designers. Yet Parker and Unwin's prescriptions were as much social as architectural. They were men of their time and of their class, preaching along with other men and women to settlement house audiences, in Fabian Society lectures, to University Extension and Workers' Educational Association students a particular brand of high-minded culture which they believed would bring about the enlightenment of individuals and the creation of a right-thinking democratic society. The nature and extent of Unwin's commitment to democracy must be understood against this insistence upon the imposition of a moral aesthetic from above. With Carpenter he could admire what was simple and honest, and disparage what was elaborated and artificial. He could celebrate the solitary dedicated artisan who produced honest work. In that sense – an individual sense – he proclaimed himself a democrat, as Carpenter and Whitman had proclaimed themselves. Yet he could not trust the people to define a worthy moral aesthetic of their own. Capitalism had imposed its gimcrack standards on a commercial society denied the education necessary to withstand them. Parker and Unwin saw their designs as just such education. Once men and women had been taught the difference between good architecture and bad, through the experience of living within healthy, liberating environments, they would be able to make choices for themselves. Until then they would need the tutelage of disinterested mentors.

The lesson the two young architects were most anxious to impart – that the way people lived must reflect the increasingly democratic nature of their changing society – encouraged them to confront the fact that for most men and women, particularly those without much economic security, change is a frightening business. In *The Art of Building*, Parker and Unwin reassured their readers of their opposition to innovation for its own sake. "Let us then," they declared in italics, "*do nothing different from what we have done before, until we feel it to be better than what we have done before.*"[20] They insisted, indeed, that many of the reforms they were suggesting were in fact rooted in the past – here echoing the pronouncements of Morris and of their Arts and Crafts contemporaries. They acknowledged the paradox implicit in their search for designs suitable for a democracy within the patterns of England's feudal past. Yet where else to look? Too often the new "strikes a note of defiance with surrounding nature." And the harmony of individual with nature remained central to their definition of democracy. Hence the appeal of an old building, which seems "almost to grow out of the ground on which it stands."[21]

Were that old building a laborer's cottage, chances are that its interior plan would, in Parker and Unwin's opinion, reflect a more wholesome – a "better" – way of daily life than that lived by workers in late Victorian cities and towns. A change dear to their hearts, reflecting their willingness to idealize the past and their determination to impose improving patterns upon the present, was the abolition of the parlor. Parlors bespoke a foolish craving for bourgeois respectability, and thus encouraged anti-democratic sentiments of class consciousness. A tiny front room, used no more than once or twice a week, robbed house-holders of desperately needed living space, often boxing them into airless kitchens facing dreary, sunless back alleys. "When mankind first took to living in houses these consisted of one room; perhaps the most important fact to be remembered in designing cottages is that the cot-tager still lives during the day-time in one room." Parker and Unwin claimed familiarity with the way working-class families lived, and an understanding of their needs. "Except by a very careful study of the life which the space is to shelter," Unwin wrote in a Fabian Society tract in 1902, "it is not possible to design the house so as to properly fit and accommodate to that life."[22] Unwin had studied that life; but he paid little heed to the ingrained – and deeply conservative – attitudes that helped give it shape. Parlors, though perhaps irrational, nevertheless embodied in an important, tangible form a family's ability to afford something beyond the minimum. The ten-by-twelve room, with its four or five pieces of all-but-functionless furniture, might supply that family with a measure of psychic sustenance as important to its well-being as fresh air and sunshine.

Unwin eventually gave up the battle. By 1919, he had yielded to the extent of acknowledging that "in order to meet the reasonable require-ments of the average working-class family, a cottage should contain three bedrooms, a living room, parlour, scullery, larder, bathroom, W.C., and coal stove."[23] He and Parker never ceased to believe in the morally therapeutic benefit of that one large room, however, and continued to design it whenever they could into houses for middle-class as well as working-class clients. With inglenooks for warmth and "cosiness" – an attribute they prized, with bay windows to catch winter light and summer breezes, it became for them an almost enchanted place where family members might experience a constant lift of spirits. Describing a "laborer's cottage," in The Art of Building a Home, they wrote of a "space for a table for meals, and a few shelves for books," then suggested that the family might find "a corner for a piano or desk." Rather than a parlor, the house should contain a study, or more probably a bedroom

5 Illustration from Parker and Unwin's *The Art of Building a Home* (1901): "An Artizan's Living Room"

large enough so that "a portion of it could be made cosy for such a purpose."[24]

Unwin was fantasizing for the laborer and his family the sort of life that he himself was living at that time, the simple, harmoniously improving life, patterned upon Carpenter's example, that he believed best suited the citizens of a modern democracy. We catch a glimpse of it in a memoir written years later by Katherine Bruce Glasier, a close friend from those early days.

> It is difficult ... to even attempt to estimate the inspiration that came in those early days from watching the Raymond Unwins translate into every detail of their daily life and of their simple five-room home ... their sincere belief in their fellow-workers' right not only to work and wage but to interest and even joy in the doing of that work and assuredly to beauty in their surroundings.... The warm curtains at the window, blankets on the bed, cushion coverings and even the hostess's frock and little son's tunic were all made from Ruskin flannel ... the joy of embroidering the strong hand-made fabrics ... working at it of an evening while one or another played or sang or read aloud from some worth-while writer – these became living experiences that could never be gainsayed.[25]

This was the life Unwin and Parker wanted for everyone, the promise of a socialist democracy. And it was a life they stoutly advocated, whenever possible, in houses designed not just to shelter but to promote a particular kind of life. "The influences which our common every-day surroundings have upon our characters, our conceptions, our habits of thought and conduct, are often very much under-rated; we do not realise the power they have of either aiding or hindering the development in us of the best or worst of which we are capable."[26] Parker and Unwin did realize the power of everyday surroundings, and determined to do all they could, by means of the houses they built, to teach men, women and children what "best" and "worst" meant, so that they might strive for the former and shun the latter.

Important though the single dwelling might be as a catalyst for moral improvement, it was but part of a larger social entity. Capitalism had promoted individualism at the expense of community, as it had competition over cooperation. Socialism taught that "independence is no end in itself, and is only good in that it sets free the individuals to form new relationships based on mutual association."[27] Unwin struggled to give that association shape and substance. Like so many of his contemporaries who despised the monotony and grimness of industrial cities, and who saw them as breeding grounds for class animosity, Unwin looked to the pre-industrial village as a model. In a chapter he wrote on "co-operation in building" for *The Art of Building a Home,* he idealized the organic unity those communities professed, not only in their collective architecture but in their social relations.

> There are houses and buildings of all sizes: the hut in which the old road mender lives by himself, the inn with its ancient sign, the prosperous yeoman's homestead, the blacksmith's house and forge, the squire's hall, the vicarage, and the doctor's house, are all seemingly jumbled together.... Yet there is no sense of confusion; on the contrary the scene gives us that peaceful feeling which comes from the perception of orderly arrangement.... The village was the expression of a small corporate life in which all the different units were personally in touch with each other, conscious of and frankly accepting their relations, and on the whole content with them. This relationship reveals itself in the feeling of order which the view induces.[28]

Unwin perceived the village as an "association for mutual help"; it was that quality that distinguished it from modern urban society, at once atomized by isolating individualism and divided by antagonistic class warfare. Not surprisingly, however, he found it all but impossible to reconcile his vision of a community whose members were "conscious of and frankly accepting" of a set of hierarchical relationships reaching from squire to road mender with his commitment to democratic socialism. He shared the dilemma with other reformers of his class who, when looking for an escape from contemporary urban disorganization and dysfunction, could see an alternative nowhere other than in an idealized, pre-industrial past. Unwin tried to wriggle free of the difficulty, but in doing so as often as not enmeshed himself further. "The relationships of feudalism have gone," he declared stoutly; but as to what exactly would take their place he was by no means certain: "democracy has yet to evolve some definite relationships of its own, which when they come will doubtless be as picturesque as the old forms."[29] Why "picturesque"? The anti-modern strain in Unwin's thinking, characteristic of Morris and Carpenter as well, encouraged him to believe that he could succeed in pouring the new wine of egalitarian socialism into the old bottles of hierarchical community.

III

In 1904, Parker and Unwin won the competition to plan Britain's first Garden City, Letchworth, in Hertfordshire. The Garden City movement in Britain was the consequence of the same combination of Utopian and conservative forces that were operating in Unwin's own mind at the time. The concept, as proclaimed by its leading evangelist, Ebenezer

6 Illustration from Parker and Unwin's *The Art of Building a Home* (1901): "Design for a Hamlet"

Howard, in his book *Garden Cities of To-morrow,* was remarkably radical. It proposed nothing less than a reform of the system of land tenure and the planning and construction of entirely new cities throughout the countryside, balanced communities for work and living in which country and city would merge together into a lively unity, as sterile suburbs disappeared along with the class division they encouraged. A number of men and women who espoused the Garden City cause, joining the Garden City Association to do so, were socialists like Parker and Unwin. And in communities that were built before the First World War – Letchworth and Hampstead Garden Suburb – schemes of communal living, such as proposed by Unwin, were in fact incorporated into the design and construction of "co-operative" housing units.

Despite the socially-advanced nature of Howard's vision and the enthusiasm of radical reformers for his proposals, the movement, as it manifested itself in the years before the war, was nonetheless backward-looking. In its expressed fear of urban life, it bespoke that hankering after an idealized past that Unwin found so tantalizing. Its goal of recreated community, far from implying a radical leveling, envisaged the rebirth of a tranquil mutuality across class lines. Its expectation that Garden Cities would encourage such worthy living was grounded in the assumption that definitions of worth should derive from values that were essentially those of a "disinterested" upper middle-class directorate of planners, patrons, architects and managers. Above all, that directorate continued to insist that however experimental the concept, it must, to establish its worth, prove itself financially sound.

Parker and Unwin were familiar with Howard's scheme, and were enthusiastic supporters of the Garden City concept. "I remember well," Parker later reminisced, "how attracted to Howard I was, and how completely sympathetic we were in our aims and views."[30] Unwin had spoken at conferences on the subject in 1901 and 1902; he and Parker had recently completed plans for the design of New Earswick, a working-class estate commissioned by the Rowntree family on a tract outside York. Their commitment was manifest, their credentials impressive. Their design, which won out over two others, departed from Howard's schematic plan in several respects – most notably as a consequence of mainline railway tracks which bisected the site. Whereas Howard made no specific mention of the way classes were to be distributed throughout his city, Parker and Unwin proposed, from the start and at the insistence of the developers, distinctive middle- and working-class neighborhoods. Within the latter, houses were in many cases plotted around quadrangles or greens, in a manner reminiscent of a scheme proposed by Unwin in *The Art of Building a Home,* and reflective of his admiration for the social "unity" of village life. A recent historian has remarked that the overall design reflected a determination that

Letchworth take shape as "a cooperatively organized community of equals." Yet he observes as well that "Unwin's aesthetic glorification of the traditional village was also a glorification of the stable social relations he imagined existed there, and an implicit critique of the modern quest for change."[31] Letchworth was a "community of equals" to the extent that its patrons and planners were determined to provide a pleasant, healthy environment for all its citizens. To ensure "stable social relations," however, they took few chances.

Unwin's intention to create community was thwarted by more than his employers' unwillingness to integrate working and middle classes. So anxious was he to provide every Letchworth citizen with green grass, trees and gardens, that he imposed a housing density below that necessary for healthy existence, and thereby inhibited the growth of neighborly interaction. The formula – twelve houses to the acre – was lower than Howard had proposed. But Howard was far more comfortable with the tight urban landscape that Unwin shied from. The overall effect was of isolated housing clusters and solitary dwellings, rather than of a unified whole. In this, early Letchworth reflected its designer's equation of democracy with individualism. Unwin himself recognized the problem. "Spaces in the garden city tend to be too large in proportion to the buildings," he wrote in 1907, "and we have much yet to learn as to the best treatment."[32]

Unity – and hence, by implication, a sense of community – was to be achieved by means of aesthetic control, most notably in the imposition of regulations as to the use of building materials. Here the individual was to give way to the communal. In a typed list of "suggestions" submitted to the city's promoters, Unwin insisted on "simple, straightforward buildings, suitably designed for their respective purposes and honestly built of simple and harmonious materials." There were to be no "artificial attempts at the picturesque" nor any "useless ornamentation." In order to ensure "unity of effect," roofs were to be of local red tiles, rather than of the cheaper blue or purple slates used elsewhere in England, and bricks whitewashed or stuccoed if they were of an inharmonious color.[33] Unwin fought a constant, and losing, battle on this front. First Garden City Company, Ltd, anxious – at times nearly desperate – to avert financial disaster, was unwilling to allow aesthetic authoritarianism precedence over fiscal responsibility. In addition, Unwin's fierce desire for unity of design often stood opposed to his equally unequivocal determination to provide workers affordable housing. Thomas Adams, the Company secretary, took a characteristic shot at Unwin in a speech to the Letchworth men's club, arguing that "it was possible to provide a well built cottage with slated roof at less cost than the tiled one, although he might be laying himself open to the charge of inartistic taste." He noted as well that the maximum of twelve houses to the acre, because it drove up costs, "was bound to place some burden on the poor" – a remark greeted by a round of "hear, hears."[34]

None of these conflicts were peculiar to Letchworth; these fights had been fought before and are fought today. What makes the argument worth noting is the fact that Unwin relied to such an extent upon aesthetic harmony to produce a sense of community. Deprived of the former, the latter suffered far more than might have been the case had Unwin found other ways to center his conception and his design.

In fact, the town was not to have a proper "center" until at least a decade following its founding. Space was allocated in the original plan, but the Company believed it a mistake to lease land for shops and public buildings until the population reached a point that would persuade builders to erect something well-designed and substantial. Despite Unwin's admiration for the work of the Continental planner Camillo Sitte, who extolled the virtues of enclosed town squares, he proposed instead an open park as the city's hub, bordered by poplar trees. This scheme, he explained, "while it tends to emphasize the centre and concentrate the life of the town there ... entails perhaps some loss of the sense of enclosure and cosiness which are attractive features of the medieval *place*."[35] That was indeed the case. Nor did the park "concentrate the life of the town," since its residents had considerable greensward upon which to enjoy themselves adjacent to their own houses. Shops would have encouraged that concentration – as they do at the present time. But Unwin appeared unconscious of the role that shops and public forums of various sorts might play in drawing people – and people of different classes – together. Even in the subsidiary "villages" that were the hallmark of early Letchworth, there were few if any neighborhood stores, though in the case of the Pixmore estate, a tract of working-class houses designed by Parker and Unwin, an institute, tennis courts and bowling green encouraged common activity, while testifying to the architects' determination, where possible, to provide workers and their families with amenities hitherto understood as privilege rather than right. Men, women and children, to the extent that they lived in such clusters, were all but actively discouraged by Unwin's plan to move beyond the confines of their closes and quadrangles, to mingle with each other as citizens of a community greater than the sum of its disconnected parts.

For the citizens of Letchworth, Unwin did his very best to design housing expressive of his democratic convictions. He and Parker struggled, and urged other architects as well, to provide the sort of accommodation they had advocated in *The Art of Building a Home*, and that the Rowntrees had promoted at New Earswick: commodious living rooms; three bedrooms and separate bath, where cost permitted; orientation so as to catch the maximum amount of sunlight, even if this meant placing coalstore and larder toward the street. Though rate of return on investment was of concern to the Rowntrees, they were, as a recent commentator has observed, "always prepared . . . to abandon the idea of low-cost housing, rather than lower aesthetic standards."[36] Not so the trustees of First Garden City Company, Ltd. From the start Unwin was forced to compromise. He argued that the minimum dimensions authorized for Letchworth living rooms – twelve feet by twelve feet six inches – were too small, providing for a family of four less cubic footage per person than that required in provincial common lodging houses and New York prisons. "Surely what is deemed essential for the inhabitants of prisons and common lodging-houses is not too generous for the inhabitants of Garden City, which seeks to set an example to the country of what the homes of the people should be like."[37] Even as built to less-than-ideal standards, workers' cottages commanded rents that put them beyond the reach of many of those employed in the factories and workshops that had begun to locate in the town.

When house plans did embody the ideal, workers remained unimpressed. The parlor debate continued a heated one. The first issue of *Garden City*, published by the Association in 1906, put the matter squarely before its readers: workmen and their wives did not want daily life lived in one room – even if that room was a comparatively large one. "They like the parlor and they mean to have it. They give many reasons for their preference. Such as the necessity of having a place into which to show the casual visitor when the woman of the household is cooking; the need for a place of retirement for the husband when he requires it, and as a sort of storeroom for souvenirs and select pieces of furniture as they possess."[38] A spokesman for W.H. Smith, which had moved its printing operations to Letchworth, complained of the difficulty the company faced as it attempted to convince workers of the advantages of Garden City housing. In addition to the matter of parlors, bedrooms were too small; and tenants complained that "some of the cottages had doors and latches like chicken houses. They were told that they would get to like the new arrangements, but they declined to try them." The cottages were "good enough as scenery," the report concluded, "but were not designed to suit the needs or prejudices of the London workman."[39]

To all of this, Unwin replied with undeniable truth that while Letchworth was not Utopia – or even Utopia Limited – it was a city far more appropriate to a truly democratic society than any other in the nation. "Has it ever occurred to you," he asked in a speech in 1912:

> to go down a street of workman's cottages in almost any other
> town in this country and assume the same critical attitude [as that
> of Letchworth's detractors]? Do we know any other town where
> there is not and never can be another slum? Do we know any

other where every house has had some thought and care bestowed on it, to adapt it to the needs of its occupants and its position? I know of none such ... [and] going as I do constantly to other places, I feel that Letchworth has given a very good lead.[40]

To the extent that Letchworth provided its individual citizens the opportunity to enjoy healthy lives in an environment in sympathy with aesthetic refinement and in touch with natural beauty, it corresponded to Unwin's own definition of democracy. Democracy meant a society of equals, in which men, women and children shared access to what was "best." If Letchworth had not entirely achieved that lofty goal, it had come closer than any other community in the nation.

Yet Letchworth's individuals did not shed the skin of class consciousness as they emerged into the sunshine of their environmental springtime. This had been the hope – as it remained, for a time, the claim. "We have no feudal survivals, no slums, no snobbery," one resident proclaimed in Letchworth's monthly journal, *The City*. "There is no storied tradition behind us which might with dead hand benumb the multifarious enterprise of to-day...." H.D. Pearsall, president of the Residents' Union, welcomed newcomers in 1911 with the injunction to "break away from the ordinary mould of English town life with its 'class' distinctions."[41]

Putting "class" in quotation marks could not diminish the reality of its presence, however. The city's governmental structure did little to promote democratic participation across class lines. Despite the existence of various councils and committees, composed in the main of elected middle-class representatives, the constantly intrusive presence of the Company in the affairs and decision-making of the community cast a paternalistic pall over the enterprise. Factory workers experienced the tensions of industrial relations that were not markedly different at Letchworth from those in any other English town or city. With factories came trade unions, and with trade unions, strikes. A member of the militant Church Socialist Union, who visited Letchworth in 1913, declared with some truth that it was "no more than Leeds whitewashed. In Letchworth the same system obtained, but it happens to be painted in more beautiful colours. There is the same division of classes, the same separation of members of the human race into masters and men." As the manager of the Phoenix Motor Works proclaimed: "It was no good him saying that they came [to Letchworth] to build a factory for the benefit of the working man; they came ... to make money."[42]

Unwin, who understood class as the enemy of democracy, undoubtedly found the evidence of such antagonism distressing. Thwarted by Company policy and by his own difficulties in conceiving an urban environment that would encourage the dissolution of class boundaries, he directed his energies at Letchworth to the establishment of a school system he hoped would accomplish that end. He was an active member of the Letchworth Education Committee, he and Parker having settled in the town with their families and built themselves adjacent houses there. In an article written in 1905, Unwin outlined plans his committee had drafted which had as their goal "the development of the individual, to fit him or her for the common life." Boys and girls of all classes would be taught together "and share the same training and experience, so that they might be prepared to meet and cooperate in civic and business spheres." The expectation was that "from the common discipline of different classes of children a more thorough and complete understanding of, and respect for, the different spheres of life would be likely to grow; and further that in this way alone, could anything like equality of opportunity be given." Though eventually some sort of streaming would be necessary, in order to accommodate students going on to university, "the whole educational system, elementary, technical, and secondary, should as far as possible be made homogeneous as regards management, quality of teaching and social status," to ensure that all children shared "in the same school life." Nor was it to be supposed that children of the working class would automatically leave school at fourteen; assistance would be provided to "the specially gifted children of less well-to-do parents."[43]

Here was concrete expression of Unwin's democratic ideals. Contrary to the philosophy of social segregation enshrined in the Education Act of 1902 and its implementation under Robert Morant's elitist code,[44] Unwin's scheme would actively encourage the nurture of individual "best selves" from whatever class, fitting them for their role in "the common life" of a genuinely democratic society. Despite his commitment to educational equality, however, Unwin could not help but express the condescension that so often colored the well-intentioned thoughts and plans of turn-of-the-century social reformers. While "the children of the well-to-do" would gain "widened experience and sympathy" from the scheme, he wrote, those of the "less well-to-do" would profit "by mixing with children who have had a more refined upbringing, and may be expected to have more refined habits and manners."[45] Tell that to respectable working-class parents, and then wonder why they might turn away in anger and resentment.

Letchworth, in its early years, was a vision as well as an emergent city, a vision that accorded with Unwin's own sense of the way in which a democratic society should be fashioned. It was a middle-class vision, shaped and articulated by men and women who had made the personal choice to live as pioneers. Unlike the majority of working-class residents of Letchworth, whose jobs had required their relocation, people like Unwin and Parker settled at Letchworth to partake of an experiment that promised something better for England and its citizens. In 1914, the Letchworth Arts Club engaged themselves in that quintessentially high-minded, middle-class pursuit, the production of a masque. Entitled "The Garden of the Leech," it derived its theme from the etymology of the word Letchworth – the leech's garden. "The town's name," the printed foreword declared, "considered as signifying the Leech's Holding, or Garden of Healing Herbs, gave the masque its point of departure. Garden City is in effect a place of healing, an experiment-ground for solutions to social ills and sores, and one where constructive thought may generate and bear fruit."[46] So it was to the masquers; and so it was to Unwin.

IV

Though in sympathy with the message the masque proclaimed, Unwin almost certainly never saw it. By the time it was performed, he no longer lived in Letchworth. In 1906, he and his family had moved to Hampstead, where he assumed the post of consulting architect and surveyor to the Hampstead Garden Suburb Trust. He remained in partnership with Parker, and continued to design for Letchworth. But his efforts were now concentrated on this new scheme – the Garden Suburb.

Although Unwin's work at Hampstead resulted in a delightful semi-urban space, the suburb project did not afford him much opportunity to design for democracy. He was constrained by the personality of the scheme's founder, the redoubtable Henrietta Barnett. Co-founder, with her husband, of Toynbee Hall, she was a power in her own right. A neighbor once remarked that "she was the only person I've ever known who could recite the Ten Commandments as if she had just made them up."[47] She had written and spoken extensively and with characteristic certainty for over a quarter of a century on problems associated with poverty, and of ways to solve them by means of programs and prescriptions to which she and her husband attached the label of "practicable socialism." Hampstead Garden Suburb was to address the urban housing problem by providing affordable workers' houses within a two-penny fare of the city. In their attractive, well-designed "cottages" and salubrious gardens, workers' families "would develop a sense of home life and an interest in nature which form the best security against the temptation of drink and gambling." The estate was to be laid out as a whole, with houses and gardens for rich and poor arrayed in a manner that would encourage community, and thereby promote better understanding between the classes living in proximity within its boundaries. Finally, the suburb would be planned so as to preserve the natural beauty, not only of the Heath extension, but of the land on which it was itself built.[48]

Once again, the ideal of the hierarchical village was extolled: "The English system of government," Henrietta Barnett wrote, "is based on the belief that there is in every district a leisured and cultivated class able to give time and thought to municipal and other public duties, and when such a class is absent the whole suffers both financially and ethically." Toynbee Hall had been founded in the 1880s to provide East London with such a leisured class. Now, twenty-five years on, Henrietta Barnett was prepared to acknowledge that the Hall had been no better than an "artificial protest against the massing in one locality of the poor." The Suburb, which would bring the classes together as genuine neighbors, would encourage the kind of social intercourse that its founders fondly believed had existed before the advent of industrialization and the uncontrolled growth of towns. "The old-fashioned village"; "the big house and the cottage"; "the cottage and the manor-house of the English village": over and over the image was evoked.[49] And with it, the expectation that class antagonisms would gradually vanish.

Nowhere in the literature surrounding the establishment of the Suburb was there much mention of democracy. At the groundbreaking ceremony, Henrietta Barnett proclaimed that "the money of democracy" – that is the contributions she had received from philanthropists and various public bodies around the country – was purchasing "the homes of the democracy." But on the same occasion, Alfred Lyttelton, Barnett's right hand and chairman of the Trust, spoke of its desire "to gather together in natural sympathy various classes so that each should take part in the common duty of good neighbourship": not, be it noted, good citizenship; rather, good neighborship. Life in the Suburb would encourage rich and poor to learn from each other, and the rich to "minister" to the poor as well.[50]

This was without question a conservative agenda. Yet it is a measure of the congruence of conservative and radical goals within the Garden City movement that a convinced socialist such as Unwin would have found the proposal an appealing one. He, too, understood the need to create new, liberating environments for workers and their families. He, too, looked to the past for models upon which to construct the communities of the present. And, along with the Barnetts and so many others of similar temperament and point of view, he subscribed to the belief that "disinterested" reformers recognized what was best for England's sadly deprived citizenry.

Unwin's democratic impulses were inhibited by more than Henrietta Barnett's agenda. He was confronted, as well, by the formidable presence of Edwin Lutyens as a second consulting architect, an appointment engineered in all likelihood by Lyttelton, whose country house Lutyens had remodeled. Lutyens's grand design for the Suburb's central square superseded one by Unwin which, unlike his scheme at Letchworth, would have encouraged community by placing shops and a working-men's club in close proximity to church, chapel and institute. Unwin intended, as he wrote in a brochure advertising the Suburb's purposes, "to bring together the best that the English village and the English city have to give."[51] Yet Lutyens wanted something different: a far more formal setting for buildings that would impress – as, indeed, they do. But their impressiveness, and the square designed to enhance that impressiveness, discourage human intercourse. The greensward lies mostly empty. People pass through the space, but seldom linger there.

Much of Unwin's socialist zeal appears to have evaporated by the time he undertook the Hampstead consultancy. The working-class housing he and Parker designed for the Suburb was of good quality, and continued to reflect the principles the two had espoused in *The Art of Building*. Their most creative work was in those sections reserved for the more affluent – not altogether surprising given the fact that budgetary constraints necessarily limited the scope of what could be attempted for workers and their families. What is surprising, however, given Unwin's earlier democratic enthusiasms, is the fact of his willingness to calm the fears of prospective middle- and upper-middle-class residents worried that pronouncements about the virtues of communitarian association between rich and poor might result in uncomfortable proximity to working-class neighbors. In order for the Suburb to succeed financially, well-to-do leaseholders wanted to know that they were not sacrificing financial – or social – security to some hastily conceived do-good improvement scheme. To that end, Unwin and his fellow Suburb architect M.H. Baillie Scott wrote a slickly produced, heavily illustrated pamphlet, in which they reassured potential householders of the estate's respectability and of the soundness of first-rate architecture as an investment. Only once were the "industrious classes" mentioned, and in such a way as to suggest that the Suburb was to become not one community but two:

> At one end of the estate where the Hampstead Golf Course forms a boundary, only houses of a larger type with good gardens are under erection. At the northern end, in pleasant contrast, cottages are being built, public greens and open spaces are being laid out, and the charm of an old English village is being recreated by Barry Parker and Raymond Unwin.[52]

Note the implication that the village idea is not to be imposed on the Suburb as a whole, but only on that portion of it at one remove from the houses of the wealthy. If rich and poor were to mingle, the pamphlet appeared to say, it would be only at the behest – and on terms established by – the former.

V

Unwin did nothing to challenge Henrietta Barnett's authority at Hampstead or to campaign there for community on more democratic lines. Whether his own youthful ardor had faded (by 1913 he was fifty years old), or whether he simply recognized the futility of such a challenge, he contented himself with laying out what is certainly one of the most pleasing urban landscapes in Western Europe or America, and with the designing of housing for all classes that, after eighty years, retains both integrity and charm. In 1914, he left his Hampstead post (and a year later dissolved his partnership with Parker) to accept appointment as Chief Town Planning Inspector to the Local Government Board, and then, four years later, as Chief Housing Architect to the Ministry of Health.

The significance of the history of Unwin's first fifty years does not consist so much in his progression from late Victorian socialist visionary to pre-welfare state reforming bureaucrat. Its importance, instead, lies in the evidence of the difficulties he encountered when he set out to design for democracy. In his writings, he hymned the virtues of community. Yet the community he tried to imagine lay tangled in the myth of the pre-industrial village, and in the ideal of an "Englishness" appealing to upper-middle-class Victorian reformers.[53] It was to that "Englishness" that they turned when frightened by evidence of class division and threats of class conflict, or by the apparent inevitability of democracy. That myth replaced the reality of class consciousness and democratic advance with the "cosy" village, where all lived healthy lives, cultivated their gardens, and accepted their place within a hierarchy ruled by an elite that understood its obligations to those whom it both ruled and served.

This was Henrietta Barnett's vision. And it was one that Unwin found seductive. Yet in the end he could not use it to solve the vexing puzzle of how to bring people together in social harmony. Whether because of a commitment to democracy at odds with the conservatism of "English" community, or because of the practical difficulties involved in its physical recreation, Unwin never succeeded in bringing such a village to life. Instead he devoted his energies to the design of houses and groups of houses for the individual families he believed were the bedrock of democratic society. Without foresaking community, he hoped that by providing what was best for individuals, their common healthy and high-minded experience might create a bond among them that would transcend class as it celebrated democracy.

NOTES

1 George Orwell, *The Road to Wigan Pier*, London, Victor Gollancz, 1937, p. 169.
2 Freda White, "Raymond Unwin," Unwin Papers, Manchester University Archives (hereafter UP), "Personal Papers," 8 September 1962.
3 Michael Day, "Sir Raymond Unwin and R. Barry Parker: A study and evaluation of their contribution to site-planning theory and practice," MA Thesis, Manchester University, 1973, pp. 3–10.
4 Raymond Unwin, Journal, entry for 26 July 1887, UP.
5 Ibid., entry for 18 July 1887.
6 Raymond Unwin, "The Architect's Contribution," *RIBA Journal*, 7 November 1931, p. 9.
7 Ibid., p. 10.
8 Unwin, Journal, entry for 4 July 1887.
9 Raymond Unwin, "Edward Carpenter and 'Towards Democracy'," in Gilbert Beith, ed., *Edward Carpenter: In Appreciation*, London, George Allen and Unwin, 1931, p. 235.
10 Edward Carpenter, *Towards Democracy*, 2nd edn, London, John Heywood, 1885, pp. 46, 48.
11 Unwin, Journal, entry for 6 May 1887.
12 Unwin, "Edward Carpenter and 'Towards Democracy,' " p. 239.
13 Edward Carpenter, "Transitions to Freedom," in *Forecasts of the Coming Century*, Manchester, Labour Press, 1897, p. 186.
14 Unwin, "The Dawn of a Happier Day," n.p., UN 9/2.1, ii, UP.
15 Raymond Unwin, "Scrambling," an essay written for *Commonweal* in 1886, "Publications and Articles," UP.
16 R. Barry Parker, speech on the occasion of the presentation of the Royal Gold Medal of the RIBA to Raymond Unwin, 12 April 1937, "Publications and Articles," UP.
17 R. Barry Parker and Raymond Unwin, *The Art of Building a Home*, London, Longman, 1901, p. iii.
18 Ibid., p. 27.
19 Samuel A. Barnett, introduction to *Toynbee Hall Annual Report*, 1892, pp. 13–14.
20 Parker and Unwin, *The Art of Building a Home*, p. 9.
21 Ibid., p. 86.
22 Raymond Unwin, *Cottage Plans and Common Sense*, London, Fabian Society, 1902, p. 11.
23 Raymond Unwin, ed., *The Nation's New Houses*, London, *Daily News* pamphlet (1919), p. 6.
24 Parker and Unwin, *The Art of Building a Home*, p. 64.
25 Katherine Bruce Glasier, "Labour's Northern Voice," August 1940, UN 13/2, UP.
26 R. Barry Parker, "Some Principles of Domestic Architecture," *British Architect*, vol. 43, 1895, p. 242.
27 Parker and Unwin, *The Art of Building a Home*, pp. 107–8.
28 Ibid., p. 92.
29 Ibid., pp. 95, 100.
30 Interview with R. Barry Parker, *Letchworth Citizen*, 5 March 1943, n.p.
31 Robert Fishman, *Urban Utopias in the Twentieth Century: Ebenezer Howard, Frank Lloyd Wright and Le Corbusier*, New York, Basic Books, 1977, p. 69.
32 Raymond Unwin, "The Beauty of Towns" (1907), reprinted in *Town and Country Planning*, vol. 22, October 1954, p. 528.

33 "Suggestions," UN 12/24/i, iii, UP.
34 *Letchworth Citizen*, 22 March 1912, p. 4.
35 Raymond Unwin, "The Planning of Garden City," Appendix B, in C.B. Purdom, *The Garden City: A Study in the Development of a Modern Town*, London, J.M. Dent and Sons, 1913, pp. 228–9.
36 Frank Jackson, *Sir Raymond Unwin: Architect, Planner and Visionary*, London, A. Zwemmer, 1985, p. 56.
37 Raymond Unwin, "Cottage Planning," in First Garden City Company, Ltd, *Where Shall I Live?*, London, First Garden City Company, Ltd, 1907, p. 105.
38 *The Garden City*, vol. 1, October 1906, n.p.
39 D.B. Cockerall, "A Workshop in London and in Letchworth," *The City* (a monthly magazine published in Letchworth), vol. 1, February 1909, p. 35.
40 *Letchworth Citizen*, 5 January 1912, p. 4.
41 G.P. Nowers, "The Call of the Future," *The City*, vol. 1, February 1909, p. 28; *Letchworth Citizen*, 22 April 1911, p. 5.
42 Ibid., 14 March 1913, p. 3; 13 December 1912, p. 5.
43 Raymond Unwin, "Education at Garden City," reprinted in the *Bedfordshire Express*, 30 December 1905, from *The Journal of Education*, in press clipping book for 1905, p. 103, Letchworth Garden City Museum (hereafter LGCM).
44 See Brian Simon, *Education and the Labour Movement, 1870–1920*, London, Lawrence and Wishart, 1965, ch. 7.
45 Unwin, "Education at Garden City."
46 Foreword, "The Garden of the Leech, A Masque of Letchworth" (1914), "Event programmes, scripts" file, LGCM.
47 Brigid Grafton Green, *Hampstead Garden Suburb, 1907–1977*, London, Hampstead Garden Residents' Association, 1977, p. 8.
48 Henrietta O. Barnett, "Science and City Suburbs," in J.E. Hand, ed., *Science in Public Affairs*, London, George Allen, 1906, pp. 55–7.
49 Henrietta O. Barnett, "A Garden Suburb at Hampstead," *Contemporary Review*, vol. 87, February 1905, pp. 234, 239–40.
50 Quoted in Barnett, "A Garden Suburb at Hampstead," p. 344.
51 Raymond Unwin and M.H. Baillie Scott, *Town Planning and Modern Architecture at the Hampstead Garden Suburb*, London, T. Fisher Unwin, 1909, p. 2.
52 Ibid., p. 27.
53 See Raphael Samuel, ed., *Patriotism: The Making and Unmaking of British National Identity*, London, Routledge, 1989; Robert Colls and Philip Dodd, eds, *Englishness: Politics and Culture, 1880–1920*, London, Croom Helm, 1986.

7 Eleanor Rathbone around the time of her election to Liverpool City Council (1909)

4

Eleanor Rathbone 1872–1946
The Victorian family under the daughter's eye

Susan Pedersen

Sometime in 1895 or 1896, two women in their early twenties walked in the gardens of Somerville College, debating whether it was possible for them to reconcile their ambitions with their womanhood. The two were Eleanor Rathbone and Margery Fry, both born into wealthy, liberal, dissenting clans – the Liverpool Rathbones, the Bristol Frys – who dominated the economic and political landscape of their mid-Victorian towns. Families like the Rathbones and the Frys took the call to public service seriously, but they expected their daughters to express such service through voluntary and philanthropic activities and in concert with domestic duties. It was their sons who were able to mesh private ambition and public duty through careers in Parliament or the civil service. Such spheres were still closed to women, a fact that left Eleanor and Margery, on that unspecified day, wondering whether in fact "there was anything worthwhile to be ambitious about." Eleanor, Margery remembered, thought that it might be worth wishing to be the Warden (or Principal) of Somerville, but Margery felt that just wasn't good enough, and the two young women concluded that as "Parliament was shut to us, and practically everything was shut to us," "[t]here was nothing worthwhile to be ambitious about."[1]

Fate was kinder; or perhaps their ambitions stronger than they knew. Margery Fry did in fact condescend to become Principal of Somerville, and Eleanor Rathbone spent sixteen years in the House of Commons, where, Harold Nicolson remembered, she lobbied for her particular reforming causes so relentlessly that junior ministers scurried for shelter when they saw her coming.[2] But Rathbone's years in Parliament were only the culmination of a long and influential career as a social reformer. Those doors so firmly closed in the 1890s seemed to open just as she reached them, and if the jambs were frozen she didn't mind giving them a push. From Somerville she became a leader in Liverpool social work; when women became eligible for election to borough councils, she became Liverpool's first woman councillor. Her work as a social investigator and social thinker earned her the right to present evidence on distributive social policy to a bewildering array of Government and private committees, while her position as Millicent Garrett Fawcett's successor at the head of the principal non-militant suffrage organization made her a logical choice for the League of Nations' committees on social policy. By 1929, when Rathbone won election to Parliament as an Independent for the seat of Combined English Universities, she was not merely another philanthropically-inclined daughter of a prominent family, but a well-known political figure in her own right, eclipsing her brothers and cousins as the most distinguished Rathbone of her generation.

As a person, however, she remains extraordinarily elusive. By her own admission "the most undemonstrative member of an undemonstrative family," she was so reticent that even her close friend Mary Stocks admitted that her "contacts with people were impersonalized."[3] She left no diaries or introspective works, and the Rathbone papers in Liverpool and London contain little personal material. Her letters to even her closest political allies and friends – the Duchess of Atholl, Nancy Astor, Barbara Hammond – are affectionate but unforthcoming. Her correspondence with her lifelong companion Elizabeth Macadam, which could alone have given us a glimpse of the woman behind the public figure, was destroyed after her death.

What is a biographer to do with a woman who so emphatically believed that by her works we must know her? I suggest that we take her at her word, and look first to the politics to tell us something of the beliefs that drove her. If we examine the causes for which Rathbone became nationally known – especially the campaigns for "family endowment" and against child marriage in India – we will discover a characteristic obsession with the domestic subjection of women, and an equally consistent determination to use state institutions and the powers of enfranchised women to mitigate it. We can then turn to the far less documented private life, and find there some of the sources for a style of social action not uncharacteristic of the daughters of the Victorians.

I

Eleanor Rathbone is remembered today primarily for her long campaign for family allowances, a campaign that received its most cogent justification in her 1924 classic, *The Disinherited Family*, and that finally came to fruition with the passage of the Family Allowances Act in 1945.[4] Family allowances seem a moderate enough goal, something social reformers from a range of political views would have been likely to favor in the period between the wars. Eleanor Rathbone did much to promote this view, arguing her case in the 1930s quite as much on the grounds of child welfare, or even population increase, as on the grounds of feminism. Historians, not surprisingly, have often claimed she moved the feminist movement in a conservative direction, judging her attitudes towards motherhood to be "anti-feminist," "functionalist," "very traditional" or even a "betray[al]" of "the independent woman."[5]

Yet Rathbone began thinking about the problems of distribution well before the war, and from the standpoint of women in the labor market, and not the family. Sometime around the turn of the century she wrote a theoretical piece, quite unlike the careful social investigations which established her early reputation. *The Problem of Women's Wages* sought to answer a straightforward question: why are women's wages so much lower than men's wages, both absolutely and in relation to any particular type of work? She surveyed many of the classic explanations – women's unskilled and ununionized status, and their willingness to work for "pocket money" – but concluded that these were only manifestations of a deeper "cause of causes." "[A]ll the factors in the problem of women's wages," she wrote:

> have their root in the one set of facts common to women as apart
> from men; viz., their functions as childbearers and housewives,
> and the economic dependence of themselves and their children on
> the male parent which, under present social arrangements, the
> proper performance of those functions entails. In simpler words,
> the difference between the wages of men and women is due to the
> different consequences which marriage has for the two sexes.[6]

We have here a first principle, central to all of Rathbone's work. She is arguing, in essence, that the familial ideal at the very heart of Victorianism made the equality of women impossible. The social investigations she conducted over the next ten years into the living conditions of dockers, seamen and casual laborers in Liverpool gave some empirical support to her views. These men were often the main family "breadwinners," her investigations found, but their wages were often too small and too irregular to support their families adequately. Yet the consequences of irregular earnings were felt quite unequally, with wives and children bearing the brunt of the hardship. Families of merchant seamen were particularly hard hit, since while seamen could have half of their wages paid to their wives, such payments were made only monthly and were in any case not mandatory. Although wives did seek to supplement family income themselves, there was little waged work open to married women in Liverpool. More common solutions, then, were the money-lender, the pawnshop or, as a last resort, poor relief.[7]

Rathbone had already concluded from her study of wages that "the arrangement by which the cost of rearing fresh generations is thrown as a rule upon the male parent, is not the only possible, nor even the only existing one"[8] her social investigations convinced her that it was not a particularly good "arrangement" either. Initially she proposed only that the state enforce men's obligation to maintain, but after watching (and helping to administer) the system of separation allowances for soldiers' and sailors' wives during the First World War she came to a different and far more radical solution.[9] State services, preferably administered by activist women like herself, could help to support mothers and children directly.

Thus was born the campaign for "family endowment" (or family allowances), which absorbed Rathbone from 1918 – when a Family Endowment Committee first made a proposal for the support of children and all mothers with children under age five – until the passage of the Act in 1945. She let no occasion pass on which to defend her pet proposal, arguing to the Sankey Commission on the Coal Industry in 1925 and the Unemployment Assistance Board in 1934 that only allowances could help lift all children out of poverty.[10] She was willing to consider virtually any type of program and any method of finance, whether tax-based, contributory or industrial. On one point, however, she held firm: family allowances must be paid directly to women, hence effecting a redistribution, however modest, from men to women.

It is important to recognize the nature of Rathbone's argument: essentially, she supplemented the "New Liberal" focus on the structural causes of poverty with an analysis based on sex. Of course, Charles Booth, Seebohm Rowntree, William Beveridge and others had also recognized that the burden of dependent children as well as low or irregular earnings were an important cause of working-class poverty; unlike these social reformers, however, Rathbone refused to treat the family as an indisseverable unit, insisting that, in the home as in the labor market, income intended for the support of whole families was monopolized by men. The belief that the male breadwinner norm was often a shield for male selfishness pervaded *The Disinherited Family*; indeed, she attributed men's reluctance to support family allowances to a desire to maintain women in dependence – to what she notoriously called a "Turk complex."[11]

Rathbone's focus on a sex-based redistribution and her tart views on the behavior of working-class men drew her into conflict with trade unionists and the Labour Party on more than one occasion. "You are rather hard on the single man," Herbert Morrison protested when he grasped that Rathbone was indeed willing to tax men's wages to pay for children, but what really outraged at least some Labour men was their suspicion that Rathbone did indeed hope to reduce the authority of the husband and father.[12] What, exactly, was the "fierce" and "never married" feminist proposing, Rhys Davies of the National Union of Distributive and Allied Workers asked?

> If she were frank with us she would say that the husband must go out to work; he should have a modicum at the end of a week for his tobacco, the employer to hand over the balance of his wages to the State, leaving the Civil Servant to dole it out to the wife and children – a sort of Truck system more objectionable than anything we have ever experienced before.[13]

He was not, actually, entirely off the mark, and other men grasped this as well. In 1922, when Rathbone first ran for Parliament as an Independent in the East Toxteth constituency of Liverpool, her Conservative opponent resorted to scare tactics, warning bachelors that they would see their wages docked to pay for other men's families.[14] Rathbone's focus on the unreliability of working men also made her a difficult ally for Labour women, many of whom preferred to argue for family allowances on the grounds of child health rather than women's rights.[15]

Yet the feminist identification Rathbone imprinted on family allowances did not go away. In 1944, with allowances legislation before Parliament, civil servants and some Ministers were still bristling at the suggestion that allowances could raise the status of married women and elaborating specious legalistic justifications for payment to the father.[16] The fact that giving even five shillings a week to a mother in her own right could be seen as so subversive is evidence that Rathbone was on to something. In an impassioned speech in the House, the woman who had campaigned for allowances for over twenty-five years threatened to oppose the measure if payment were not made by right to the mother.[17] Family allowances were advocated in Britain explicitly as a means of curtailing men's domestic authority: in their history of underfunding and neglect we find the response to that feminist identification.

II

If we can read Rathbone's long campaign for family allowances as an attempt to mitigate the husband's economic power, her campaigns in the area of colonial policy, to which she devoted much of the 1920s and 1930s, can be seen as an attempt to circumscribe his sexual rights.[18] Here Rathbone was on shakier ground, not only because of her deep suspicion of all forms of male sexuality, but also because her belief in the commonality of women's interests across national lines made her slow to understand the degree to which the complex politics of empire – and indeed her own position and loyalties – divided women as well as men.[19] Rathbone's decision that the status of women in the British colonies was

109

a matter for her concern stemmed from her reading of a work that caused one of the greatest popular controversies of the interwar period. The book was Katherine Mayo's *Mother India*, a lurid and misleading diatribe on the social conditions of Indian women. Child marriage and female seclusion were the consequence, according to Mayo, of the degeneracy of Hindu teachings and the lusts of Indian men. Such social conditions, Mayo explicitly stated, made national independence impossible, since a populace incapable of governing their passions could scarcely govern a nation. Prurient, simplistic and impassioned, *Mother India* sold like wildfire, outraged many Indian (and some British) readers, and left years of controversy in its wake.[20]

Rathbone had brought *Mother India* with her to read on holiday in 1927 and, friends recalled, was distressed almost to the point of illness by Mayo's graphic account.[21] She responded to the ensuing outcry over the book by, typically, turning to official publications to examine its claims. The short article she wrote summarizing her views is interesting not only because Rathbone did by and large defend the findings, although not the tone, of *Mother India*, but also because its analysis mirrored that developed in the family endowment campaign. As in the case of family endowment, Rathbone elided the problems of children into those of women, and defined both groups as relatively powerless. Their subjugation, seen largely as sexual, was dissociated from broader relations of class, religion or empire, and attributed in the first instance to men. While she professed to understand Indian revulsion against a book that found no merit in Indian civilization, she nevertheless asked, "which is the more important – the hurt feelings of the race-conscious, educated, articulate Hindu, or the millions of tortured bodies and wasted lives upon whose secrets Miss Mayo's book has shed its ray?" Her own answer was clear, and, just as she insisted that middle-class feminists had an obligation to aid working-class women, so too she looked to British women, "the natural custodians of that portion of the Imperial burden," to protect Indian women from Indian men.[22]

Yet when Rathbone began exercising her "custodianship," she discovered that her ostensible charges were less than receptive to her oversight. One of Rathbone's first actions was to organize a conference under the auspices of the National Union of Societies for Equal Citizenship (of which she was President) on "constructive schemes for improving the condition of women in India." "Experts" were to present papers on topics like child marriage and the caste system, and participants were to devise strategies for furthering Indian social reforms. No Indian women were scheduled to speak, although several, including Dhanvanthi Rama Rau – who had been one of the first women students at Madras University and had been active in social campaigns (including that against child marriage) within India – were in London in connection

110

with the Simon Commission. Rama Rau attended the conference and vividly recalled her feelings of outrage at the lack of Indian speakers, the prominent place given to Rathbone's article on child marriage, and the reiteration of the view that "the eradication of social evils in Indian society was the responsibility of the British – the White Man's Burden." In a brief intervention, she disputed the right of British women to speak on subjects they knew little about, and insisted that "educated Indian women were working in every province of their country to eradicate social evils and outmoded customs and prejudices." While Indian women would be grateful for British women's moral support, she explained to the conference the following day, the practical work of reform had to be undertaken by Indian women themselves. She won over a good portion of her audience, which refused to pass Rathbone's carefully-framed resolutions.[23]

This confrontation did not lead Rathbone to abandon the issue, although she became less patronizing and politically more astute. She began an extensive and frank correspondence with the leaders of the All-India Women's Conference and the Women's Indian Association and, as negotiations over constitutional reform progressed in the early 1930s, campaigned to have Indian women placed on the bodies framing the new constitution, and to win reserved seats for women in the provincial legislatures and a wider women's franchise. Yet her fundamental concern did not change. She continued to believe the "barbarity" of Indian social customs to be the main problem besetting Indian women,[24] and her efforts were based less on a commitment to Indian self-government *per se* – about which she continued to have complicated and ambivalent feelings[25] – than on the conviction that the interests of Indian women were by no means safe in the hands of Indian men. This latter view was shared by Nancy Astor, who wrote to ask Sir Samuel Hoare – then Secretary of State for India – whether he could "sleep easy in [his] bed and think of India governed only by Indian men."[26] And Rathbone told her correspondents about her reservations: when Rajkumari Amrit Kaur, then President of the All-India Women's Conference, told Rathbone that she "almost wished" that they hadn't raised the franchise issue "until we had gained a substantial backing from our men," Rathbone retorted that she was afraid "that men all the world over are much the same" and would only listen to women when they could back their opinions with votes.[27]

But the Indian women's organizations she consulted had their own political concerns and proved difficult to convert to her point of view. They had turned against the reservation of seats in 1932 – although largely, Rathbone felt certain, because they were "thinking in terms of Congress rather than in terms of women"[28] – and were disinclined to compromise on their initial demand for adult suffrage. Rathbone's correspondents did not deny the existence of social problems within India, but many insisted that independence was the prerequisite for their solution, unable to accept that a maternalist alliance with British feminists would be a more effective guarantor of women's rights than joint self-determination with Indian men. Women were "too nationally minded now to accept any favours for themselves to the detriment of their country's interests," Amrit Kaur wrote back to Rathbone; she could not agree that either the Congress Party or Indian men, rather than the British, were the problem. Against Rathbone's plea to accept those partial improvements she and other British women had been able to insert into the new constitution, Amrit Kaur argued that while such a gradualist approach might work "in a free country like yours," "in a subject country . . . a start on the wrong basis means disaster *ab initio*."[29]

Some of Rathbone's correspondents also resisted her view that relations between women could be untouched by the wider politics of colonial domination. Rathbone does seem genuinely to have believed this to be possible: as she told Amrit Kaur, "where sufferings and injustices affecting women are concerned, I as an old suffragist simply cannot remember or bother about national distinctions."[30] This perspective did lead her to criticize Mayo's denigration of Indian efforts at social reform in fairly harsh terms and to repudiate the pleas of successive Secretaries of State for India to desist from an agitation that could destabilize British rule[31] – but it sometimes made her insensitive to other hierarchies besides those of sex. Rathbone found it hard to accept that in an imperial context her Britishness was as immutable as her womanhood, that her decision not to "bother about" relations of imperial power was, effectively, a decision to accept – even exploit – an imperial status quo that divided women as well as men along racial and national lines. True, Rathbone's interventions into working-class women's lives also tended to presume shared interests from a position of superior social power, but here the democratic institutions to which she was strongly committed held her accountable to those she sought to represent. No such check constrained her activities involving women in the colonies, and sharing much of the late Victorian liberal's faith in the "civilizing" effects of British rule, she could not understand a feminist movement that insisted that women's emancipation and social reform could not be dissociated from national independence. She did what she could to convince Indian feminists that they must establish their rights against men as well as against the British. Most (but not all) resisted her interpretation;[32] and as the international situation worsened, she herself became caught up in new issues, new campaigns.

112

III

There is a pattern, then, to Rathbone's work for the two causes that absorbed her in the years between the wars. Although she became involved in issues at the heart of the New Liberal project (distributive social policy, Indian constitutional reform), in both cases her activism was based on her fear that reformers might leave untouched inequalities *between* the sexes, especially those rooted in an ostensibly natural domestic sphere. She then proposed to deal with such inequalities in two ways. First, she presented herself and the feminist movement with which she was allied as the champions of subjugated women. Second, she sought to use state institutions to redistribute power and resources between men and women within every given stratum of society and every region where British law held sway. Hers was an extraordinary vision, by no means merely the expression of the philanthropic conscience of the Victorians adapted to the twentieth century. How was Eleanor Rathbone able to recast Victorian ideals so thoroughly and so astonishingly? What can we find in Rathbone's life to help us explain it? Let us return now to her youth and early womanhood in the 1890s, to that era in which female ambition was scarcely possible.

IV

We know relatively little about Eleanor's childhood, but it does seem to have been marked by that combination of high-minded self-denial and emotional repression typical of many dissenters' upbringings. She was, family members recalled, a strong-willed and even wayward little girl, but she may have been lonely as well.[33] Eleanor loved and admired her father, the redoubtable William Rathbone (the sixth of this name), but he was more than fifty when she was born, and there were already grown children from a first marriage. Her own capable mother, who raised both the five children from the first wife and her own five, was almost as intimidating – so formidable that Eleanor's letters to her, even as a girl, were signed with her full name: your loving daughter, Eleanor Florence Rathbone.[34] She was close to her elder sister Evie, but Evie married her second cousin Hugh Rathbone when Eleanor was sixteen. There is no record of any close childhood friendships, and the family's annual pilgrimage between London and Liverpool may have made the cultivation of emotional ties difficult for this intense and earnest young girl.

Somerville made all the difference. To go to Somerville in 1893 was not an obvious course of action – not only was the college only fourteen years old, but the mere act of seeking a university education could seem an unwarranted piece of selfishness for young women raised (as William

Rathbone's daughters were) to place duty and family before self. Eleanor agonized over this decision for nearly a year, until her father unexpectedly set her free. In a remarkable letter (always his preferred means of communication when strong emotions were involved), the man who in 1866 had told his eldest daughter that "[t]here is no happiness & no peace except in denying ourselves and taking up our daily cross,"[35] in 1893 told his youngest that: "What your mother & I are most anxious you should do is that you should go to Oxford, Cambridge or stay at home exactly as you may think best for *yourself & your future happiness*; that is what we wish & what ought to decide you." Her own hope of "be[ing] of good to" her brother was, he said, "too uncertain to be allowed to weigh against whichever is most likely to promote your own improvement & happiness." It was her indecisiveness – and not any particular choice – that concerned him, and he warned her that she would lead "a very unhappy wasted life" if she did not cure herself of it.[36]

Licensed to achieve, Eleanor went to Somerville without further ado; nor did she ever merit her father's rebuke again. And Somerville gave her just what she needed: a room of her own and the chance to exercise what her first-year philosophy tutor called her "considerable power of independent thinking."[37] Perhaps more importantly, it gave her friends – her first taste of a community of educated women. Eleanor and some of the most determinedly intellectual soon formed a discussion group, the APs, understood by insiders to stand for "Associated Prigs." In the records of the APs, we see this first generation of women students struggling to define both an ideal of social service and their own place as independent women. Their set topics were fearsomely socially-conscious: the Fabian Essays and the Factory Acts, parish work and the disestablishment of the Church. True, in 1895 the group spent a session discussing dress, but did so only with reference to rival interpretations of duty: while the minority held that they should dress simply in order to make clear their disapproval of frivolity and extravagance, the majority supported the view "that we as women students should dress as well as possible, lest, among other considerations, carelessness in this matter should bring discredit on the cause of women's education."[38]

She had, then, the education of a "new woman": but how could she put it to use? Return to Liverpool in 1896 did offer her the chance of a life in public service, but it was a life in her father's footsteps. The sixth William Rathbone had helped to found many of the voluntary and municipal services of Liverpool: the development of district nursing had been his special accomplishment, but he had also helped set up the Central Relief Society and the University College, served on the Cotton Famine Relief Fund and been a local MP. By the time Eleanor returned from Oxford, he was old and quite infirm, but still wrapped up in schemes of philanthropic and social service. He relied on Eleanor for help, and such was her admiration that she humbly bent her will to his. "It is a real and unmixed pleasure to me to work for you," she wrote to him; "I have seen so much of your work now that I think I could manage a fair imitation."[39] She worked as a visitor for the Central Relief Society, and produced for him a memorandum criticizing its operation as, essentially, not sufficiently in keeping with those moralizing principles that had always informed his work.[40]

She tried to be happy with this, with life as a laborer in her father's vineyards. Work that makes "a great difference to a very few lives" was "quite as important, quite as interesting," as work that makes "a very small difference to a great many lives," she wrote to her old Oxford friend Hilda Oakeley, and "that is why I like the despised [Charity Organisation Society] work so much."[41] Yet there are hints that her daughterly role did not completely content her, that a purely "imitative" form of social service was not enough. There is, for example, her immediate assumption of a key role within the local constitutionalist suffrage society; there is also the letter she wrote to Margery Fry, now the Somerville college librarian, urging that the terms of the new Mary Somerville Fellowship oblige its holder to be resident at the College for a full three years. "I don't think the Council realizes quite the position many women are in towards their families," she wrote, "nor what advantage to the Fellow herself strict regulation may be, to enable her to resist domestic pressure."[42]

This is the classic dilemma of the daughters of the Victorians – but with a twist. Eleanor Rathbone was not denied a useful life; her father encouraged her, even saw her as his heir. But her energies outran the place he had carved out for her; more important, her mind had begun to reject the assumptions of the naturalness of marriage and wifely dependence on which much of the Victorian moral economy, and indeed her parents' own lives, were based. Tied to her father by admiration and love, Eleanor could not voice her reservations; she fulfilled her daughterly duties in a Victorian mode. Even the memoir she wrote of him after his death was cast in his terms. Sir Edward Fry, her friend Margery's father, remembered that many found its impersonality shocking; more shocking, perhaps, is the fact that Eleanor's mother was mentioned only in passing and never by name. This is an odd omission given that Eleanor spent most of her life trying to win public recognition for wives and mothers, but also a suggestive one. Perhaps Emily Rathbone insisted on her own exclusion; perhaps Eleanor's own convinced spinsterhood made her unable to see marriage as an institution that could allow, as Seth Koven argues in this volume, not merely for complementarity but also for the subversion and reworking of gender roles.[43] Certainly she identified with her father rather than her mother and felt his loss deeply: she confessed her loneliness in letters to an old Oxford friend.[44]

She determined, however, to carry on in the spheres of social work to which he had devoted his life, and something intervened to help her. Shortly after his death in 1902, Eleanor met Elizabeth Macadam, a trained Scottish social worker in her early thirties who had just been appointed Warden of the Victoria Women's Settlement in Liverpool. Within a year, Eleanor and Elizabeth were companions and collaborators. Rathbone helped Macadam set the finances and services offered by the Victoria Settlement on a more solid footing; together, they helped to establish a program with Liverpool University for the training of social workers.[45] They cemented the links between the voluntary agencies and women's organizations like the Women's Industrial Council and the National Union of Women Workers, one result of which was the string of social investigations that revealed the condition of the city's working class. By 1915, when the old and crusty Executive Committee of the Liverpool Central Relief Society decided it might be wise to open the committee to women, the two friends were seen as almost interchangeable, the committee agreeing to invite "either Miss Macadam or Miss Rathbone" to join.[46] When Macadam's work on government welfare committees and Rathbone's work for women's suffrage began to take them to London, they bought a house there. They lived together for the rest of Eleanor's life.

It is hard to capture the essence of this friendship from a distance of fifty years and across the Freudian divide, and certainly misguided to interpret it primarily in sexual terms. Rathbone's secretaries and friends all remembered that sexuality – even physicality – made her distinctly uncomfortable; one of her secretaries told Brian Harrison that Rathbone confessed herself raised to be shy of the nakedness even of young children.[47] What Macadam offered, rather, was an affirming mirror, a confirmation that the life of an independent woman could be both active and emotionally fulfilling. Macadam was a counterpoint to her family as well, and certainly the two women's friendship made the large and loving Rathbone clan uncomfortable. Elizabeth Macadam and Eleanor's sister "Mrs Hugh" "rather fought over Eleanor," B.L. Rathbone, Eleanor's favorite nephew, remembered.[48] Yet Macadam – and not her family – did become the emotional center of Rathbone's life: "Except when I am with you," Eleanor wrote to her, "I am always alone."[49]

Elizabeth Macadam also helped to mediate Rathbone's intellectual pilgrimage from a Victorian belief in the "demoralizing" nature of public assistance towards a new optimism about statutory state intervention. Rathbone did not owe Macadam her ideas, but there are points of contact: Macadam had begun to investigate the problem of child poverty even before Rathbone began studying casual labor; she shared

Rathbone's horror of "hap-hazard" philanthropy, and wrote on the need for "partnership" between the voluntary and government services.[50] It is unlikely that Eleanor's father could have made this pilgrimage with her: raised in the ideals of the Charity Organisation Society, he would have argued (as Mrs Fawcett did) that "indiscriminate" state aid would deprive men of their sense of responsibility and self-respect. But after more than ten years of social investigation in Liverpool, Eleanor was no longer willing to sacrifice women and children to preserve male work incentives. With perhaps excessive confidence in the benevolent intentions of professional women social workers, she came to believe that local services and activist government could uplift rather than demoralize families.

It was, then, during the first decade of the twentieth century, when Rathbone and Macadam were busy establishing a model for social work among the Liverpool working class, that Rathbone worked out her analysis of the causes and consequences of women's inequality, and her ideas about what was to be done. All the elements of her later campaigns were present in these early writings and investigations – the location of women's subjection in the domestic sphere, the insistence on the need for some independent support of mothers, and the call to feminist action (and sometimes supervision) across the lines of class. Her optimistic belief that the state could be made responsive to women reflected, once again, her own experience: it was the community that she and Macadam built up among educated middle-class women in Liverpool that gave her a basis for entry into electoral politics. When she contested Granby Ward as an Independent in a by-election in 1909 – two years after women received the right to stand – Patricia Hollis notes, "her secretary, election agent, canvassers, party workers, and supporters were all women." The settlement workers and suffragists worked the district for her, and in the end she owed her victory to the fact that women came out to vote for her in record numbers: fully 74 per cent of women but only 43 per cent of men turned out to vote.[51] Rathbone held Granby Ward until 1935; in 1963 the seat was won for Labour by Margaret Simey, whom Rathbone and Macadam had trained as a social worker some four decades earlier.

We can find, then, in Rathbone's experiences as a social worker in a reforming community in Liverpool, the roots of her analysis and politics. What she embodied was a particular moment in social action: the moment – well described by Martha Vicinus – in which the educated daughters of the Victorians began to push their analysis and their ambitions beyond the rhetoric and institutional framework of complementarity, demanding that they and the "womanly values" they articulated be incorporated into the spheres of national politics and administration itself.[52] This was a distinctly Edwardian moment, dependent as it was on a still-powerful Victorian ideal of personal social action, the existence of a network of separate and sometimes cross-class women's institutions able to articulate a distinct "women's point of view," and suffragist optimism about the malleability of the state.

Times changed, but Rathbone's analysis did not. Neither the disillusionment with politics that followed the Great War, nor the sexual revolutions of the interwar period, influenced her. Her focus remained extraordinarily woman-centered, but for all her preoccupation with mothers, the sexual side of marriage – indeed the very question of female sexuality – remained strictly out of bounds. She was uninterested in birth control, and unlike (say) Dora Russell or even Vera Brittain, she never adopted a rhetoric of women's sexual fulfillment in marriage. And while psychoanalysis would have offended her, she remained convinced that men's hostility to women was a potent force, based on prejudices that "lie very deep down in masculine human nature."[53] It was her distrust of "male values" – and not a belief in complementarity – that underlay both her non-party status and her much-misunderstood espousal of a "new" and "difference-based" feminism in the 1920s. Usually very guarded, she never expressed these reservations more clearly than in her presidential address to the National Union of Societies for Equal Citizenship in 1923. She argued:

> It is a fatal thing for a woman's organisation to get the reputation of being "anti-man," and I would not for worlds bring that reproach on the NUSEC. But I knew a wise old lady who was fond of repeating: "The more I see of some people the better I like my dog"; and after every experience of men's politics and administration my feeling is: "The more I see of some men, especially politicians, the less I want women to adopt all their methods and standards of value."[54]

Rathbone had no intention of restricting women to roles ancillary to men. Rather, she hoped to extend women's capacity to define their own ideals – a freedom she had first experienced at Oxford, and which she remembered with gratitude for the rest of her life.

V

Only during the last years of her life did Rathbone adopt causes and develop arguments that transcended an analysis based on sex-antagonism. Although her shift in focus was probably inevitable given the urgency of international crises in the 1930s, it may also have been influenced by her increasing contact with men. When Rathbone entered Parliament as an Independent MP in 1929, after years of work largely among women, she walked into what was still a very exclusive male

118

club. She was surprised to find that she loved the House of Commons, finding its masculine rituals and antics less threatening and more amusing than she had anticipated.[55] Not that she slacked in her feminist commitment: she spoke more than any other woman in the Commons during the interwar period except Nancy Astor, Brian Harrison tells us, and a good deal more than any other MP on issues of women's rights.[56]

Yet problems of the rise of Fascism and the threatened peace increasingly absorbed her. Her initial appraisal of these questions was not unrelated to her feminist concerns: she and other MPs were alarmed in 1933 by the Nazi dismissals of women from government service.[57] She came to realize, however, that Fascism could not be interpreted only as another attempt to circumscribe women's independence; nor was she able to view the prospect of a defensive or isolationist Britain with equanimity. What was at stake by the mid-1930s, she realized, were the liberal values with which she had always identified, and the national identity she had been loath to admit. Already a harsh Commons critic of the Government's effective acceptance of the Italian conquest of Abyssinia (a fellow League member) in 1935, during the next four years she did what she could to combat what she saw as an abdication of Britain's moral responsibilities. She traveled to Spain, Czechoslovakia and Romania with the Duchess of Atholl and Ellen Wilkinson in cross-party efforts to draw attention to the plight of these threatened or divided countries; she tried to convince her colleagues in the League of Nations Union to abandon futile hopes of world disarmament and campaign for a workable program of collective security; and she helped to organize a cross-party ginger group aimed at waking the Government up to the dangers of appeasement.[58] When the worst happened anyway, she was devastated: her nephew recalled her lapsing into tears over tea in the Commons soon after the declaration of war; she only wished, she told him, that old people like herself could serve and young men's lives be spared.[59] Long active in organizations aiding refugees from the fascist and occupied countries, she became a persistent critic of Britain's wartime internment of many refugees as "enemy aliens" and of its inaction in the face of revelations of the Nazis' adoption of a policy of wholesale murder of Jews.[60] By the middle of the war, she was working through a "National Committee for Rescue from Nazi Terror," and in May 1943 led an attack on the Government for failing to attempt to save those threatened with annihilation.[61]

In some ways these last years were merely a continuation of her earlier work. She was as busy as ever, absorbed with Parliament, with her endless work with refugees, with attempts to bring the long campaign for family allowances to fruition. In another sense, however, they were a decisive break, for she did jettison her earlier mode of reasoning, and especially her tendency to reduce political problems to the domestic rivalries of women and men. Her sympathies, in consequence, widened, but she also became more vulnerable. Her feminism had provided Rathbone with an analysis of power, that most essential of tools for political action. Her close identification with the wrongs of her sex – the sole element of self-consideration that she allowed herself – had sustained her through her youth and middle years. When she could no longer see the world primarily in these terms, her sense of personal responsibility proliferated beyond measure. By the mid-1940s, Mary Stocks recalled, she seemed often "unbearably oppressed by the magnitude of that sea of suffering in relation to the puny efforts of such human endeavour as could be mobilized for its redress."[62] Yet whatever her own feelings of inadequacy, when she died suddenly in January 1946, tributes from refugees and fellow workers proliferated in the papers.

VI

The Rathbones remained a presence in Liverpool: in business, on the City Council, on the governing bodies of the University. There is still a Rathbone in Parliament, and although he sits as a Conservative, he has been known to cross party lines to support the family policies his distinguished relative campaigned for so long to bring about. Eleanor's concerns and accomplishments have been recognized by her city and by the wider world: there is an Eleanor Rathbone Memorial Lecture devoted to questions of social policy, an Eleanor Rathbone building at the University of Liverpool, and an Eleanor Rathbone cultural center for refugee children in Israel. Yet memory is mixed with distortion, and, as her old friend Margery Fry shrewdly noticed, in the case of Eleanor Rathbone orthodoxy set in early.[63] Her seriousness of purpose, her public-spiritedness, even her feminism, were all recognized, but somehow the life itself – and the ideals that drove it – have been lost to view.

I believe this is because the two sides of Rathbone's politics have too often been seen in isolation, the innovative heir of the Rathbone political legacy divorced from the national advocate of family allowances and a "new" feminism.[64] Yet the private and the public, I hope to have shown, were integrally connected. Rathbone indeed brought from her family a weighty, almost debilitating, sense of social responsibility, but she expressed it in new ways. Her imagined transformation of Victorian or even New Liberal ideals not only recognized the possibilities for a positive use of state power; it was driven by a desire to use that power to increase women's autonomy, even within the domestic sphere. This core goal pervades all of Rathbone's work from her early years as a volunteer social worker in Liverpool through her parliamentary campaigns of the mid-1930s. The simplicity of her analysis was the source of her strength but also of her limitations, and the outcomes of her interventions depended heavily on the context in which they occurred. The skepticism of "male values" and the belief in women's shared interests that made Rathbone such an effective figure in domestic social policy debates also led her to assume that British women could protect the interests of women across the empire – even when the very existence of that empire (and hence their own authoritative position) was viewed as illegitimate by those they sought to represent. She had the courage of her convictions, however, leaving us a wealth of writings and speeches which reflect her own experiences but also capture many of the characteristic ideals of a unique and vanished coterie of women: the educated, economically independent, celibate and socially-conscious daughters of the Victorians.

NOTES

I am grateful to Dr B.L. Rathbone, Jenny Rathbone and Margaret Simey for sharing information and memories about Eleanor Rathbone, and to the University of Liverpool and the Principal and Fellows of Somerville College for permission to cite material in their collections. Thomas Ertman, Mrinalini Sinha, Robin Kilson, Barbara Ramusack, Margaret Simey and Peter Mandler provided helpful criticisms and suggestions on various drafts, as did the participants of the Women's History Seminar at the Institute of Historical Research in London. A grant towards research and travel expenses was provided by the Milton Fund of Harvard University.

1 Margery Fry, "London Calling Asia" (BBC Broadcast), 26 March 1956, quoted in Enid Huws Jones, *Margery Fry: The Essential Amateur*, London, Oxford University Press, 1966, p. 47.

2 Harold Nicolson, obituary in *The Spectator*, 11 January 1946, quoted in Mary D. Stocks, *Eleanor Rathbone: A Biography*, London, Victor Gollancz, 1949, pp. 142–4.

3 Eleanor to her sister "Evie" (Emily Evelyn Rathbone), n.d. (1945), Rathbone Papers XXIIA.116, Sidney Jones Library, University of Liverpool; Stocks, *Eleanor Rathbone*, p. 181.

4 There is an extensive literature on family allowances in Britain. The standard work, which covers Rathbone's campaigns closely, is John Macnicol, *The Movement for Family Allowances, 1918–1945: A Study in Social Policy Development*, London, Heinemann, 1980; also, for a study of the place of family policy within the development of the welfare state, see Susan Pedersen, *Family, Dependence, and the Origins of the Welfare State*, Cambridge, Cambridge University Press, 1993.

5 Harold Smith, "British Feminism in the 1920s," in *British Feminism in the Twentieth Century*, Amherst, University of Massachusetts Press, 1990, p. 48; Susan Kingsley Kent, "Gender Reconstruction After the First World War," in ibid., p. 78; Olive Banks, *The Biographical Dictionary of British Feminists*, vol. 1, London, Harvester Press, 1985, p. 168; Sheila Jeffreys, *The Spinster and her Enemies: Feminism and Sexuality, 1880–1930*, London, Pandora, 1985, p. 152.

6 Eleanor Rathbone, *The Problem of Women's Wages*, Liverpool, Northern Publishing Co., 1912, pp. 20–1.
7 Eleanor F. Rathbone, *Report of an Inquiry into the Conditions of Dock Labour at the Liverpool Docks*, Liverpool, Northern Publishing Co., 1904; *How the Casual Labourer Lives: Report of the Liverpool Joint Research Committee on the Domestic Condition and Expenditure of the Families of Certain Liverpool Labourers*, Liverpool, Northern Publishing Co., 1909; E. Mahler and E.F. Rathbone, *Payment of Seamen: the Present System*, Liverpool, C. Tinling, 1911.
8 Rathbone, *The Problem of Women's Wages*, p. 21.
9 Susan Pedersen, "Gender, Welfare and Citizenship in Britain during the Great War," *American Historical Review*, vol. 95, October 1990, pp. 983–1006.
10 Royal Commission on the Coal Industry, *Minutes of Evidence*, vol. 2, London, HMSO, 1926, pp. 862–79; "Memorandum. . . . by E.F. Rathbone," July 1934, Markham Papers, Part I, Item 7/9, British Library of Political and Economic Science [BLPES].
11 Eleanor F. Rathbone, *The Disinherited Family*, 1924, 2nd edn, London, George Allen and Unwin, 1927, pp. 268–74.
12 Trades Union Congress, Joint Committee on the Living Wage, Rathbone Evidence, 26 January 1928, p. 10, TUC Archives, File 117.32, Congress House.
13 Rhys Davies, "Family Allowances – Good or Bad," *New Leader*, vol. 15, 2 November 1928, p. 8.
14 See the scrapbook of presscuttings on Rathbone's candidacy, and especially the two articles, "Miss E. Rathbone Misrepresented," *Liverpool Daily Post*, 14 November 1922, and "An Insult to Bachelors," *Liverpool Daily Courier*, 15 November 1922, Rathbone Papers (Liverpool) XIV.3.90.
15 For Labour women's campaigns around family endowment, see Pedersen, *Family, Dependence*, ch. 3; Pat Thane, "Visions of Gender in the Making of the British Welfare State: The Case of Women in the British Labour Party and Social Policy, 1906–1945," in Gisela Bock and Pat Thane, eds, *Maternity and Gender Policies: Women and the Rise of the European Welfare States, 1880s–1950s*, London: Routledge, 1991, pp. 92–118.
16 On these machinations, see Pedersen, *Family, Dependence*, ch. 6.
17 408 *H.C. Deb.*, 5th ser., 8 March 1945, col. 2283.
18 Barbara Ramusack has written extensively on Rathbone's campaigns and, more widely, on British feminists' interventions in India. See her articles: "Women's Organizations and Social Change: The Age of Marriage Issue in India," in Naomi Black and Ann Baker Cottrell, eds, *Women and World Change: Equity Issues in Development*, London, Sage, 1981, pp. 198–216; "Catalysts or Helpers? British Feminists, Indian Women's Rights, and Indian Independence," in Gail Minault, ed., *The Extended Family: Women and Political Participation in India and Pakistan*, Columbia, Missouri, South Asia Books, 1981, pp. 109–50; and "Cultural Missionaries, Maternal Imperialists, Feminist Allies: British Women Activists in India, 1865–1945," *Women's Studies International Forum*, vol. 13, 1990, pp. 309–21.
19 For a sophisticated account of the ways in which British feminists' interventions, by constructing Indian women as the "Other" to be protected by their more "advanced" western sisters, themselves crucially sustained the ideology of empire, see Antoinette M. Burton, "The White Woman's Burden: British Feminists and 'The Indian Woman', 1865–1915," *Women's Studies International Forum*, vol. 13, 1990, pp. 295–308.
20 Katherine Mayo, *Mother India*, New York, Harcourt, Brace, 1927.

21 Stocks, *Eleanor Rathbone*, pp. 124–5; interview with Margaret Simey, 7 January 1993.

22 Eleanor Rathbone, "Has Katherine Mayo Slandered 'Mother India'?," *The Hibbert Journal*, vol. 27, January 1929, pp. 197, 207.

23 Dhanvanthi Rama Rau, *An Inheritance*, London, Heinemann, 1977, pp. 170–2.

24 For the reference to "barbarity," see Rathbone's letter to Wedgwood Benn of 27 March 1931, Rathbone Papers 92/2, Fawcett Library.

25 Rathbone's views on Indian independence are complicated and deserve more extensive treatment than I can give them here. Although she did support devolution, she tended to identify the independence movement as a sideshow to the more central task of social reform: "I do feel rather distracted at the thought of all the wretched little brides who are likely to be sacrificed on the altar of India's political aspirations during the next few years," she wrote to Lady Hartog in 1930 (Rathbone to Lady Hartog, 26 May 1930, Rathbone Papers 93/4, Fawcett Library). Like many liberal intellectuals, Rathbone had an implicit faith in the Millian paradigm whereby self-government would be granted to those sections of the population (or empire) who demonstrated a sufficient level of education and "civilization," and had trouble even understanding Nehru's objections when she entered into correspondence with him during the Second World War. Both Barbara Ramusack and Mary Stocks treat Rathbone's Indian interventions at some length.

26 Astor to Sir Samuel Hoare, 25 July 1933, Astor Papers 1416/1/1/1013, University of Reading Library.

27 Rathbone to Amrit Kaur, 9 January 1935, Rathbone Papers 93/12, Fawcett Library.

28 Rathbone to Lord Lothian, 9 April 1932, Rathbone Papers 93/7, Fawcett Library. In some ways Rathbone's concerns were prescient. Barbara Ramusack (personal communication, 20 October 1992) points out that the 1974 landmark report by the Government of India, *Towards Equality: Report of the Committee on the Status of Women in India*, contains a discussion of the problems of women's underrepresentation in political bodies, and recommends that seats be reserved for women in local government – as Rathbone had suggested.

29 Amrit Kaur to Rathbone, 11 February 1935, Rathbone Papers 93/12, Fawcett Library.

30 Rathbone to Amrit Kaur, 29 February 1934, Rathbone Papers 93/12, Fawcett Library.

31 See especially Rathbone's letter to Mayo, probably written in 1928, in which she criticized Mayo's failure to pay tribute to the courage of reformers within India and her tendency to assume that their attempts to end child marriages were mere "window-dressing," Rathbone to Mayo, n.d., Mayo Papers, 345/11/97, Yale University Library. For attempts to "silence" Rathbone, and her responses, see Sir Samuel Hoare to Rathbone, 7 November 1933, Rathbone Papers 93/6; also Wedgwood Benn to Rathbone, 15 May 1930, 15 July 1930 and Rathbone to Wedgwood Benn, 22 May 1930, 17 July 1930, 27 July 1931, Rathbone Papers 92/2, Fawcett Library.

32 Indian feminist opinion was not, of course, monolithic, and political arguments about constitutional and social change divided women as well as men. Some Indian women activists were supportive of Rathbone's proposals, but had trouble pursuing these issues as the nationalist movement solidified (Barbara Ramusack, personal communication, 20 October 1992).

33 Script of a BBC broadcast on Eleanor Rathbone by Margery Fry, 18 March 1952, Rathbone Papers (Liverpool), XIV.3.92.

34 Eleanor Rathbone to Emily Lyle Rathbone, c. 1890, Rathbone Papers (Liverpool), XIV.1.1.

35 William Rathbone to Elizabeth Rathbone, 12 August 1866, Rathbone Papers (Liverpool), IX.4.188.

36 William Rathbone to Eleanor Rathbone, 6 September 1893, Rathbone Papers (Liverpool), IX.9.9a.

37 Report by Mr Ritchie, Philosophy, for the Lent Term 1894, Somerville College Archives.

38 Minutes Book of the AP Society, Meeting 22, 23 June 1895, Somerville College Archives.

39 Eleanor Rathbone to William Rathbone, 15 May 1901, quoted in Stocks, *Eleanor Rathbone*, p. 56.

40 Ibid., pp. 50–1. Eleanor also read a paper, probably by her father's invitation, on ways of encouraging providence in wage-earners at an Executive Committee meeting of the CRS. See, Liverpool Central Relief Society, Executive Committee Minutes, 14 October 1897, Liverpool Record Office.

41 Rathbone to Hilda Oakeley, n.d., quoted in Stocks, *Eleanor Rathbone*, p. 55.

42 Rathbone to Margery Fry, quoted in Huws Jones, p. 61. It is likely that Rathbone was thinking here not of herself, but of her older, unmarried half-sister Elizabeth, who kept house for her family and for Eleanor in Liverpool but was enough of a feminist to leave the bulk of a very substantial estate (valued at over £100,000) to Eleanor upon her death in 1920, to the exclusion of her own brothers.

43 Her insistence on treating her father as an individual, rather than as part of a couple is particularly striking, since she quotes (in a footnote) her father's own statement that he and his wife acted together in all things, and adds that "those who knew them best know how almost literally true this is." See, Eleanor F. Rathbone, *William Rathbone: A Memoir*, London, Macmillan and Co., 1905, p. 187.

44 Stocks, *Eleanor Rathbone*, p. 57.

45 Margaret B. Simey, *Charitable Effort in Liverpool in the Nineteenth Century*, Liverpool, Liverpool University Press, 1951, pp. 132–5; Eleanor F. Rathbone and Elizabeth Macadam, "Schools for Training for Social Work," in Somerville Students' Association, *Twenty-Seventh Annual Report and Oxford Letter*, November 1914, pp. 41–4.

46 Liverpool Central Relief Society, Executive Committee Minutes, 12 August 1915, Liverpool Record Office.

47 Brian Harrison, *Prudent Revolutionaries: Portraits of British Feminists Between the Wars*, Oxford, Clarendon Press, 1987, p. 100.

48 Interview with Dr B.L. Rathbone, Liverpool, 16 August 1989.

49 Rathbone to Macadam, n.d., quoted in Stocks, *Eleanor Rathbone*, p. 181.

50 Victoria Women's Settlement, *Annual Report*, no. 9, 1906, pp. 10–13; [Elizabeth Macadam], "Victoria Women's Settlement" [leaflet, 1904], p. 3; both held in Victoria Settlement Papers, Liverpool University Archives. On Macadam's writings on social work, see, Jane Lewis, *Women and Social Action in Victorian and Edwardian England*, Stanford, Stanford University Press, 1991, pp. 280–1; obituary of Elizabeth Macadam, *Manchester Guardian*, 12 November 1948.

51 Patricia Hollis, *Ladies Elect: Women in English Local Government, 1865–1914*, Oxford, Clarendon Press, 1987, pp. 408, 418.

52 Martha Vicinus, *Independent Women: Work and Community for Single Women, 1850–1920*, Chicago, University of Chicago Press, 1985.

53 Rathbone, "Put Not Your Trust in Parties," Fifth Presidential Address to the NUSEC, 26 March 1924, in *Milestones: Presidential Addresses at the Annual Council Meeting of the National Union of Societies for Equal Citizenship*, Liverpool, by the Union, 1929, p. 24.

54 Rathbone, "Patience and Impatience," Presidential Address to the 1923 Annual Council Meeting of NUSEC, in *Milestones*, p. 16.

55 Stocks, *Eleanor Rathbone*, p. 141.

56 Brian Harrison, "Women in a Men's House: The Women MPs, 1919–1945," *The Historical Journal*, vol. 29, 1986, pp. 632, 641.

57 Harrison, "Women in a Men's House," p. 653.

58 Stocks, *Eleanor Rathbone, passim*; Donald S. Birn, *The League of Nations Union, 1918–1945*, Oxford, Clarendon, 1981, pp. 174, 184–5. See also the volume Rathbone wrote for the Left Book Club advocating a strong (and well-armed) policy of collective security, *War Can Be Averted*, London, Gollancz, 1938.

59 Interview with Dr B.L. Rathbone, Liverpool, 16 August 1989.

60 For the Government's policy – and opposition to it – see François Lafitte, *The Internment of Aliens*, 1940, new edn, London, Libris, 1988.

61 Eleanor Rathbone, *Rescue the Perishing*, London, National Committee for Rescue from Nazi Terror, 1943; Bernard Wasserstein, *Britain and the Jews of Europe*, Oxford, Clarendon Press, 1979, pp. 186, 203–4.

62 Stocks, *Eleanor Rathbone*, p. 314.

63 Fry, quoted in Huws Jones, *Margery Fry*, p. 222.

64 Recent feminist work has tended to focus on the latter to the exclusion of the former, and it is worth returning to the memorial lectures given by T.S. and Margaret Simey, who place their subject in the context of Beveridge, Rowntree, Booth and the development of sociology and social policy (if at the cost of treating her feminism rather as an adjunct). See T.S. Simey, *Social Purpose and Social Science*, Liverpool, Liverpool University Press, 1964; Margaret Simey, *Eleanor Rathbone: A Centenary Tribute*, Liverpool, Liverpool University Press, 1974.

8 E.M. Forster, portrait by Roger Fry (1911)

5

E.M. Forster 1879–1970

Connecting the prose and the passion in 1910

Peter Stansky

I feel it is particularly appropriate to write about E.M. Forster in a book of essays devoted to the memory of John Clive. There were some similarities of interests between Clive and Forster. The founders of the Clapham Sect, from whom Forster was descended, and the figures in Clive's first book, *Scotch Reviewers* (1957), although separated geographically, occupied to a degree the same world. Macaulay, Clive's great subject, and like Forster descended from Clapham, was hardly the sort of Cambridge man beloved by Forster, but he and Clive both had an affection for Cambridge. Both had a life-long love for music, and one might also hazard a guess that Australia played a role in Clive's life somewhat similar to the role of India in Forster's.

I met John during my senior year at Yale, 1952–3, through my teacher, Charles Blitzer, who had been a contemporary of his at Harvard. John had just received his PhD from Harvard, but although he was not yet thirty, in the eyes of an undergraduate he was already a formidable scholar. He was wonderfully charming and friendly; this was also true when I became a graduate student at Harvard in 1956, but then John's love of the role of rank had to be factored in. I was already interested in Bloomsbury. I believe that on the occasion of our first meeting John was singing the praises of Noel Annan's splendid study of Leslie Stephen. That year, 1953, I had already been accepted to do a second BA at King's College, Cambridge. Noel Annan told me some years later that he and his colleagues were amused that a young American should be interested in Bloomsbury. The dons of King's regarded the group as friends and practically contemporaries, hardly topics for academic study. In any case, I put aside my own academic interest in the Bloomsbury Group in favor of more traditional history for some years. But living in Cambridge, so important in the history of the group, and at King's in particular, was of continual interest and fascination in terms of acquiring some sense of their legendary world – a case, one might say, of "And did you once see Shelley plain?"

Of course, one of the sources of excitement at being at King's was that, since 1947, E.M. Forster had been living in the College. His was an unassuming presence, though he was fully conscious of his own worth. King's had a tradition of dons being far friendlier than was true at other colleges and quite a few of them would have lunch with the undergraduates and then repair to our rooms for coffee. Sometimes, Forster did this too, and he would certainly respond to invitations to tea; he resisted any attempt to treat him in any special way. And so it happened that when John visited me, probably in the late spring of 1954, I had the opportunity to introduce him to Forster. Or at least so I remember. "Only connect," as he counseled in the epigraph to *Howards End*, and thus it gives me particular pleasure, although the occasion is sad, to write about Forster in this collection dedicated to John's memory.

I

In many ways Forster was a Victorian inside out. The abiding sin of the Victorians, at least as seen by members of Bloomsbury, most notably by Lytton Strachey in *Eminent Victorians* (1918), was their willingness to allow public values to intrude upon and determine the private values by which they lived. With his emphasis upon personal relations, and his famous (notorious?) overly quoted remark about choosing, if one had the courage, friendship over country, it is easy to misunderstand the position of Forster and his friends. Thus, although they believed in a freer sexual life – Forster himself would not put theory into practice until his mid-thirties – they were far from self-indulgent or unreflective in their thoughts and actions. They did not deny themselves the obligation (also a pleasure?) to judge others: Forster could be severe with his friends if he felt they had lapsed. There is that tendency to moralism (very British) which has survived the Victorian age, and which for Forster was a true testimony of friendship. But what was different for him and his friends from the thoughts and actions of their Victorian forebears was that such feelings and actions were on behalf of *private* values. In that sense they were quite contrary to the age in which Forster had been born in 1879. As the editors of the present volume point out, the Victorians did not make a distinction between private conscience and public duty. Forster did. But he accepted the obligation to speak out in public (within realistic limits) on behalf of what one believed. This is not to transform him into a premature activist – he valued the privacy of private life and he was not upset that his homosexual novel, *Maurice*, begun in 1913, finished in 1914, and "dedicated to a happier year," could not be published during his lifetime. Yet decade by decade manners and mores were changing in England and that novel (not among his best work) probably could have appeared there before he died in 1970. By then, however, he had grown accustomed to assuming that it was not to come out until after his death, though he had circulated it to chosen friends earlier. His unwillingness publicly to reveal his homosexuality – illegal in England until 1969 – had nevertheless an important effect upon him: it was a contributing factor in his stopping writing fiction after the publication of *A Passage to India* in 1924. In his masterly biography of Forster, P.N. Furbank uses as an epigraph a quotation from a letter Forster wrote to T.E. Lawrence in 1928: "But when I die and they write my life they can say everything." Bloomsbury did not believe, during its lifetime, in the revelation in public of its private life. It is a nice touch that it was Michael Holroyd's biography of Lytton Strachey (1967/68) that heralded the arrival of the nothing-held-back biography. Forster was not uncomfortable with the English compromise which provided personal liberty at the price of a certain measure of public conformity. Yet he did not hesitate to use his considerable authority to speak out on controversial issues of the day, particularly against censorship for sexual reasons, as in the cases of *The Well of Loneliness* and *Lady Chatterley's Lover*.

Since I believe that much that formed the modern public and private persona began to take a decisive shape in 1910 and in the remaining years before the Great War, it seems appropriate that this essay should be illustrated by a "post-impressionist" portrait of Forster painted by his friend Roger Fry in 1911. Although not too pleased with it, Forster did purchase the portrait and hung it for a short period in the house he shared with his widowed mother. While it was still being painted, in December 1911, he wrote to his great friend and confidante, Florence Barger:

> It is too like me at present, but he [Fry] is confident he will be able to alter that. Post-Impressionism is at present confined to my lower lip which is rendered thus ... and to my chin, on which soup has apparently dribbled. For the rest you have a bright healthy young man, without one hand it is true, and very queer legs, perhaps the result of an aeroplane accident, as he seems to have fallen from an immense height on to a sofa.[1]

Forster was not especially sympathetic to the artistic convulsion that Fry had orchestrated only the year before in his landmark exhibition, "Manet and the Post-Impressionists," on view at the Grafton Galleries in London from November 1910 to January 1911. But Forster's remark demonstrates how easily the term coined by Fry for the exhibition, "post-impressionism," had already entered the language. And whatever his feelings about "post-impressionism," Forster's lack of ease about his sexuality is suggested by the fact that he gave the portrait to Florence Barger when a clergyman friend of his mother's remarked to her after looking at the portrait that he hoped her son wasn't "queer."[2]

The portrait of Forster, to my mind, delineates an "arrived" person: a young man in his early thirties who had, in 1910, with the publication of *Howards End*, been recognized as a major novelist. But that year, 1910, was important to him also for a number of reasons apart from the novel. It was then that he had declared to his young Indian friend, Seyd Ross Masood, his great passion for him. Even though that declaration was rebuffed, it represented a significant step towards the resolution of his sexual identity. However painful, his continuing affectionate friendship with Masood set him on the course that led ultimately to his writing *A Passage to India*. It was in 1910, also, that he had come closer to Bloomsbury, although his relation with the group would always be characteristically tangential – a meeting of cool congenial spirits, one might say, in contrast to the passion for Masood. All these events – the publication of *Howards End*, the declaration to Masood, the association with Bloomsbury – were to have lasting effects upon him and mark the year as one of the most important in his life.

II

By 1910, Forster was already a fairly well-known writer, but it was *Howards End* which established him in the front rank of his generation. *Where Angels Fear to Tread* was published in 1905, *The Longest Journey* in 1907, and *A Room with a View* in 1908. In 1906, he had met Masood through a friend of his mother's in Weybridge, Sir Theodore Morison, who was Masood's guardian. A strikingly handsome Muslim, ten years Forster's junior, Masood was the grandson of the founder of the well-known school at Aligarh in India which had played a major part in the Muslim "Awakening." Masood had come to England to be educated, and it was arranged by Morison that Forster should be the young man's tutor in Latin to help prepare him for Oxford. Thus began the most influential friendship in Forster's life. Largely thanks to Masood, he would develop a life-long interest in India, where Masood would be his guide for a good part of his first visit there in 1912. Masood was thereafter a continuing focus of Forster's deepest feelings, though the two would see each other only infrequently over the years till Masood's comparatively early death in 1937.

To judge by his letters, Masood was all expansiveness, charm and unrestrained affection. His teasing Forster about the English unwillingness to express emotion helped to liberate him, unlocked the "undeveloped heart" which Forster himself saw as the besetting English sin. His own letters to Masood at first were rather jokey. But he became increasingly fond of him, and Masood, in his warmhearted way, reciprocated. In late 1909, they went to Paris together, Forster's first visit. When he returned to London ahead of Masood, his young friend chided him (in a letter) for the coldness of his farewell at the Paris train station. Forster replied: "We mustn't quarrel about sentiment. We agree that it is the greatest thing in the world, and only differ as to how it's to be made most of."[3]

The two were in frequent correspondence and seeing one another regularly while Masood was a student at Oxford.[4] In the early spring of 1910, Forster had gone to Italy with his mother, where he finished the manuscript of *Howards End*. In a letter to Masood commenting about the death of Edward VII and the English ladies buying mourning in Florence, he burst out:

> Masood, I am sick of all these formalities: they are stifling all the heart out of life. Nothing but gossip & millinery, and all real feeling crushed into the background. Well, I suppose the Purdah is worse. Women are a bad drag on civilisation up to now.[5]

Despite this disparaging comment about women in his letter from Florence, Forster was aware of feminine aspirations for the future. The women's suffrage campaign was becoming ever more exigent, and the role for women was, in a sense, very much a theme of *Howards End*. He was more a cautious supporter than an enthusiast, which disappointed his great friend Florence Barger, whose commitment to the cause was ardent. But in December 1910 when he was moving into the orbit of early Bloomsbury he delivered a paper on "the feminine note in literature" at a meeting of the Friday Club, and won high praise from Virginia Stephen who told him "it was the best paper the Club had heard so far."[6]

With the publication of *Howards End*, worldly success, about which Forster would always have ambivalent feelings, appeared to be coming his way – another problem to be dealt with, but the Masood problem was much more disturbing. For there was Masood proclaiming his love for him, and at the same time confiding the difficulties that beset his evidently active heterosexual life. It would appear that Forster was finding it somewhat hard to cope, but he was improving in coming to terms with this most un-English effusiveness. By now, he fully understood the nature of his own sexual urges – very different from Masood's – but he had not brought them to a physical resolution, despite some kissing and hugging one evening on a sofa with his old friend, the married H.O. Meredith. (He was not to have a lover in the physical sense until his affair with Mohammed el Adl in Alexandria during the war.) Masood wrote in mid-November, urging that they should travel together to Turkey.

> What a dear fellow you are, & your letter shows me that you love me as much as I love you. . . . Whatever happens, don't let us give

up Constantinople. I shall go alone with you.... Dearest boy if you knew how much I loved you & how I long to be alone with you in that romantic part of the world, you would never dream of changing our original plans. England is all right but it does not possess a romantic or even a pathetic atmosphere.... But this next time we will be alone, for I want to have you as much to myself as ever I can.... I only wish that you & I could live together for ever & though that is a selfish wish yet I feel sorry that it will never come to anything.... And now I have nothing more to tell you except the old fact that I love you more than almost any other man friend of mine & so kiss you au revoir.[7]

In Forster's rather "tutorial" letter to him on 21 November he seemed to be replying to an issue involving some woman:

It [what Forster meant precisely by "it" is not clear] is such a difficult subject and we shall not make anything of it until we talk together even more freely than we have before. There are two sides to it – firstly it is an experience for you; secondly, you may do good to her. Now, in this latter side I don't think there is any point at all. You will not do any good to her. I am absolutely certain of it. It is not your fault, or hers; but because you are the age you are, you will always be arousing hopes of another kind in her. This is natural. The only good you do is indirectly – through men. Vice can only be suppressed through men. Tell every one you know that it is a horrible, disgusting notion that love can be bought for money. The more men believe this, the fewer poor women will be forced into a life of debauchery and disease.

But the minatory tone lightens with news of *Howards End*: "My book is selling so well that I shall probably make enough money by it to come to India. There will not only be an American edition, but a Canadian, and perhaps a translation into French."[8]

On 20 December, Masood was urging him not only to visit India but to write about it: "You are the only Englishman in which I have come across true sentiment & that, too, real sentiment even from the oriental point of view. So you know what it is that makes me love you so much, it is the fact that in you I see an oriental with an oriental view of life *on most things*."[9]

Emotions frequently run high at holiday times; perhaps they were even more intensified for Forster as his birthday fell on 1 January. He and Masood had arranged to go together to see Richard Strauss's *Salomé*, an opera that throbbed with sexuality. Although it had had its première in Germany in 1905, it was not performed in London until December 1910, as part of a season of two Strauss operas being conducted at

Covent Garden by Thomas Beecham – the other was *Elektra*, which had had its world première in Germany the year before. The first perform-ance of *Salomé* was on 8 December, and it aroused great advanced interest: potential ticket buyers had started to queue at 6:30 a.m., and once the box office was open, tickets had sold out in an hour and twenty minutes. *The Times* delivered itself of a burst of wonderment at the fashionable audience assembled for the opening performance:

> During the progress of a General Election and at a time when the London season is not in existence [it is surprising that] an audience so distinguished and representative should have gathered together. Among those in the audience: the French Ambassador, the Duchess of Rutland and [her daughters] the Ladies Violet and Diana Man-ners, the Duchess of Manchester, the Ranee of Sarawak, Lord Rib-blesdale, Lady Cunard, Lady Jekyll, Mrs George Cornwallis-West, Mrs Willie James.

It was the height of Edwardian luxe. For the next performance, the audience was equally grand: "Princess of Monaco, Duchess of Westmin-ster, Colonel Sir Herbert Jekyll, Duke of Rutland, with Ladies Marjorie and Diana Manners, Lord Robert Manners, Baron and Baroness de Meyer, Lady Lytton."[10]

These new operas, powerful as they were, being performed in December of that year, might well provide further evidence to support Virginia Woolf's later comment that human character had changed in December 1910. Certainly they had a violence and sensuality quite different from the genteel tradition of well-bred art in post-Victorian England – hence, the furious reactions to the Post-Impressionist exhi-bition going on concurrently with the Strauss season. There was also a quite characteristic English aspect of the performance: the peculiar relation of the state to the theatre through the role of the Lord Chamber-lain. In 1892, Wilde's play itself (the text for the opera) had been banned. There had been some advance since then in what was or was not deemed permissible for the English to see in the theater, but one senses that England was still behind the Continent in its artistic sophistication. Harley Granville-Barker, the great theatrical figure, wrote to *The Times* on 17 December:

> If in his [the Lord Chamberlain's] precious opinion, *Salomé* is a noxious thing, is it not his duty to use his autocratic power to crush it? If he has come to his senses on the subject, then let him set the play free.

The Lord Chamberlain had insisted that John the Baptist be called the Prophet instead:

And what is this foolishness – and worse than foolishness – of forbidding the use of the severed head, compelling Mme Ackté to make dramatic nonsense of the most poignant passages of the tragedy by addressing them to a bedaubed tea-tray? ... It is an insult to the public, an insult to the work of Oscar Wilde, and an insult to a great composer. How much longer is this inept official to make our theatre the laughing stock of Europe?[11]

Forster found *Salomé* disappointing, but its passionate music was likely to have added to the intensity of his feelings. The year, after all, had been one of great tension in his and Masood's relations. As early as the previous 15 January he had written in his diary: "Joyful but inconclusive evening with him. I figured an unbearable crisis, but we only care for each other more than before, each in his own way." There was a somewhat odd note of sublimation on 21 July: "However gross my desires, I find that I shall never satisfy them for the fear of annoying others. I am glad to come across this much good in me. It serves instead of purity." The climax came on 29 December: "Yesterday, in the O[xford] & C[ambridge] Musical Club, I spoke. He had been praising my insight into Oriental things, & I could bear no more. He answered 'I know' easily."[12]

Afterwards, there were a few days of misery for Forster at home in Weybridge. To compound his distress, he was not happy with his birth-day gift from Masood, a painted tray with candlestick and matchbox. On the day, 1 January, he wrote to thank him, but added: "My real need is a letter. If you will use your imagination, you will see that I am not having much of a time."[13] Forster was feeling ill, and feared that he might have tuberculosis. A letter did arrive, but Masood apparently had no intention of dealing directly with Forster's love and distress. Forster replied:

Dearest Boy, Your letter arrived. There is nothing to be said, because everything is understood. I agree. But oh you *devil* – ! Why didn't you write at once? I was in an awful stew all Satur-day & Sunday. You may say that this was not sensible of me, but when all that one is and can feel is concerned, how can one be sensible?[14]

Emotions continued at a high pitch in early January, when Forster's grandmother died, causing his mother to go into a depression from which she never completely recovered, and making her more dependent than ever upon her only child.

The close friendship with Masood, if not the relationship as Forster would have wished, survived both the passionate declaration and its tactful rejection. In 1912 the first visit to India took place. (The success of *Howards End* made it possible for Forster to pay for the trip.) He became more systematic in his reading about India, including a biography of Masood's grandfather, the founder of Aligarh, and was increasingly drawn to it as a subject. After Oxford, Masood returned to India, married, and made his life there. But the correspondence between them, though sporadic, was for some years as intense as ever. In 1923, Forster wrote to him: "You are the only person to whom I can open my heart and feel occasionally that I am understood."[15] And in February 1924: "Yours is the only affection that remains with me as a solid unalterable truth."[16] After Masood's death in 1937 Forster acknowledged: "My own debt to him is incalculable. He woke me up out of my suburban and academic life, showed me new horizons and a new civilisation and helped me towards the understanding of a continent."[17] Perhaps his final feeling about the relationship is suggested at the end of *A Passage to India* – the novel dedicated to Masood – with its famous sentence " 'No, not yet,' and the sky said, 'No, not there.' "

III

But this is to anticipate. In August 1910 Forster, on a walking tour on his own, wrote to Masood:

> It isn't bad being alone in the country – the nearest approach we Anglo Saxons can make to your saints. There's such a thing as *healthy* mysticism, and our race is capable of developing it. . . . Now I have proofs to correct, and with luck I shall finish them next week.[18]

It was as if he were taking the "thingness" of the Victorian and Edwardian novel and, without scorning it, going behind it to the more transcendent and mystical aspects of life. As he wrote in his diary the previous February: "Am grinding out my novel into a contrast between money & death – the latter is truly an ally of the personal against the mechanical."[19]

In England, *Howards End* made him well known, something of a celebrity, and it was ranked, alongside Arnold Bennett's novel, *Clayhanger*, as one of the two most significant books of the season. There is a certain irony that *Howards End* should share honors with *Clayhanger*. Bennett was rich and famous, and as a leading Edwardian novelist was customarily bracketed with H.G. Wells and John Galsworthy. In 1924, in the high tide of modernism, Virginia Woolf would launch in her essay "Mr Bennett and Mrs Brown" a sardonic attack on those three most famous practitioners of Edwardian fiction. It was in the same essay that she observed that human character had changed in December 1910. Significantly, Woolf's chief complaint against the three was that in their realistic, externalized descriptions of character they failed to penetrate to its essential reality. Forster she placed with the modernists; in fact he was less that than either Joyce or Lawrence. But in his attempt to "connect," to probe further inside his characters, to be more symbolic, perhaps to be more mystical, to achieve a greater sense of the essence of his characters, he was a newer sort of novelist. There is little question that Bennett, Galsworthy and Wells were attached to the "thingness" of life. Forster had even published a short story, "The Machine Stops," in 1909 which parodied Wells's science fiction. The argument over the nature of literature was not new, as the correspondence between Wells and Henry James, a rupture between master and pupil, had painfully made clear. But its postwar direction is more pertinent in the contrasts between Wells, Bennett and Galsworthy – triumphant middle-brow novelists – and the great outsiders, Lawrence and Joyce, and those who were much more securely within the middle class than they, Forster and Woolf herself.

Howards End marked the transition of Forster from minor to major novelist. Could one call *Howards End* a Post-Impressionist novel? Possibly, yes – at least to the degree that it broke with conventional models then in favor, much in the way the Post-Impressionist pictures being shown in London in December 1910 had done. In contrast to Bloomsbury, still in the process of formation, Wells and Bennett were happy Philistines. Bennett judged the reviews of his books by how many inches they were. As he wrote to his agent J.B. Pinker while in the process of writing *Clayhanger*, "My first draft is always also the final writing. I would much sooner write a complete fresh novel than rewrite two chapters of an old one."[20] Fine in many ways as *Clayhanger* is, *Howards End* does penetrate further into its world and its characters.

It is intriguing to note how books that have become classics were first received. In the case of *Howards End*, there were ardent reviews. The *Daily Telegraph* noted that "his stories are not about life. They are life." And R.A. Scott-James wrote in the *Daily News*: "the novel rises like a piece of architecture full-grown before us. It is all bricks and timber, but it is mystery, idealism, a far-reaching symbol." But there were demurrers. *The World* felt that *Howards End* was unfairly receiving more attention than *Clayhanger*. "There is no doubt that this novel has been one of the sensations of the autumn season, and in that respect, it has been made – not wisely – to overshadow Mr Arnold Bennett's *Clayhanger*, which is a much greater book." Bennett himself reviewed the book in the *New Age*, favorably but rather grudgingly: "I am in a position to state that no novel for very many years has been so discussed by the *elite* as Mr Forster's *Howard's*[sic] *End*." In America the *New York Times* compared the book with Galsworthy, but felt that Galsworthy was better, while Elia W. Peattie of the *Chicago Tribune* insisted that the author must be a woman.

> In feeling the book is feminine; but it is not to be gainsaid that a number of the strongest masculine writers of our times have been able to represent the feminine mind, with its irrational yet dramatic succession of moods, better than any woman can do it. It may be that E.M. Forster is one of these, but my impression is that the writer is a woman of the quality of mind comparable to that of the Findlater sisters or to May Sinclair.[21]

More complex than Forster's three previous novels, *Howards End* is a great Edwardian novel that has won a place among the enduring novels of this century. It shares with the Edwardians their obsessive interest in money, but with a profound difference. The possession of money, we are shown, matters only to the degree that it may make possible the freedom to live a fulfilled life. Even then it does not follow as an immutable law: money is no more than a starting point – essentially, the without-which-nothing. The book is candid in recognizing the role of money and its importance in making England and those who lived there powerful. Forster's great theme was the need to connect – "only connect" – the prose and the passion, the world of the rich Wilcoxes and the sensitive Schlegels, money itself and what money could make possible. The materialism of the Wilcoxes is not sufficient as an end; it needs to be combined, to connect with the more spiritual interests of the Schlegel sisters and that of the first Mrs Wilcox – a change in human character so that it will become capable of connection. There are both elements of hope and despair in the book; connection has mostly failed. But the illegitimate child of Helen Schlegel and Leonard Bast, the lower middle-class clerk, will be the inheritor of the house, Howards End. The child is, perhaps, evidence of a more democratic and classless society that may be coming, something good amidst the defects that are part of the new age, the red rust of building that is creeping into the country-side from London.

Although there is little specific discussion of the politics of the period, the sense of turmoil and disorder, the goblins of Beethoven's Fifth Symphony, is present in the book, an unspoken reminder, perhaps, that Forster was doing his final work on the manuscript in 1910, that year of great political upheaval, and of the growing militancy of the women's suffrage movement. (Although the suffrage question is not discussed, one feels that Helen would be a militant, and Margaret a moderate – increasingly so – but both would have believed in votes for women.) But as Forster wrote to Edward Garnett about the novel: "It is devilish difficult to criticise society & also create human beings."[22]

Forster felt uneasy about his success, and had the common reaction of not agreeing with the praise, much as he enjoyed it, and taking the criticism too seriously. He wrote to Eddie Marsh about a captious review in the *Spectator*: "I haven't seen the Spectator, but it was to be expected. They would find the thing both irritating & easy to slate, and I shall agree with the strictures I fear, though I wish the paper to the devil."[23] As his biographer, P.N. Furbank, has noted, he reacted to his success by returning to his evangelical roots in his attitude, writing in his diary on 8 December.

> Prayer. Not to imagine people are noticing me.... Let me not be distracted by the world. It is so difficult – I am not vain of my over-praised book, but I wish I was obscure again. If I come an unholy smash let me never forget that one man and possibly two [Meredith?] have loved me. In old age I shall look back enviously to this year which gave me so much, but is the material for happiness rather than happiness. I knew I shouldn't and I don't enjoy fame.[24]

He wrote to his great friend, Goldie Dickinson, in November: "I go about saying I like the money, because one is simply bound to be pleased about something on such an occasion. But I don't even like that very much.... I am another Harmsworth darling. No, it *is* all insanity."[25] It was hard for a Cambridge Apostle such as Forster to handle worldly success, for Apostles tended to believe that that was really the world of illusion.

Success is rarely as satisfying as one might hope, and he felt it hard to return to creativity. *Howards End* argues the importance of money for providing an income to give one the freedom to do what one likes; yet in the end the freedom may be tainted. Forster recognized that the income from the novel would allow him to visit India, increasingly important to him in terms of his relation to Masood. As he wrote to his friend Malcolm Darling in September: "My novel will be out in October, and you will receive a copy, if you will undertake not to dislike me for having written it. I am afraid it will give little pleasure to anyone. But the money, my boy! It helps me to get to India."[26] One might have expected Forster to have a sense of purpose similar to Margaret Schlegel's: she came to know what she wanted. But in his own life, he seemed more unsure and tentative, and felt awkward about his great success. In 1912 he began work on a novel, *Arctic Summer*, which he abandoned, and then during the next two years he wrote *Maurice*, his novel of an idealized, fulfilled, ultimately happy homosexual love, a "daydream book," so to speak, which could not be published.

IV

Forster needed to come to terms with his success; he needed to come to terms not only with Masood's rejection of him as a lover, but also with the continuation of their intense friendship. Less significant but vexing (and not without its comic aspect) was still another question that arose in 1910: whether or not he should be the godfather of the newly-born son of his friend, Malcolm Darling. Darling's elder brother had been an exact contemporary of Forster's at King's. Malcolm Darling, who entered the college two years later, became a great friend of Forster's. In 1904 he had joined the Indian Civil Service and had acted as a tutor to the Raja of Dewas State Senior, where Forster would visit in 1912, and return to in 1921 to act as secretary to the eccentric Maharajah. Darling described Dewas as "the oddest corner of the world outside Alice in Wonderland. Dewas has 16,000 inhabitants, two Rajas, each with a salute of 15 guns, each with a Minister & a Palace."[27] Forster corresponded with Darling regularly, reporting on a variety of things ... politics ... publishing ... the election over the House of Lords in January 1910 ... a walking tour with their Cambridge contemporary, Hilton Young, who had proposed, unsuccessfully, to his childhood friend Virginia Stephen in May 1909. ...

His ever-deepening love for Masood furthered and nurtured his interest in India; so too did his very different friendship with Darling, sustained by the flow of letters between them. There are suggestions in *Howards End* of moving away from western rationality, which would become so much more decisive an element in *A Passage to India*. When Darling wrote to him of some incident involving an illogical yogi, Forster replied:

> Wealth, success, friendship, love, are all one illusion, and reality, (what it may be) is obscured by them. But in practice one shrinks from this conclusion. The western world, and in particular the Latin races, have too vivid a sense of surface-values. How wonderful – and how comforting – that the yogi should be illogical at the last moment too![28]

Darling wrote to Forster in May: "The English Mail is about the most romantic thing of this very romantic country. At Rajanpur it came to me on the camel's back; at Dewas a horseman would bring it to the door." He added as a postscript, pointing out that he was writing at nearly midnight from an encampment in a grove of apricot trees in the Himalayas:

> Shall I tell you? Yes, I think I must, but you will be secret. We expect a third in July or early in August – most unwillingly at first, for it is pleasant to be two together, also Josie has suffered

cruelly these last 6 months, almost unceasing sickness & other things. . . . Neither of us had really the least wish for a child. But it will at least be interesting. Write me another letter from Italy if this finds you there. I would barter the whole Himalayas for one little Umbrian hill.[29]

Forster didn't take his friend's doubts too seriously, replying: "You say that neither of you have been anxious for a child; when it comes surely you will feel differently, and realise it is the greatest of blessings. Children are so delightful – and something more besides."[30] The baby, John Jermyn, was born on 14 July, and Forster wrote about him on 12 August very much in the spirit of *Howards End*. "I am pleased about the baby, of course, and more pleased than I can say that his coming has made other things better. He is the future, & our love for him is still hidden in it." In this letter, too, began the tiny rather Forsterian comedy of whether or not he would be a godfather to the boy. Forster at first refused. "I have only once said yes, and that was to parents whose atheism was even more pronounced than my own."[31]

Ten days later he wrote again, as the Darlings had written meanwhile assuming that he would be a godfather.

I do trust and think that you will both understand why I have refused. . . . I couldn't be of less use to him than my own official godparents have been to me, and perhaps it's the emptiness of my own experience in this direction that makes me behave like such a prig now. . . . The only present I ever feel inclined to give babies is to take away some of their toys. I do wish I could see him. . . . I am very fond of babies. Though I can't help laughing at them – they will more than pay me out for that in the future.[32]

It may have been that Forster's initial refusal had not reached the Darlings in time; a mutual friend who saw him thought that he was the godfather.

Goodall thinks that I am already a god father willy nilly. . . . The fault of the bishop of Lahore, and his surpliced minions. Not my fault. I should have all the pleasure of authority with none of its responsibilities, if this report were true.[33]

The issue continued on 22 September, when Forster wrote: "Your letter about the godfather just received, & it is a comfort to know that you do not think I have been a pedantic ass."[34] Darling had suggested that Forster write a "catechism" for the child; Forster proposed that Darling and his wife write it themselves. But he became increasingly captivated by the idea, and finally did write something for the child on 20 November. On the 21st he appeared to consent to be a godfather, but on his own terms, and if the Darlings approved of what he had written out: "I was not the least ashamed of my conduct in refusing & prevaricating at first, but felt that I had done quite the proper thing throughout. . . . For it is difficult to accept such a post quickly when one is definitely not a Christian."[35]

He changed his mind again, and decided not to act in the role. But he did pass on the "catechism" to Josie Darling when she came to Britain in December because of the death of her father, Lord Low, a Scottish Law Lord, and also, presumably, to show the baby to her friends and relations. Before seeing the baby and her family, Forster, who had not met his good friend's wife before, wanted to see Josie on her own. There is a splendid series of notes from him – as if it were out of one of his own novels – arranging a meeting with her at the Tate Gallery to talk before going to tea at Malcolm Darling's mother's, where the baby would be shown.

> So do let us meet at the Tate at 2.30, opposite Ulysses (Schlegel) defying Polyphemus (Wilcox) . . . I will bring the catechism with me – a meagre little thing which will not take two minutes. . . . If Ulysses [a painting by Turner] should not be at the Tate – I forget if he is still at N.G. – we meet in the room where the biggest Turners are. I shall not recognise you – it is not my habit to recognise people – and you will have to have a shot at me. I am now very stout.

He wrote again on 20 February:

> King Cophetua [Burne-Jones] 2.30, Wednesday, then. In case of disaster, parties shall not dash feverishly about, but shall repair for recriminations to the turnstile, and leave messages about each other with the man who guards it.

On the 22nd he wrote to Malcolm: "I have at last seen J.J., and approve entirely. He is not a baby, but a very dear little boy."[36]

What of the catechism itself? Forster called it "Liking Being Alive" and entitled it as if it had been written by the Darlings, and then "Written out by E.M. Forster 20/11/10." It was in the form of a dialogue between the son and his mother, when the boy is eight or so – and he is asking her what a godfather might be, but he doesn't want the questioning to go on so long that it will delay his going riding. The boy says that he enjoys being alive, and the mother points out that his father does too, and when young "He liked to walk all night, sometimes with a friend, sometimes alone. As he grew older he began to care for other things, he read books." He became more and more aware of nature, and of the importance of friends. But his greatest discovery was love:

141

there came a thing that was more wonderful than all the other things put together, a thing that made his life – oh! – bigger than all the stars and the sun, brighter than any light you can think of, a thing so glorious so beautiful, so overwhelming that it was almost frightening to him.

The mother also talks about herself:

In some ways I have not been as happy as he has, because people think that girls ought not be as happy as boys, and instead of helping me to like life, they would give me orders about it, and this is never any help, never.

For the parents "the wonderful thing was love, and out of our love you came. Because we cared about life, you are alive. You are the sign that we have loved, and all the beauty that we have seen." God is the name of all the good things that made the child. This is hard to understand, and godparents are to help:

They are to tell you about the things that they have liked in life.... They want you to be an inheritor of the Kingdom of Heaven. No one knows where the Kingdom of Heaven is – whether it is the place that the sun is flying to, or whether it is far behind that place or whether it is actually here on this beautiful earth.[37]

Anne-Marie Roman, in an interesting article on the catechism, puts more weight on a rather slight piece than it can comfortably manage, but her claim about its significance is intriguing. Its few pages do suggest the importance of nature, and of personal relations, for Forster, and also "the luminous revelation of love."[38] These, like many of the other elements that figure in the catechism are already in place in *Howards End* – nature, connection, personal relations, the role of a baby. Even a more mystical approach to life has been adumbrated there, though it will become of far greater importance in *A Passage to India*. Perhaps in the catechism, Forster was half-consciously striving towards some sort of symbolic resolution to his personal dissatisfaction, as in his declaration a month later to Masood.

"Until 1910," Roman tells us, "the ultimate reconciliation of the seen and the unseen, the inner and the outer, appears only as an aim; but by way of writing out the catechism, Forster approached his ultimate goal: the formation of a link between art and life, the connection between the ideal and the real."[39] That, of course, had been an aim of *Howards End*, where Forster was arguing for a change in human character that would make possible a union between the ideal and the real. In a very simplified, even naive or childlike fashion, he was making the point again in his catechism for a godchild.

Finally, by contrast, Bloomsbury and the grown-ups. With the success of *Howards End*, Forster began to move into the wider world. As an Apostle he had always maintained very strong ties with Cambridge, but being somewhat older than the generation of Bloomsbury Apostles, he had not yet established a bond with them in London. In 1910 the principal Bloomsbury figures were Keynes, Strachey, Virginia Stephen (who would marry Leonard Woolf two years later) and Clive and Vanessa Bell. At that point they were more significant for what they promised to become than for what they had yet achieved. In that year, Roger Fry met a number of them in the course of organizing the Manet and the Post-Impressionist exhibition, established personal relationships with them – for a time he was to be Vanessa Bell's lover – and became a central figure in their group. Older by more than a decade, he had done more than those younger friends who had "begun" Bloomsbury, which was still pretty much a private social cluster rather than a congregation of high intellects who would influence the values and artistic activities of Britain in the twentieth century.

Forster too was slightly older than Keynes and Strachey and like Fry had already accomplished more far earlier than they. Although he knew them both, he did not actually see much of them or of the other post-Cambridge Bloomsbury figures in London – he did not even meet Virginia Stephen until 1910. The crucial event that would lead to his becoming on friendly terms with the group took place in December, when he was asked to give a paper to their Friday Club. The suffrage movement was by then at its most intense; "Black Friday" – the demonstration that turned violent in front of the Houses of Parliament – had occurred on 18 November; feminine questions were taking on a more immediate urgency. Forster gave a paper "On the Feminine Note in Literature" on 9 December in which he argued in favor of a special feminine sensibility.[40] While he granted that differentiations between men and women were lessening, he rejected what he understood to be J.S. Mill's claim that there were no distinctions to be made between them. (Mill's *Subjection of Women* had been discussed at the previous meeting of the Club.) Forster acknowledged, "A freer atmosphere is at hand, and the artificial products of the past – the Chatelaine, the Grande Dame, the Blue stocking – will be blown away and give place to the individual." But, despite Mill, he felt that "women ... live nearer the truth of human nature.... The feminine note is – preoccupation with personal worthiness. The characters try not so much to be good as to be worthy of one of the other characters.... Men have an unembodied ideal. Women embody their ideal in some human being, be it a woman or a man. . . . Women have this strong practical vein, the desire to set up a sensible visible standard of righteousness."[41]

Thus, in 1910, through several comparatively private events of varying intensity – ranging along a spectrum from his impassioned relation to Masood to the social/literary pleasures of Bloomsbury and the Friday Club to the catechism for the Darling baby – and one great public event, the publication of *Howards End*, Forster had taken considerable steps forward in 1910. His character may not have changed, but his life had changed in public and private ways, and he had in *Howards End* made his private values shape the public world of his fiction.

NOTES

I would like to express my gratitude here to P.N. Furbank, S.P. Rosenbaum and William Abrahams for their reading of this essay, and for their suggestions. I am also indebted to Peter Jones, the Librarian of King's College, Cambridge, and to Michael Halls and Jacqueline Cox of its Modern Archive Centre, to Cathy Henderson and the Harry Ransom Humanities Research Center at the University of Texas at Austin, and to the Centre of South Asian Studies, Cambridge University. Published Forster material copyright The Provost and Scholars of King's College, Cambridge, 1985. Unpublished Forster material copyright The Provost and Scholars of King's College, Cambridge, 1993.

1 Forster to Florence Barger, 24 December 1911, quoted in P.N. Furbank, *E.M. Forster: A Life*, New York, Harcourt Brace, 1977, vol. I, p. 206.

2 Ibid., p. 208. See Evert Barger, "Memories of Morgan," *New York Times Book Review*, 16 August 1970, pp. 2, 32–5. It should be noted that at this point "queer" simply meant peculiar. According to the OED, it did not come to mean homosexual until the 1920s in the United States and the 1930s in Britain.

3 Jalil Ahmad Kidwai, ed., *Forster–Masood Letters*, Karachi, Ross Masood Education and Culture Society of Pakistan, 1984, p. 56.

4 Many of Forster's letters to Masood have been published in Jalil Ahmad Kidwai, ed., *Forster–Masood Letters*. Some are to be found in Mary Lago and P.N. Furbank, *Selected Letters of E.M. Forster*, vol. I, *1879–1920*, Cambridge, Mass., Harvard University Press, 1983.

5 Forster to Masood, 9 May 1910, Forster papers, King's College Library.

6 Furbank, *Forster*, p. 193.

7 King's College; also in Furbank, *Forster*, pp. 193–4; Kidwai, *Forster–Masood Letters*, pp. 101–2.

8 King's College; also in Kidwai, pp. 61–2.

9 Kidwai, p. 103; Furbank, p. 194.

10 *The Times* (London), 20 November, 8 and 12 December 1910.

11 *The Times* (London), 17 December 1910.

12 Copy of Forster's locked diary, 21 July, 29 December 1910, King's College, Cambridge. Forster did make another declaration the following August when Masood and he were vacationing together in Tesserete in Switzerland. He commented on the trip in his diary in the last entry for 1911. "The first week was incoherent joy, though the detail escapes me. Towards the end Masood grew tired of the place and it was less pleasant, but it was clear he liked

me better than any man in the world, so I did not mind. Near the beginning, I spoke, seeing that after all he did not realise. He was surprised and sorry and put it away at once. It has made either no difference, or a good difference." Diary, 31 December 1911, quoted Philip Gardner ed., *E.M. Forster Commonplace Book*, Stanford, Stanford University Press, 1985, p. 350.

13 Forster to Masood, 1 January 1911, King's College.
14 Forster to Masood, [?] January 1911, King's College.
15 Forster to Masood, 23 May 1923, in Kidwai, p. 81.
16 Forster to Masood, 13 February 1924, King's College.
17 E.M. Forster, "Seyd Ross Masood," in *Two Cheers for Democracy*, London, Edward Arnold and Co., 1951, p. 299.
18 Forster to Masood, 18 August 1910, King's College.
19 Copy of locked diary, 19 February 1910, King's College.
20 Letter of 9 February 1910, in James Hepburn, ed., *The Letters of Arnold Bennett*, London, Oxford University Press, 1966, p. 133.
21 Philip Gardner, ed., *E.M. Forster: The Critical Heritage*, London, Routledge and Kegan Paul, 1973, pp. 130–60.
22 Forster to Edward Garnett, 12 November 1910, Forster papers, Harry Ransom Humanities Research Center, The University of Texas at Austin. Published in Lago and Furbank, eds, *Selected Papers*, p. 117.
23 Forster to Edward Marsh, 6 November 1910, Berg Collection, New York Public Library.
24 Furbank, *Forster*, p. 191.
25 Forster to G.L. Dickinson, 21 November 1910, King's College.
26 Forster to Malcolm Darling, 22 September 1910, Forster papers, Humanities Research Center.
27 Darling to Forster, 11 May 1907, Malcolm Darling papers, Box 51, Centre of South Asian Studies, Cambridge University.
28 Forster to Darling, 10 February 1910, in Lago and Furbank, *Letters*, p. 104.
29 Darling to Forster, 3 May 1910, Darling papers, Box 51. As Darling wrote to his mother on 15 February: "India is hard enough on married couples, but it is downright cruel to the children. This is in fact no country for them." Lago and Furbank, *Letters*, p. 109.
30 Forster to Darling, 29 June 1910, in Lago and Furbank, *Letters*, p. 108.
31 Forster to Darling, 12 August 1910, ibid., p. 110.
32 Forster to Darling, 22 August 1910, ibid., p. 114.
33 Forster to Darling, 4 September 1910, Humanities Research Center.
34 Forster to Darling, 22 September 1910, Humanities Research Center, part quoted in Lago and Furbank, *Letters*, p. 111.
35 Forster to Darling, 21 November 1910, in Lago and Furbank, *Letters*, p. 111.
36 Forster to Josie Darling, 17 and 20 February 1911, Forster to Malcolm Darling, 22 February 1911, Humanities Research Center.
37 E.M. Forster, "Liking Being Alive," *The Library Chronicle of the University of Texas at Austin*, New Series, no. 23, Austin, 1983, pp. 75–9. The words indicated as crossed out in the text are not given here. See also Anne-Marie Roman, " 'Liking Being Alive' and E.M. Forster's Aestheticism," in ibid., pp. 63–73. Contrary to Lago and Furbank, Roman assumes that Forster did finally consent to be a godfather. I have not found an explicit statement in which he finally declines, but I would hesitate to disagree with Forster's biographer.
38 Roman, "Liking," p. 68.
39 Ibid., p. 73.

40 Material from Furbank, *E.M. Forster*, pp. 192–3.
41 E.M. Forster, notes for paper "Feminine Note in Literature," 90–106 ff., King's College.

9 Leonard Woolf

6

Leonard Woolf 1880–1969
The conscience of a Bloomsbury socialist
F.M. Leventhal

In September 1938 Maynard Keynes presented *My Early Beliefs* to the Memoir Club, the name given to those regular encounters at which Old Bloomsbury shared recollections and attempted to clarify the record for posterity.[1] Keynes recalled that he and his fellow Cambridge Apostles, adopting G.E. Moore's "religion" while discarding his morals, recognized neither moral obligation, nor "inner sanction to conform or to obey." Describing his circle as "water-spiders, gracefully skimming, as light and reasonable as air, the surface of the stream without any contact at all with the eddies and currents underneath," he helped to foster an image of Bloomsbury as self-absorbed and frivolous, preoccupied with the enjoyment of romantic and aesthetic experience.[2]

Such a characterization was totally inapplicable to Leonard Woolf, a pillar of Old Bloomsbury who differed from his friends in certain crucial respects. While the antecedents of prominent Bloomsbury figures were evangelical and Nonconformist, Woolf was a Jew; while many of them were either apolitical or congenitally liberal, he was a socialist; while several of them were homosexual and promiscuous, he was neither. This essay will attempt to trace the sources of Woolf's distinctiveness, to determine the way in which his private conscience shaped his sense of public duty, and to describe his transformation from Cambridge aesthete to political activist.

I

In *Culture and Anarchy* Matthew Arnold, elaborating Heinrich Heine's dictum that all men were either Jews or Greeks, identified two opposing forces, each striving for man's salvation, which he described as Hebraism and Hellenism. Hebraism was concerned with obligation to duty, obedience, self-control and strictness of conscience; Hellenism, by contrast, was associated with spontaneity of consciousness, with beauty, sweetness and light. Whereas Hebraism, rooted in a sense of human sinfulness, was skeptical about the possibility of attaining perfection,

Hellenism was imbued with an optimistic faith in rational intelligence.[3] If Bloomsbury endeavored to realize the Hellenist ideal of beauty, rationality and spiritual perfection, Leonard Woolf embodied both Hebraism and Hellenism, and it is the tension between them that provided the dynamic for his intellectual and moral development.

Woolf observed that before the age of sixteen he would have described himself as a gentleman, while recognizing that "society was rigidly divided into a world of gentlemen and a world of cads."[4] Yet a more significant dichotomy for him was that between Jews and Gentiles. In contrast to the cultivated Stracheys and Stephens, his family had only recently risen from the stratum of Jewish shopkeepers.[5] One generation removed from Regent Street tailoring, the Woolfs were Victorian *arrivistes*, their prosperity resting precariously on Sidney Woolf's professional fees at the bar. Young Leonard's gentility had not yet acquired the patina of age that most of his St Paul's and Cambridge contemporaries wore so effortlessly. To complicate matters further, family fortunes collapsed when Sidney died prematurely, leaving his wife and nine children in reduced, although hardly penurious, circumstances, obliged to sacrifice a large South Kensington establishment for more modest Putney.

But it was not merely the financial deprivation that affected Leonard. After all, he won a scholarship to St Paul's, a tribute to his cleverness no less than to the greater tolerance in late Victorian England that enabled an impecunious Jewish boy to secure admission to a prestigious public school. The death of an idolized parent when Leonard was only eleven, rendering his father's legacy all the more precious, tempered his generational rebelliousness towards Victorian values. Relating his own experience to Sophocles' recognition of reversal of fortune as the essence of tragedy, he observed that,

> his death meant not only the disaster of his death, the loss of him, but also the complete break-up and destruction of life as I had known it. . . . The reversal of fortune had had, I am sure, a darkening and permanent effect. In my own case I can only describe it as this sense of fundamental insecurity, and a fatalistic acceptance of instability and the impermanence of happiness.[6]

Whether it was the experience of parental loss or the Jewish tradition imbibed from his forebears, Woolf came to appreciate as one of his ingrained characteristics a "kind of fatalistic and half-amused resignation,"[7] a distinctly non-Hellenist trait which he identifies elsewhere as "the inveterate, the immemorial fatalism of the Jew."[8]

In both his autobiography and in his *roman à clef The Wise Virgins* (1914), Woolf's portrait of his mother is unflatteringly patronizing, but the memory of Sidney remained untarnished. What he derived from his father was, I suggest, a sense of Jewish identity. It was partially associated with an emphasis on education, gained from his grandfather as well, which turned Leonard into an incorrigible intellectual at a young age. Coupled with this commitment to learning was industriousness, a Victorian no less than a Jewish trait:

> To work and work hard was part of the religion of Jews of my father's and grandfather's generations. . . . I think that my father had absorbed this tradition and instinctively obeyed it, and that, young as I was when he died, I had observed it and again, in my turn, instinctively obeyed it.[9]

Beyond the stereotypical Jewish zest for knowledge was Sidney's tolerant conviction, based on the teachings of the prophet Micah, that the proper rule of conduct was to do justly and love mercy. As a practicing Reformed Jew, he added the injunction to "walk humbly with thy God," a precept that Leonard abandoned as readily as he clung to the rest of his father's ethos. At the age of fourteen he declared himself a non-believer, refusing thereafter to attend synagogue, somewhat to the chagrin of his more conventional mother. He claimed to feel neither sense of sin nor need to worship a God. While he may have been too young to grasp its meaning, his father's creed "entered into and had a profound effect upon my mind and soul." In later years Woolf came to regard this "Semitic vision" of justice and mercy as "the foundation of all civilized life and society." It was, he recognized, only a limited prescription, but when he later found that the Greeks had added to it "the vision of liberty and beauty" – when, in other words, he coupled Micah's injunction with the speech of Pericles as recounted by Thucydides – he discovered what became his ultimate ideal of civilization.[10]

Shortly before he died, Woolf confirmed that Judaism had had "little effect" upon his life. Although always "conscious of being a Jew," frequently encountering "the common or garden antisemitism," Judaism had "not touched me personally and only very peripherally."[11] It is true that his career was not obviously hampered by being Jewish: he suffered no disabilities at St Paul's or Cambridge, where he was elected as the first Jewish Apostle, in Ceylon or in the Labour Party. Most of his friends, in and out of Bloomsbury, were non-Jews. His independent literary career, to be sure, shielded him from institutional prejudice, which he might have encountered had he remained in the colonial service.

Woolf regarded his intelligence and temper as an inheritance from his father, but his austere, obstinate personality might also be attributed to his Jewish upbringing, to the Hebraist side of his nature. Although grief-stricken when Virginia died in 1941, her suicide did not destroy him spiritually. He associated this resilience, his acquiescence in the impermanence of happiness, with a Jewish belief that fate could be mastered through self-control and unremitting labor.[12] If he was accepted at Cambridge by the scions of the intellectual aristocracy, he remained in certain ways an outsider, personally detached, socially somewhat aloof, perhaps fearful of overstepping the bounds of propriety. The young self-hating Jewish hero of *The Wise Virgins* says to Camilla, the character patterned on Virginia: "We aren't as pleasant or as beautiful as you are. We're hard and grasping, we're out after definite things, different things, which we think worth while."[13]

Woolf doubtless felt ambivalent about his background, if not about his father's values. In his story entitled *Three Jews* one character comments tellingly, "We're Jews only externally now, in our black hair and our large noses, in the way we stand and the way we walk. But inside we're Jews no longer."[14] He might imagine himself a non-believer, but he was nonetheless a Jew to the outside world, even to intimates. Virginia, who described her future husband as "a penniless Jew," remarked at one family gathering, "Let the Jew answer."[15] Their marriage, which created a breach with his own family, made him more conscious of his distinctiveness as a Jew. While friends like Harold Nicolson, Vita Sackville-West and T.S. Eliot moderated their anti-Semitism in his presence, he could hardly have been impervious to it. He might dismiss it as an irrational survival, part of an atavistic communal psychology, but it demanded that "carapace," that facade of indifference cultivated while a student at St Paul's "as a protection to the naked, tender, shivering soul."[16] Only when confronting Nazi racism was his equanimity shaken, his carapace discarded. Denouncing Fascism as "a reversion to the primitive quackery of superstition," he identified Jews with the progress of civilization. Jews might not boast superiority to Aryans, but they need not be ashamed of a lineage "which produced the Ten Commandments, Job, Ecclesiastes, the Song of Solomon, the Psalms, Isaiah, Christ, Montaigne, Spinoza, Heine, Marx, Einstein, Proust, and Freud."[17] While Judaism might prove, at least minimally, a social liability even in England, it nonetheless spurred his political awareness, especially at the time of the Dreyfus case, and his moral sensibility.[18]

II

If Woolf revered his father's memory and took pride in inherited Jewish values, if not in its familial pieties, he felt much more resentful about his public school. A born "swot," he could only survive its anti-intellectualism by excelling at games and by "the concealment or repression of a large area of my mental life."[19] What St Paul's gave him, despite – or because of – its regimentation and narrow curriculum, was an extraordinary grounding in ancient languages and literature which enabled him to gain entry as a classical scholar to Trinity College, Cambridge.

It was this immersion in Greek civilization which was also to define his further intellectual development, challenging, if not effacing, his Hebraist cast of mind with Hellenist ideals.

Frederic Spotts contends that Woolf suffered a spiritual crisis during his first year or so at Cambridge. The intellectual excitement, the friendship of kindred spirits, the freedom to explore literary interests, must have proved both exhilarating and intimidating to one whose background had been so circumscribed. This new iconoclasm, associated particularly with his friend Lytton Strachey, seems to have left him temporarily bereft of moral signposts. Increasingly convinced that there was neither reason nor order in the universe, he despaired that "everything seemed slipping from my grasp / And the whole world was vanity."[20] It was only later that he could face with equanimity, sustained by his assimilation of Greek stoicism, the notion that "I can find no place for and no explanation of my life or my mind in this fantastic universe."[21]

Certainly the tension between the values of his home and the astringent rationality and camaraderie of Trinity contributed to a sense of malaise. His sister Bella, distressed that "the 'unanswerables' of life take such hold of you," tried to console him with the hope that he would "rise triumphant from the Valley of the Shadow of 'Doubt'."[22] Writing from Putney during one vacation, he confided to Strachey his need "to break through this hen-coop of an existence and do something inordinately outrageous," lamenting that "the worst of it all is that one *never* does."[23] Envious of the more refined postures of his friends, but aloof from their homosexual escapades, Woolf saw himself as "a mere spectator with my hands in my pockets."[24]

The publication of G.E. Moore's *Principia Ethica* in 1903 has frequently been identified as a milestone in the emergence of Bloomsbury.[25] If Keynes believed that the philosopher sanctioned sexual license and aesthetic self-indulgence, Woolf regarded him differently. In his eyes Moore was the moral exemplar, who filled the void left by the death of his father. What attracted Woolf to Moore, whom he described as "the only great man whom I have ever met," was his goodness and innocence, his pursuit of truth "with the tenacity of a bulldog and the integrity of a saint."[26] If he taught his disciples to question received truth, he was no less fascinated by the problem of moral conduct, by the consequences of actions. It was not that duty and virtue were irrelevant, but rather that they must be justified as means towards the realization of ultimate ends. Moore, Woolf noted, "gave us a scientific basis for believing that some things were good in themselves," indefinable or intuited though they might be.[27] If such doctrines liberated Woolf from his Hebraist conscience, it also led him to believe that a life of public activity could be reconciled with the selfless pursuit of truth, a conviction that drew him back to his image of classical Greece. Moore brought clarity, freshness and common sense to the analysis of moral and political questions, but he did not, as Keynes seemed to imply in *My Early Beliefs*, deny their importance. When he left Cambridge to take up his cadetship in the Ceylon colonial civil service, Woolf had come to believe that it was "not merely my right, but my duty to question the truth of everything and the authority of everyone, to regard nothing as sacred and to hold nothing in religious respect."[28]

III

Woolf's seven-year interlude in Ceylon was a lonely and, in many ways, intensely unhappy period. He was separated from his beloved Cambridge, and Strachey's gossipy letters merely heightened his isolation. He found the resident English community snobbish, preoccupied with daily tennis and social trivialities. He assuaged his misery by reading the ninety-volume edition of Voltaire brought from England, bemoaning his fate in letters to friends, but, above all, by work:

> I practically do nothing but work & ride & shoot. This sort of work becomes an obsession; I do about 12 hours a day. . . . I think really what makes it pleasant is that one has no time to think at all about anything but work & food & facts; one is perpetually doing something. Of course if it weren't for that, one would probably go mad. . . .[29]

What was more remarkable, however, was his professional success and rapid promotion. An efficient, conscientious, if somewhat rigid administrator, he developed an affection for those under his authority and for the scenery, heat and physical discomfort notwithstanding. Responsibility brought out his strongest Hebraist tendencies – unremitting labor, obedience to his superiors, the imposition of stern justice. He enjoyed wielding power, gratified to play, while still in his twenties, the role of imperial consul.

Yet devotion to duty could not keep disenchantment at bay. However beneficial the regulations he tried to enforce, they were resented by the native population, calling into question the moral basis of imperialism. To the villagers, he was "part of the white man's machine, which they did not understand. I stood to them in the relation of God to his victims." If he could not himself worship any God, neither could he willingly play God to those cast in the role of inferiors. Without doubting the fairness of his actions, he came to realize "the absurdity of a people of one civilization and mode of life trying to impose its rule upon an entirely different civilization and mode of life."[30] While colonial peoples might be unfit, as yet, to rule themselves, there was no necessary corollary that the British ought to govern them.[31] By the time Woolf came to write about imperialism after the First World War, he was prepared to disavow it as immoral, injurious to native culture, and economically irrational. The correct approach would be gradually to introduce local self-government, conceding home rule once a people had attained "the necessary degree of civilization."[32] His commitment to rationality and civilized values, even among "backward peoples," transformed this diligent colonial official into an outspoken critic of imperialism.

By 1928 he had moved from the quasi-Marxist economic critique of his early writings to one which harked back to the Hellenist model. Ancient Greek civilization had been a paragon of tolerance, neither acquisitive, proselytizing nor militaristic. Despite its unaggressive posture, it "had the greatest influence upon its neighbours and profoundly affected every civilization." By contrast the European seizure of African territory, savage and unscrupulous, had turned the native into "the economic slave of the white man."[33] The only way to safeguard native interests was to reserve the land for their use, preventing its expropriation by predatory foreigners. Once European powers abandoned the selfish pursuit of their own economic interests, surrendered their authority to an international system of mandates, and educated the Africans, imperialism would have made some restitution to civilization.

IV

Woolf was professionally at a loose end when he returned from Ceylon. The Dreyfus case and his later exposure to imperialism aroused his moral outrage without providing either a political focus or an ideological perspective. While Moore's philosophy did not preclude involvement in public affairs, many Apostles interpreted his otherworldliness as disapprobation of "the life of action generally, power, politics, success, wealth, ambition."[34] Attempting to explain their indifference to social problems, Woolf told Kingsley Martin many years later,

> The social conditions did not seem quite so frightful or menacing before 1900 as they do today in retrospect. Things were improving and therefore we did not think so much about them.[35]

It was ironic that Woolf, whose education and outlook had been entirely shaped by men – especially his father and Moore – and by exclusively male institutions – St Paul's, the Apostles, Trinity, the Ceylon civil service – should owe his transformation into a socialist to three women. In 1912 Virginia's cousin, Margaret Vaughan, recruited him into the Charity Organisation Society, where his experience of poverty in Hoxton opened his eyes to the devastating effects of capitalism. Deploring the feeble palliatives of paternalistic philanthropy, convinced that social reconstruction alone could alter the situation, he proclaimed himself a socialist.

Shortly thereafter he fell under the influence of the redoubtable Margaret Llewelyn Davies, a friend of Virginia's and the secretary of the Women's Cooperative Guild. Attending its congresses, lecturing to members, investigating the structure of the movement, Woolf became a proselytizer for the organization. Cooperation not only offered an alternative to the obsessive profit-making that he abhorred in capitalism but seemed to be a means to apply democratic principles to the economic system. Beyond its fundamental goal of non-competitive production and distribution, eliminating the profit motive, lay an ideal of democracy in which the individual as a consumer would make choices that would determine what was produced. Inspired by Llewelyn Davies, he envisioned the Guild as an agency for educating working-class wives and mothers, elevating them from the poverty to which the capitalist economy had subjected them. He was soon disheartened to discover that the cooperative movement was as parochial as trade unionism, its members impervious to the appeal of consumer democracy.

The process that Vaughan and Llewelyn Davies began, Beatrice Webb completed. After reading his article on the Newcastle congress of the Guild in June 1913, Beatrice, always on the lookout for promising young men who might prove politically useful, invited Woolf to lunch, enlisted him in the Fabian Society, and later persuaded him to undertake an inquiry into "the whole arrangements of international control over Foreign Policy, Armaments and methods of warfare."[36] Financed initially by a grant from Joseph Rowntree, Woolf's investigation went through several incarnations, beginning as a report to the Fabian Society, subsequently appearing as a *New Statesman* supplement, and eventually being published as *International Government* in 1916. In the course of his research Woolf gained expertise in a field in which he had been a novice; assiduous study and a talent for drafting reports enabled him to produce a document that exerted considerable influence on British proposals for a League of Nations. His basic premise was that the only way to prevent war was to establish international machinery for the peaceful settlement of disputes. His inquiry cited existing institutions, such as the Universal Postal Union, to refute the notion that inherent conflict among nations made international cooperation impossible. His scheme adumbrated a supranational authority consisting of an International High Court, a Council of member states and a Secretariat. Skeptical about the viability of world government, Woolf disavowed any abrogation of national sovereignty as long as states were willing to submit justiciable disputes to the International High Court. Above all, signatories to the proposed treaty should consent to undertake common action, "even to the extent of war," against any country which violated the fundamental agreement.[37]

By the end of the war Woolf had become fully engaged politically, his contribution acknowledged by his appointment as secretary to the Labour Party's Advisory Committee on International Questions. A member of the Independent Labour Party, he had come, somewhat reluctantly, to acknowledge Labour as the only party he could support, even while disliking its timorous leadership, its petty squabbling, its lack of vision. When Arthur Henderson resigned from the Cabinet in 1917 over its veto of participation in a proposed international socialist gathering in Stockholm, Woolf grumbled, "I suppose it's too much to expect of the Labour Party that they would have the sense to come out of the Government."[38] The Left was no better: ILP members were

> so bitter and truculent that they can see nothing except a tiny segment of the horizon. . . . Anything more childish one can hardly imagine. What a bore it all is: extremists hopeless because they are as blind as mad bulls, and moderates hopeless because they are moderate![39]

In later years his exasperation grew, as Labour repeatedly compromised principles for the sake of electoral advantage, failed to deliver on promises to colonial peoples, and vacillated over the League of Nations and collective security.

Despite his frustration, Woolf remained loyal, serving uncomplainingly on innumerable Labour and Fabian committees. As in Ceylon, the commitment to duty, even where he disagreed with the authorities, reflected the Hebraist cast of his personality. If Labour did not embody British socialism, it was nonetheless the only plausible vehicle for its promotion. Not that his own socialism was ever very orthodox. Although he claimed to be a "Marxian-Socialist – but only up to a point,"[40] he remained "a socialist of a rather peculiar sort."[41] Blaming the system of private property for the conflict of interests, he doubted whether modern society could become civilized without greater community control of industry:

> If the individual is not always pursuing his own interest, he goes under unless he belongs to the very small class which has been born with private wealth. . . . Personally I think that the class war and the conflict of class interests are the greatest curses, and that the first things that one should aim at is to abolish this conflict and class war.[42]

Since class conflict was inimical to civilization, the only way to reconcile divergent interests was through socialism. He denied being anti-Bolshevik, admitting that "they're the only people who've made an honest and serious attempt to practise what I believe in."[43] Unlike the Marxists, he felt that socialism was not an end in itself, but rather the means to a civilized society, based not on the dictatorship of class, state, or even organized producers, but on consumer democracy. Woolf spelled out his own idiosyncratic agenda in *Socialism and Cooperation*, a book written in 1921 at the behest of the ILP which he later dismissed as "even more futile than most of my books."[44] It was socialism derived at least as much from Moore as from Marx, a transposing of Hellenist values to the struggle between capital and labor.

Unconsciously permeated with the competitive, profit-making ideals of capitalism, the worker had been induced to pursue his own self-interest at the expense of others in his class. In the "capitalistic industrialized State the individual is compelled to carry on a perpetual struggle, not against nature, but against his neighbour."[45] Both capital and labor were attempting to sell their commodities and services at the highest price with scant regard for cooperation or commonality. Socialism would replace individual acquisitiveness with communal objectives, but these must not be achieved by sacrificing individual autonomy. Democracy meant "acting together on an equality for a common end," but it also signified

> a desire to express one's own individuality freely combined with a very large tolerance of the free expression of their individuality by other people; and finally a conception of society as composed not of competing individuals and classes, but of citizens making individually or collectively their distinctive contributions towards the common life.[46]

The cooperative movement, by organizing industry on the basis of consumption, enabled the community, constituted as consumers, to control production. It was motivated by the principle that goods should not be produced for the sake of profit or work, but simply to furnish essential commodities. The value of a product ought to be determined by its social or aesthetic worth or the mental attitude of the producer, much as the ancient Greeks, recognizing intrinsic value in beauty, intellectual activity, leisure and happiness, made the "good life" rather than profit maximization their goal. "We shall not begin to be civilized," he affirmed, "until, both individually and socially, we realize that the value of production and work depends upon the value of the product and the quality of the productive activity."[47]

As long as most of the population was obliged to spend at least eight hours a day in manual labor, society would remain an oligarchy based on industrial slavery. The goal should be to reduce industrial production to a minimum consistent with material comfort. Only those goods required for the community to partake of civilization or the good life should be produced. If everyone performed a share of unpleasant but essential toil, the individual would be left with nine months a year to devote to other activities. Those who refused to perform their share of industrial work would be debarred, as consumers, from receiving its products. It was, he felt, preferable for members of the community to enjoy a book or picture, play football, dance, or cultivate their gardens than to manufacture some article that was useless or ugly. Woolf, like William Morris, was convinced that beautiful objects would be produced, but not by industry: it was in leisure time that creative expression could be given free rein.[48] Once the citizen was organized solely as a consumer, rather than as a member of a class, and private ownership was abolished, the way would be cleared for an end to exploitation. So radical a conception of society, in which tolerance and individuality were elevated above class solidarity, in which industrial production was reduced to a minimum, in which organized labor willingly sacrificed higher wages to leisure and culture, and in which compulsory work was imposed on everyone, however briefly, was clearly too visionary to be regarded seriously within the ILP. *Socialism and Cooperation* was his first extended foray into socialist theory, and it also proved to be his last.

V

Until the 1930s Woolf, without harboring many illusions, believed that the prospects for peace were auspicious. The League of Nations represented an effective means for achieving disarmed internationalism, renunciation of war, peaceful resolution of conflicts, and pooled security. Yet he remained both a realist and a skeptic, realistic in recognizing at an early stage that "an alternative to armed nationalism requires that every state should assume some obligations to stand by the side of the victim of aggression and to resist the aggressor,"[49] skeptical about the willingness of European powers to comply with the provisions for pooled security.

As late as 1933 Woolf opposed mandatory sanctions against an aggressor as "much too dangerous in the world of today."[50] By the next year he had adopted an intermediate position, admitting to Philip Noel-Baker that "nothing but [collective security] can stand between the world and war," but disclaiming both the "disorientation" of the pacifist Left and the "sanctions madmen."[51] With the League's failure to contain Japanese expansion and the collapse of the Disarmament Conference, he began to warn that

only a drastic revolution in the League itself, in the aims and policies of the existing governments, and in the whole European situation could make the League of today an effective international instrument for peace and justice.

Labour's foreign policy, in his view, should aim at restoring an effective system for ensuring international accord and preventing war without reliance on national armaments. To pursue a policy of rearmament in the face of League impotence would be to "throw power into the hands not of socialists, but of fascists."[52] Defending collective security to the point of armed sanctions against an aggressor, he quarreled with Kingsley Martin, the editor of the *New Statesman*, who was apprehensive lest military action, even under League auspices, degenerate into a capitalist, imperialist war. Having long argued that pooled force did not constitute old-fashioned war, Woolf admonished the pacifist Left for lack of realism. The notion, he added, that it was possible to select a policy which would result in absolute good was a political delusion:

> In 999,999 cases out of a million, the choice is between two evils and two courses both of which will lead to evil; the wise man is he who by reason or instinct chooses the less evil course leading to the lesser evil.[53]

The Spanish Civil War convinced him that, since the League had been irretrievably damaged, it was time for Labour to revise its entire international policy. He advocated a coalition of democratic and socialist states prepared not only to satisfy legitimate grievances, but to oppose encroachments on the integrity of non-fascist governments. Although mutual defense involved risks, he was convinced that "the only conceivable way of dealing with the force problem" was "a system of collective resistance to any state resorting to war."[54] Despite his animosity towards the National Government for appeasing the dictators, he reluctantly conceded that, if Britain were to deter Hitler and Mussolini, "mere negative opposition to a policy of rearmament would be sterile and ineffective,"[55] thus tacitly endorsing rearmament provisions. By the time of the *Anschluss* he was advising Labour to espouse a Churchill-led coalition and immediate introduction of conscription.

The crisis of the 1930s gave a new twist to Woolf's literary endeavors. In addition to analytical articles for the *Political Quarterly* and memoranda for the Advisory Committee, he became, to use Stefan Collini's term, a "public moralist."[56] In several polemical works he excoriated the forces of barbarism, while extolling the ancient Greeks, who, by applying ethics to society and by secularizing government, had made European civilization possible.[57]

In the oddly-titled *Quack, Quack!* (1935) Woolf contrasted past civilizations with primitive societies in order to depict Fascism as a recrudescence of barbarism and quackery. Only two peoples – the Greeks and the English – had made significant contributions to political culture, devising a system in which "freedom, tolerance, and compromise – the foundations of a civilized life – have been slowly and painfully substituted for irresponsible power, violence, privilege, and superstition."[58] Civilization, dependent upon the repression of instinct and the application of reason, was inimical to notions of race superiority and national assertiveness. He described Nazi anti-Semitism and communist persecution of the bourgeoisie as equally symptomatic of political quackery and the revolt against reason.

Even in England, periods of crisis encouraged charlatans and fanatics to exploit savage instincts. But the defects of contemporary society lay deeper than transitory economic or national ills: the cancer afflicting the West was the refusal of the minority to share their advantages with the majority, thereby creating an unwitting alliance between the elites and the dictators.[59] It was not merely the assertion of reason against quackery and freedom against despotism, but of equality against privilege that was essential to sustain civilization against barbarism.

Increasingly in the 1930s Woolf began to perceive communism as no less a threat to western culture than Fascism. In view of his more strident tone, it was somewhat surprising for Victor Gollancz to invite him to write a defense of western civilization for the Left Book Club. While Gollancz had begun to rethink his own earlier defense of Soviet repression, his editorial colleagues, John Strachey and Harold Laski, had fewer qualms.[60] Woolf demanded a guarantee that he be permitted to express his views without constraint, but Gollancz's acquiescence did not preclude serious misgivings once the book was submitted in May 1939. Strachey and Laski both objected to the manuscript, and even Gollancz admitted that it contained statements liable to be misconstrued by anti-Soviet propagandists.[61] Woolf, unrepentant, refused to modify his argument on grounds that criticism of the Soviet Union was inopportune. Nor was he dissuaded by the editor's speculation that publication might jeopardize the delicate Anglo-Soviet negotiations or provoke resignations from Left Book Club members. Since Woolf would not relent, Gollancz postponed publication rather than renege on his contract. In the end, after the signing of the Nazi–Soviet pact dramatically altered the situation, *Barbarians at the Gate* appeared as the November 1939 Left Book Club selection.

As in *Quack, Quack!* four years earlier, Woolf defined civilization by reference to the achievements of fifth-century Athens, where the government sought to enhance freedom, equality and tolerance, and where the standards of value were compromise, truth and knowledge. Europe before 1914 had also made strides in extending liberty and equality of opportunity, but, even so, economic power remained concentrated in the hands of a small class of capitalists and financiers, unlike ancient Greece, where the distribution of wealth had been reasonably equal and economic distinctions irrelevant. Despite the concession of political rights, western society fell short of genuine democracy: "under the capitalist system a society of free and equal citizens was no more possible without economic than it was without political democracy."[62]

If he deplored the resurgence of barbarism, Woolf tried to distinguish among the dictators. Stalin was the heir of western civilization, acknowledging the same egalitarian ideals of rights and duties as Pericles. Hitler's regime, on the other hand, relied on subordination to a leader, a concept closer to the Spartan view of communal life than the Athenian. He challenged the notion that there was nothing to choose between the dictatorship of Stalin and that of Hitler or Mussolini:

> The Soviet Government, whatever may be the results of its practice, is in its ultimate objective on the side of civilization, whereas Fascist dictatorships are on the side of barbarism.[63]

But if the Bolshevik revolution had been imperative in order to impose socialism, the liquidation of capitalism and the triumph of the proletariat should have obviated the necessity of further autocracy. Instead, with the death of Lenin, the regime became stabilized as a tyrannical despotism. In the exercise of power rather than ultimate goals, there was little difference between the Soviet commissars and the fascist rulers. The fault lay with Stalin and his subordinates, not with the underpinning ideology:

> There is nothing in Marxism which requires that the central government should be a dictatorship or that there should be no communal control of the controllers of power or that personal liberty, freedom of speech, humanity and tolerance should not exist.[64]

Western culture was menaced not only by despots who resorted to violence, but by those who betrayed the civilized ideals to which they owed allegiance. These included those socialists and communists in England willing to condone cruelty and intolerance in a socialist government which they condemned in a fascist state. The greatest danger to civilization, he concluded, was

> not in Hitler, Mussolini, and the Nazi and Fascist systems, not in the barbarian at the gate, but within the citadel; it is in the economic barbarism of France and Britain and the ideological barbarism of Russia. For both these barbarisms destroy freedom and make the idea of a community in which the freedom of each is the condition of the freedom of all an illusion and a sham.[65]

Whether it was the exigencies of an anti-fascist alliance or a reluctance to offend his Left Book Club audience that caused Woolf to qualify his strictures against the Soviet Union, he found it increasingly difficult to conceal his repugnance after the Second World War. Stalinism was a travesty of Marxist objectives: rather than being transferred to the proletariat, power was monopolized by party functionaries, who subordinated socialist ideals to their own dictatorship. Unlike the Athenians, for whom democracy was only a means to attaining happiness, freedom, tolerance and justice, Marx's heirs made communism the supreme end of society, to which civilized values were readily sacrificed.[66] What he found so reprehensible was that, unlike Hitler and his associates, the Soviet rulers were

> not common gangsters or criminals; they [were] not paranoics or pathological sadists.... Yet in the course of a few years they have evolved a political system as frigidly inhuman, as insanely irrational as that of the fascist or nazi.[67]

They were challenging a central canon of his belief: that it was never right to do a great evil so that a greater good might result. Furthermore, the adoption of evil means for ostensible social benefits perverted social values and undermined civilization.

Nowhere do these preoccupations emerge more compellingly than in Woolf's heated exchanges with Kingsley Martin, who transformed the *New Statesman* into a vehicle for Soviet apologetics during the Cold War. A committed pacifist, prone to virulent anti-Americanism, Martin typified the left-wing tendency to equivocate on principles for the sake of socialist solidarity. At the same time he regarded Woolf as a paragon of intellectual integrity who might assuage his conscience. Instead Woolf seized every opportunity to chastise Martin by pointing out the moral defects of his position. When the *New Statesman* appeared to excuse the 1949 show trial and execution of Laszlo Rajk, the Hungarian Interior Minister, as trivial in comparison with the indiscriminate bombing of cities or the massacre of heretics, he accused Martin of condoning judicial murder and implying that "one wrong anywhere makes everything right for ever after."[68] He castigated the *New Statesman* for appearing to sanction political trials when undertaken to serve some national objective. Such a claim was inappropriate in this context:

> If our whole sense of justice had not been perverted in the last 30 years, I do not believe that you or anyone else would use that argument about a gang of low-class Hungarian politicians deliberately murdering by judicial process members of another gang, not with regard to a great issue but with regard to an internal struggle for power.[69]

The same moral issue resurfaced some years later when Martin, while absolving Mao, questioned the necessity of liquidating more than a million people. To Woolf this seemed to imply that there were circumstances under which mass political executions might be warranted.[70] Several years later, resuscitating their argument, Martin insinuated that Woolf had once admitted that Mao would be justified in authorizing the death of millions, if he believed that he was saving China from renewed war.[71] Vehemently denying the allegation, he stipulated that "under no circumstances conceivable would a government be justified in executing two million of its own subjects."[72] Where Martin differed from him, Woolf observed, was "in believing that politically you can know certainly what is good in itself or absolute truth so that it justified you in *acting* upon it melodramatically and over the dead bodies of other people."[73] Ultimately the issue hinged on Woolf's refusal to concede that purportedly worthy aims could exonerate those who employed evil means:

> I cannot pretend to believe what you believe or that any one, individual or government, Jew, Arab, capitalist, or communist, is justified in doing immense evil immediately on the excuse that he thinks it will hypothetically in the distant future prevent a greater evil or produce a very great absolute good.[74]

VI

V.S. Pritchett described Woolf as one of the "rationalist saints of our time" with "the Jewish feeling for justice and mercy, enlarged by the half-Jewish Montaigne's hatred of cruelty."[75] Despite Woolf's atheism and antipathy to dogma, it is perhaps appropriate to characterize him as a religious man.[76] Like Victorian doubters, his wife's father included, he might have said that he had ceased to believe in God but did not believe any the less in morality. That ethical structure was derived from his inherited Judaism, leavened by a strong dose of Cambridge rationalism and an idealized image of ancient Greek culture. His moral sensibility, in contrast to that of some of his Bloomsbury friends, was socially oriented, rooted in concepts like justice and mercy, tolerance and liberty, rather than focused on self. States of mind, contemplative self-absorption, meant less to Woolf than the application of ethical precepts to social questions. This was the source of his commitment first to the cooperative movement and then, more generally, to socialism, as effective means to realize those values perceived as ultimately good. His preoccupation with communal psychology and instinctual conduct was part of an effort to elucidate a more rational order, modeled on Periclean Athens, for his fellow man:

> The good life, as the Greeks called it, whether of the individual or

of the community requires ever more and more reason and rationality, a profound belief in its values tempered by the profoundest scepticism.[77]

Hence his dislike for capitalism, nationalism and communism, all of which not only violated his moral criteria of justice and equality, but also exploited irrational forces, like prejudice or superstition.

If Woolf remained suspicious of any form of ideology – religious or political – he never ceased to believe that private conscience must be brought to bear on public morality. In that sense at least he did not forsake the Victorian world in which he had come of age. Unlike Martin, he refused to subordinate principles to political expediency, however obstinate or heterodox this made him appear. If he occasionally erred on the side of self-righteousness, impatient with those who lacked his scruples, that sense of moral certainty may have been his most singular characteristic. After one of their recurrent quarrels he told Martin, "Although I always intend to follow Christ's teaching, Jehovah always breaks through."[78] He was here acknowledging not only his intolerance of disagreement, but the inflexibility of his conscience and the rigor of his moral standards. If Moore and Cambridge and Bloomsbury had converted him to Hellenism, the soul of a Hebraist survived to the end.

NOTES

I am grateful to Mrs Trekkie Parsons for permission to quote from Leonard Woolf's letters and published works and to Mrs Elizabeth Inglis of the University of Sussex Library for access to the Kingsley Martin, the Monk's House and the Leonard Woolf Papers.

1 Leonard Woolf, *Downhill All the Way*, London, Hogarth, 1967, pp. 114–15; Quentin Bell, *Bloomsbury*, New York, Basic Books, 1968, p. 74.

2 John Maynard Keynes, *Two Memoirs*, London, Rupert Hart-Davis, 1949, pp. 82, 98, 103. Woolf dismissed Keynes's interpretation of Moore and his influence on them as "distorted." Leonard Woolf, *Sowing*, London, Hogarth, 1960, pp. 124–6.

3 Matthew Arnold, *Culture and Anarchy*, J. Dover Wilson, ed., Cambridge, Cambridge University Press, 1932, pp. 129–35. Also see Lionel Trilling, *Matthew Arnold*, New York, W.W. Norton, 1939, pp. 256–8.

4 Leonard Woolf, *Principia Politica*, London, Hogarth, 1953, p. 34.

5 Leonard Woolf, *Beginning Again*, London, Hogarth, 1964, p. 74.

6 Woolf, *Sowing*, pp. 67–9.

7 Ibid., p. 12.

8 Leonard Woolf, *The Journey Not the Arrival Matters*, London, Hogarth, 1969, p. 127.

9 Ibid., pp. 128–9.

10 Ibid., p. 167. Woolf said that he never read Thucydides' rendition of Pericles' speech without "an uplifting of the heart." Also, Woolf, *Principia Politica*, p. 78.

11 Woolf to Dan Jacobson, 3 June 1968, in Frederic Spotts, ed., *Letters of Leonard Woolf*, New York, Harcourt Brace Jovanovich, 1989, pp. 565–6.
12 Ibid., p. 463.
13 Leonard Woolf, *The Wise Virgins*, New York, Harcourt Brace Jovanovich, 1979, p. 111. In a self-revealing passage he later wrote, "Most people are both proud and ashamed of their families, and nearly all Jews are both proud and ashamed of being Jews," Woolf, *Sowing*, p. 170.
14 Leonard Woolf, *Two Stories*, Richmond, Hogarth, 1917, p. 14.
15 Virginia Woolf to Violet Dickinson, 4 June 1912, in Quentin Bell, *Virginia Woolf: A Biography*, New York, Harcourt Brace Jovanovich, 1972, vol. 2, p. 2; Spotts, *Letters*, p. 470.
16 Woolf, *Sowing*, pp. 55–6.
17 Leonard Woolf, *Quack, Quack!*, London, Hogarth, 1935, pp. 197–9. A second, cheap edition in 1936 left out the appendix on anti-Semitism.
18 Woolf, *Journey*, pp. 26–8. Lord Annan remarked that the Armenian massacres and the Dreyfus affair "gave Woolf his vision of what justice and mercy meant in this world." Noel Annan, "Leonard Woolf's Autobiography," *Political Quarterly*, vol. 41, 1 (January–March 1970), p. 36.
19 Woolf, *Sowing*, p. 73.
20 Spotts, *Letters*, pp. 6–7.
21 Woolf, *Quack, Quack!*, p. 181.
22 Bella Woolf to Woolf, 4 May 1901, in Spotts, *Letters*, p. 16.
23 Woolf to Lytton Strachey, 20 March 1901, ibid., p. 13.
24 Woolf to Lytton Strachey, 25 June 1903, ibid., p. 31.
25 Rosenbaum calls *Principia Ethica* the "single most important work in Bloomsbury's Cambridge education." S.P. Rosenbaum, *Victorian Bloomsbury: The Early Literary History of the Bloomsbury Group*, New York, St Martin's Press, p. 227.
26 Woolf, *Sowing*, pp. 111, 114. Rosenbaum contends that Woolf was "the most worshipful of Moore" among the Cambridge Apostles at that time. Rosenbaum, *Victorian Bloomsbury*, p. 197.
27 Woolf, *Sowing*, p. 127.
28 Ibid., p. 131.
29 Woolf to G.E. Moore, 4 January 1909, in Spotts, *Letters*, p. 144.
30 Leonard Woolf, *Growing*, London, Hogarth, 1961, pp. 191, 193.
31 See Leonard Woolf, "The Colour of Our Mammies," *Encounter*, vol. 13, July 1959, pp. 3–8.
32 Leonard Woolf, "Colonies," Advisory Committee on International Questions Memorandum No. 23, Labour Party Archive, Manchester.
33 Leonard Woolf, *Imperialism and Civilization*, New York, Harcourt Brace, 1928, pp. 52–3, 109.
34 Keynes, *Two Memoirs*, p. 96.
35 Woolf to Kingsley Martin, 20 January 1965, Martin Papers, University of Sussex Library.
36 Beatrice Webb to Woolf, 16 December 1914, in Norman MacKenzie, ed., *The Letters of Sidney and Beatrice Webb*, Cambridge, Cambridge University Press, 1978, vol. 3, p. 45. Also see Beatrice Webb to Woolf, 21 January 1915, in ibid., pp. 48–9. Woolf told Sidney Webb that "it would be impossible to give a real idea of what you both did and meant for people of my generation, and the debt we owe you is immense." Woolf to Sidney Webb, 2 May 1943, in Spotts, *Letters*, p. 477.

37 Leonard Woolf, *International Government*, London, Fabian Society and George Allen and Unwin, 1916, p. 233.
38 Woolf to Margaret Llewelyn Davies, 4 August 1917, Monk's House Papers, University of Sussex Library.
39 Woolf to Margaret Llewelyn Davies, 25 August 1917, Monk's House Papers, University of Sussex Library.
40 Woolf maintained that Marx's ideas came to him through a fog which "consisted in part of a great deal of nonsense derived from Hegel, a certain amount of faulty economics, and the inevitable impossibility of foreseeing many developments of the capitalist industrial and financial system." Leonard Woolf, *Barbarians at the Gate*, London, Victor Gollancz, 1939, pp. 123–4.
41 Woolf, *Beginning Again*, p. 105.
42 Woolf to Lord Robert Cecil, 11 April 1921, Monk's House Papers, University of Sussex Library.
43 Woolf to Margaret Llewelyn Davies, 5 April 1920, Monk's House Papers, University of Sussex Library.
44 Woolf, *Downhill*, p. 85.
45 Leonard Woolf, *Socialism and Cooperation*, London and Manchester, National Labour Press, 1921, p. 21.
46 Ibid., p. 30.
47 Ibid., p. 55.
48 Ibid., pp. 58, 61, 66–7, 86, 95, 100.
49 Leonard Woolf, "From Geneva to the Next War," *Political Quarterly*, vol. 4, January–March 1933, p. 42.
50 Woolf to Frank Hardie, 29 November 1933, Hardie Papers, Bodleian Library, Oxford.
51 Woolf to Philip Noel-Baker, 11 March 1934, Noel-Baker Papers, Churchill College Library, Cambridge.
52 Leonard Woolf, "A New Foreign Policy for Labour," Report for the New Fabian Research Bureau, 1934, pp. 3, 6, held in Fabian Society Papers, Nuffield College Library, Oxford.
53 Woolf to Kingsley Martin, 29 September 1935, Martin Papers, University of Sussex Library.
54 Woolf to H.M. Swanwick, 1 October 1937, in Spotts, *Letters*, p. 413.
55 Woolf, *Downhill*, p. 243.
56 See Stefan Collini, *Public Moralists: Political Thought and Intellectual Life in Britain, 1850–1930*, Oxford, Clarendon Press, 1991, esp. pp. 2–3.
57 Woolf, *Principia Politica*, pp. 56–7.
58 Woolf, *Quack, Quack!*, p. 107.
59 Ibid., pp. 27–8.
60 Victor Gollancz to Woolf, 10 October 1938, Woolf Papers, University of Sussex Library.
61 Victor Gollancz to Woolf, 22 June 1939, Woolf Papers, University of Sussex Library.
62 Woolf, *Barbarians*, p. 153.
63 Ibid., p. 191.
64 Ibid., p. 190.
65 Ibid., p. 219.
66 *Principia Politica*, pp. 86–8, 176.
67 Ibid., p. 212.
68 Letter to Editor, *New Statesman*, 22 October 1949.

69 Woolf to Kingsley Martin, 24 October 1949, Martin Papers, University of Sussex Library.
70 "London Diary," *New Statesman*, 30 August 1952; Woolf, Letter to Editor, *New Statesman*, 6 September 1952. Also see Edward Hyams, *The New Statesman: The History of the First Fifty Years*, London, Longman, 1963, pp. 282–3.
71 Memorandum by Kingsley Martin, 24 April 1963, Woolf Papers, University of Sussex Library.
72 Woolf to Kingsley Martin, 26 April 1963, Martin Papers, University of Sussex Library.
73 Woolf to Kingsley Martin (memorandum), 7 May 1963, Martin Papers, University of Sussex Library.
74 Woolf to Kingsley Martin, 10 May 1963, Martin Papers, University of Sussex Library. Mrs Parsons indicated to me that Woolf frequently expressed these sentiments. Trekkie Parsons to author, 22 May 1991.
75 V.S. Pritchett, "Grace and Iron," *New Statesman*, 24 October 1969, pp. 577–8.
76 See George Spater and Ian Parsons, *A Marriage of True Minds: An Intimate Portrait of Leonard and Virginia Woolf*, New York, Harcourt Brace Jovanovich, 1977, p. 154.
77 Woolf, *Principia Politica*, p. 287.
78 Woolf to Kingsley Martin, 3 August 1956, Martin Papers, University of Sussex Library.

10 J.M. Keynes with Lydia Lopokova, portrait by William Roberts (1932)

7

J.M. Keynes 1883-1946
"The best of both worlds"
Peter Clarke

It has increasingly been recognized in recent years that Keynes's work cannot properly be appreciated if he is regarded narrowly as "an economist." Indeed an expertise in current economics may be misleading rather than enlightening. A distinction (though not always the same distinction) is now customarily drawn between Keynesianism, as a technical, professional, conventional doctrine or practice, and the thought of the historical Keynes. Keynes himself talked of his mature theoretical insights, for which he made such notoriously high claims, as simple, basic ideas. He went so far on one occasion as to claim that, while what he had to say was "intrinsically easy," it was "only to an audience of economists that it is difficult."[1] This reflected a longstanding belief that economics was "an easy subject – at which, however, very few excel!" The paradox was that the avocation of the economist required a combination of gifts: not only as mathematician and historian, but also as statesman and philosopher.[2] This paper explores the relation between these two latter roles – the one pre-eminently concerned with politics and public duty, the other intractably preoccupied with the foundations of personal morality.

A substantial body of research has recently been devoted to uncovering the philosophical underpinnings of Keynes's work.[3] Its general trend is to suggest that Keynes's *Treatise on Probability* (hereafter *Probability*), effectively begun in 1907, must be seen as one of the foundation stones of his *General Theory*, published nearly thirty years later – a thesis which, in its rigorous form, argues for a textual continuity in the treatment of the linked themes of uncertainty and probability. But it is not so easy to find agreement on how, or how securely, the economic edifice reposes upon its supposed philosophical footings. Marxian scholars will be familiar with the basic variants of this game of "What Keynes Really Meant." Thus the traditional position, as represented by Richard Braithwaite, is that there is a discontinuity between the philosophical thought of the Young Keynes and the Old Keynes.[4] This view has now met two revisionist arguments for a continuity thesis: one maintaining that the

Old Keynes was clearly immanent in the Young Keynes and the other that the Young Keynes was faithfully reproduced in the Old Keynes.

Keynes's own account of his early beliefs put into circulation two influential notions, which are intertwined at the heart of the puzzle. The first was that he, like other undergraduate Apostles who sat at the feet of G.E. Moore in Edwardian Cambridge, had "a religion and no morals."[5] The other was his declaration that "we completely misunderstood human nature, including our own," through a misplaced attribution of "rationality" to it.[6] The young Keynes was, on this reading, obsessed with questions of personal relations and private ethics but indifferent to public and civic responsibilities. This is the view persistently conveyed in volume one of Skidelsky's biography.[7]

This reading of "My Early Beliefs" is also consistent with much of the Keynesian debunking of the last two decades. For it is a short step from the impression of an apolitical young Keynes to the view of the mature economist as either an unreconstructed rationalist or an overconfident technocrat – and, in either case, betraying an impatience with, or an incomprehension of, the political processes of the real world. Now it must be acknowledged that Keynes presented such critics with plenty of ammunition, not least in the conclusion to the *General Theory*, with its assertion that "soon or late, it is ideas, not vested interests, which are dangerous for good or evil" – famous last words indeed![8] At the time A.L. Rowse denounced this as a "rationalist fallacy, the fatal defect of the liberal mind, the assumption that human beings are rational, will respond to a rational appeal, that ideas in themselves are effective and need only to be thrown out upon the waters of discussion for the right ones to prevail."[9] Fifty years on, this had become the crux of the public-choice theorists' critique of Keynesianism: "Keynes did not envisage the application of his policy views in a vulgar contemporary political setting, in which parties of all persuasions are continuously tempted to yield to such pressures as numerous private vested-interest groups, including the bureaucracy, and the necessity of vote-gathering in order to win elections."[10]

These two lines of interpretation are neatly conflated by a reference to Roy Harrod's influential concept of "the presuppositions of Harvey Road" – an assumption, which Keynes inherited from his parents, "that the government of Britain was and would continue to be in the hands of an intellectual aristocracy using the method of persuasion."[11] It would, however, be rash to suppose that Harrod and Skidelsky – let alone Keynes – were in fact subscribing to exactly the same account. This takes us back to a biographical and historical problem which has too often been treated in cursory or downright misleading ways.

Let us begin with what Keynes himself said. Part of the trouble is that his brilliant memoir, "My Early Beliefs," has been read as a document in

172

ways alien to the circumstances of its composition. Written for his friends as the Munich crisis brewed in 1938, it made a profound impression upon them as they listened to its evocative account of a lost age of innocence, while the light slowly drained out of the bleak autumnal sky. "The beauty and unworldliness of it" struck Virginia Woolf, even though it made her feel "a little flittery and stupid." Maynard had contrived his effects with an artist's sureness of touch: it made for "a very human satisfactory meeting."[12] Posthumously published, the essay has sometimes been perused in cold print without recognizing that literary artifice has its own conventions and that strict veracity is not necessarily among them.

In Harrod's interpretation, essentially from the perspective of 1938, the supposed influence of Moore in temporarily diverting his impressionable disciple from the path of public duty is not directly contested. Thus Keynes may have had a passing prepossession with the problem of the "good"; but this was countered and contained by the presuppositions of Harvey Road.[13] If Harrod was inclined to discount the iconoclasm of Keynes's account and to disclose instead an implicit recognition of public duty, to Skidelsky this stood out as another example of how the authorized biography had reflected a pious and unhistorical commitment to defend Keynes's reputation even from the self-inflicted barbs of autobiography.

Not that "My Early Beliefs" is accepted uncritically by Skidelsky, for he acknowledges that "certain liberties with strict truth for the sake of effect and amusement would have been natural."[14] Moreover, he also acknowledges that Leonard Woolf was one Apostle who directly repudiated its reading of Moore and his influence, maintaining that "we were not 'immoralists.' "[15] Yet this testimony is brushed aside by Skidelsky, on the grounds that Woolf's undisputed commitment to political objectives must have derived from "something else." Despite saving phrases, therefore, the authority of "My Early Beliefs" as a source remains integral to Skidelsky's interpretation. The point on which he fastens is that "Moore provided no logical connection between ethical goodness and political, social or economic welfare"; hence a Moorite – and "Keynes always remained a Moorite" – was consistent in evincing no interest in such matters.[16] Yet the curious feature in what Skidelsky contends about the lack of connection between Moore's doctrine and Keynes's politics is that elsewhere in his volume the author goes so far in supplying an account of the logical connection between them – through Keynes's theory of probability. It has been left to Keynes's most recent biographer, Donald Moggridge, to integrate these concerns by making out a case for "the important role of the period of the creation of *Probability* in bringing Keynes out from the inwardness and ultra-rationality of his 'early beliefs' towards a view of the world that could link 'science and art,' his duty to his friends and an active role in the wider phenomenal world."[17]

Nor can probability be safely ignored in studying Keynes's mature writings, which persistently suggest the salience of conceptions of uncertainty and risk in the formation of economic expectations. In his last major theoretical contribution, "The General Theory of Employment," published in the *Quarterly Journal of Economics* in 1937, uncertainty is a leitmotif running through the article. What was wrong with the orthodox theory was its assumption "that we have a knowledge of the future of a kind quite different from that which we actually possess." It was this "hypothesis of a calculable future," with its "underestimation of the concealed factors of utter doubt, precariousness, hope and fear" which was at the root of the trouble.[18]

Now if this were the whole burden of Keynes's message it would substitute a fundamentally irrationalist for a purely rationalist theory of the economy. This is the direction in which Shackle's suggestive insights about the role of uncertainty as Keynes's "ultimate meaning" tend to lead.[19] But Keynes gives a clear hint that a more subtle epistemology is in fact proposed. He thought it worthwhile to digress on the distinction between what is "probable" and what is "uncertain." "The game of roulette is not subject, in this sense to uncertainty; nor is the prospect of a Victory bond being drawn." What is uncertain is the outbreak of war or other matters where "there is no scientific basis on which to form any calculable probability whatever." It is this intractable lack of relevant knowledge which "compels us as practical men to do our best to overlook this awkward fact and to behave exactly as we should if we had behind us a good Benthamite calculation of a series of prospective advantages and disadvantages, each multiplied by its appropriate probability, waiting to be summed."[20]

Over the years, several economists took up this hint that readers of the *General Theory* might also turn with profit to *Probability*. But none of them, it is fair to say, turned with the requisite rigor and persistence; and only in the last decade has professional expertise in this field been allied with archival access to Keynes's writings on probability stretching back to the Edwardian period. Once we apprehend that a sophisticated concern with probability was part and parcel of the same bundle of early beliefs – of which Keynes wrote his classic account within a couple of years of dropping these ripe hints about the ubiquitousness of uncertainty – it becomes apparent that some technical understanding of his ideas in this field is likely to illuminate his more accessible beliefs about economics and policy and politics.

I

The current state of the literature has not produced a consensus. The common ground between the different accounts is, however, sufficiently extensive to permit some clear conclusions to be drawn. In the first place the significance of Moore's work can now be better appreciated. Moore asked two questions in his *Principia Ethica*: "What kind of things ought to exist for their own sakes?" and "What kind of actions ought we to perform?" His answer to the first was the basis of Keynes's "religion": that we know what is good on the basis of intuition. But with actions, as Bateman has nicely put it, we enter a field of "objective consequentialism" which is close to classical utilitarianism in insisting on the causal effects of our actions as the relevant test of whether they are good or bad. Moore's point about "moral rules or laws, in the ordinary sense" was that it was "generally useful, under more or less common circumstances, for everybody to perform or omit some definite kind of action." So it is not surprising that his system faced a critical choice between what modern philosophers dub rule utilitarianism and act utilitarianism. Should *the individual* always follow the rules? Or are individuals ever justified in judging particular cases for themselves? In his 1903 opus Moore insisted on following the rules because the probability of an individual turning out to have been correct in deciding otherwise in any particular case was unknowable.[21] These were the rule-bound "morals" which Keynes, as a principled immoralist, rejected.

The difference between them, however, was much more narrowly defined than Keynes's subsequent broad-brush picture suggests. The provocative language of "immoralism," with its suggestion that rules were only there to be flouted, masked the real point at issue, which was the caveat that rules need not *invariably* take precedence over a soundly argued objection. What the young Keynes rejected was not a consequentialist social ethic as such but the conception of probability on which Moore had implicitly relied in deciding that personal discretion could never be justified.

"My Early Beliefs" claimed that the Apostles "took not the slightest notice" of Moore's chapter on "Ethics in Relation to Conduct." But, as O'Donnell has pointed out, to gloss this as "ignored" is wildly inaccurate, since Keynes in fact devoted close attention to a discriminating critique of this chapter, notably in a paper which he gave to the Apostles on this theme.[22] The gist of Keynes's criticism was to indict Moore for employing a frequency theory of probability, which sought to measure probability by the observed frequency of subsequent events. To Keynes this seemed absurd – as though the actual frequency with which a coin happened to come down heads or tails in a series of tosses could disturb the proposition that each outcome had, on each toss, been equally likely.

Probability for Keynes was already seen as a rational judgment *ex ante*, a way of summing expectations, not a statement *ex post*.

If this were so, Keynes argued, then probability, properly understood, offered the basis for actions to be judged on the basis of their likely consequences. Moore's impossible requirement for complete certainty of knowledge in order to justify personal judgment was thus made redundant. Moreover, Bateman has shown that Moore took the point. Keynes argued out his position in his King's College Fellowship dissertation of 1908, which formed the backbone of his *Probability* as finally published in 1921. The impact of Keynes's work is demonstrated by Moore's abandonment of his earlier argument when he published a new book on ethics in 1912, and his adoption instead of a terminology about probability which avoided Keynes's criticisms. Moore now allowed for the exceptional case in which it could reasonably be foreseen that following a rule would probably lead to bad results, which ought to be avoided – even though there could be no absolute certainty that things would have turned out that way.[23] In short, by means of probability Keynes seems to have made an "immoralist" of his mentor. If Keynes was a Moorite, there are senses in which Moore became a Keynesian.

The technical dimension to this discussion is inescapable, however rebarbative it seems to connoisseurs of the deceptively easy style in which Keynes couched "My Early Beliefs." What Keynes rejected was an *aleatory* conception of probability, based on observed frequency of occurrence; what he proposed instead was an *epistemic* conception, dependent on the degree of prior knowledge of the likelihood of an event. Now aleatory theories are necessarily objective, and epistemic theories may be subjective. But the distinctive feature of *Probability* was that it presented an *objective epistemic* theory. It argued for a unique, given, determinate, calculable set of probabilities in the world, susceptible of correct perception through logical inference from the available evidence.[24]

Maybe the essential point about Keynes's early beliefs can be made without adopting such a tight taxonomy. Thus Carabelli prefers to argue that *Probability* extended the logic of probability to arguments of a non-demonstrative and non-conclusive character. Such arguments, dependent on limited rather than perfect knowledge, were part of a logic which had its own rationality while resting also on intuition.[25] Indeed, this leads Carabelli to identify a clear subjectivist element in Keynes's theory from the time he first began drafting it in 1907; and to argue that he had already broken with the sort of rationalism which he caricatured in "My Early Beliefs," which might accordingly be retitled, "My Very Early (around 1903–6) Beliefs."[26]

There is no need here to assimilate these varying emphases. More striking is their common reading of the work on probability which

Keynes had substantially completed before the outbreak of the First World War, though not published as *Probability* until afterwards. What he upheld was a probabilistic theory of ethics with a strong consequentialist emphasis. In general he acknowledged that rules and conventions had a social utility, even though he made a persuasive case against Moore's earlier insistence that they should always be obeyed. He was an immoralist in this sense rather than that which stuck in Leonard Woolf's autobiographical gorge.

There was thus no chasm in his thinking between private and public claims, even though he saw many practical dilemmas in living out his ideas in the world. Moreover, in licensing personal judgment, he implicitly assumed that it would have been formed and constrained by the same conventional morality which he refused to accept as an infallible commandment – a post-Victorian attitude in more ways than one. In this respect there is a revealing passage in Virginia Woolf's diary, recording a discussion about Christianity with Keynes in 1934.

> Morality. And JM [Keynes] said that he would be inclined not to demolish Xty if it were proved that without it morality is impossible. "I begin to see that our generation – yours and mine V., owed a great deal to our fathers' religion. And the young, like Julian [Bell], who are brought up without it, will never get so much out of life. They're trivial: like dogs in their lusts. We had the best of both worlds. We destroyed Xty & yet had its benefits." Well the argument was something like that.[27]

Recent attempts to demonstrate the continuity in Keynes's thought from the composition of *Probability* to the *General Theory* have encountered – maybe created – one major problem. This concerns his apparent shift of view in 1931, when he responded to criticism of his theory of probability from Frank Ramsey, who argued that the confidence with which expectations were formed and held depended on subjective factors and not just on logical inference from objective reality. Ramsey was a brilliant young mathematician whose premature death Keynes mourned, and personal sympathy may explain the tone which he adopted in a review of Ramsey's subsequently published papers. But can it explain away Keynes's capitulation? "So far I yield to Ramsey – I think he is right," Keynes wrote, accepting that "the basis of our degrees of belief – or the *a priori* probabilities, as they used to be called – is part of our human outfit, perhaps given us merely by natural selection, analogous to our perceptions and to our memories rather than to formal logic."[28] If this were so, then probabilities were not unique, assessed correctly or incorrectly by those who grasped or failed to grasp the appropriate logical relationships. Instead, probabilities might reasonably be assessed differently by different people – albeit on the basis of the same evidence.

This retraction has usually been taken at face value; only with the work of Carabelli and O'Donnell has it been argued – on different grounds – that Keynes's position remained substantially unchanged. For Carabelli this is obviously because she has already detected in the Young Keynes a full perception of subjectivism which the Old Keynes did not need to learn at Ramsey's posthumous knee.[29] For O'Donnell, conversely, the evidence that the Old Keynes did not abandon the logical basis of the Young Keynes's theory is sufficient evidence that no conversion to a radically subjectivist model took place.[30] It has been left to Bateman to reassert that there was a real shift, albeit within the same basic model, from an objective epistemic theory to a subjective epistemic theory. He uses this discontinuity to argue against a fundamentalist influence of probability theory in Keynes's economic thinking.[31]

The relevance of a probability model to the *General Theory* does not, however, depend on maintaining that there was continuity in Keynes's thought. It may be fruitful to ask instead whether the early 1930s saw a shift towards subjectivism in Keynes's thinking about *both* probability and economic behavior. If the first shift in Keynes's views in the early 1930s was towards recognizing a clearly subjective element in his model of rational behavior, his other shift – in economic theory itself – was complementary. It turned on the relation between expectations and equilibrium, as seen in their contrasting treatment in the *Treatise on Money* and the *General Theory*.

Keynesianism already existed as a set of practical policy axioms before Keynes sought to challenge the theoretical postulates on which, as he liked to say, he had been brought up. In 1930 the *Treatise on Money*, for all its striking novelty in expression, did not doubt that market forces tended towards an equilibrium at which all resources in the economy, including labor, would be fully employed. What the *Treatise on Money* did was to dwell on the unhappy consequences of disequilibrium. It made the point by stressing the difference between saving and investment. For if decisions to save and to invest were taken by different people, there was an obvious need to reconcile them. Interest rate classically did this job, finding a level that was not too high (for that would choke off Enterprise) and not too low (for that would fail to reward Thrift) but just right. Disequilibrium between saving and investment was a symptom of a rate of interest that was wrong. If it was too low ("cheap money"), an investment boom occurred, accompanied, of course, by inflation. But that was hardly the problem in 1930. The real issue at the time was what happened when dear money caused entrepreneurs to make losses. This was the practical problem in Britain after the return to the Gold Standard in 1925, because bank rate had to be kept high to maintain the pound at an overvalued parity.

Keynes had, of course, made his name as an economic publicist in the 1920s, disputing the Gold Standard policy on pragmatic grounds; what he did in the *Treatise on Money* was to theorize his critique. He explained the inability of interest rates to fall to their proper domestic level by pointing to the *modus operandi* of bank rate in responding to international pressure on the exchange rate. The level of interest rates required for internal equilibrium between saving and investment was precluded by external commitments. That, at least, is how Keynes preferred to put the matter. He could not, however, deny the fact that if British labor costs had exhibited the flexibility assumed in orthodox thinking, and fallen in tandem with the price level, the trick could have been turned.

The salient point in the *Treatise on Money* was that disequilibrium was a product of thwarted expectations. When entrepreneurs made their investments, they did so with an expectation of normal profit which failed to materialize. Bank rate was stuck too high to allow them to prosper. Not only did dear money raise the cost of investment and set a correspondingly high target for the returns needed to make it profitable, but it also provided savers with an excessive incentive. The excess of saving over investment measured the windfall losses which entrepreneurs suffered as a consequence. How so? Because, had this slice of income not been devoted to excessive saving but to consumption, it would have provided the slice of extra spending on consumption goods which would have allowed their producers to make their anticipated level of profit. Instead, the goods would have to be sold for knockdown prices, visiting disappointed entrepreneurs with windfall losses on a scale which exactly equaled the excess of saving over investment. Only when expectations were fulfilled was equilibrium achieved; conversely, disequilibrium was only the problem so long as expectations were not fulfilled.

This way of describing the *Treatise on Money* brings out the centrality of expectations to its model of the economy. Not only does it raise the question: why are expectations not fulfilled? It also prompts a further question: should expectations that are not fulfilled be regarded as irrational? "Rational expectations" these days are axiomatically those which are fulfilled. But for Keynes, as has been seen, an appeal to the subsequent fact of non-fulfillment would have been quite improper. It would have imported exactly the aleatory test of probability which he always rejected as appropriate to human behavior.[32] The right question was: had the expectations been reasonable at the time the relevant decisions had been taken? Not altogether, Keynes suggested.

Keynes's experience of developments in the real world from the Wall

Street crash of 1929 to the flight from sterling in 1931 brought home to him the full importance of business psychology in sustaining or undermining confidence in self-reinforcing cycles which took on a life of their own. Did such insights help prompt his sympathetic response to Ramsey's argument for the irreducibility of subjective beliefs? After all, Keynes published his review, not in an abstruse philosophical journal, but in the *New Statesman and Nation*, and he did so the week after Britain was forced off the Gold Standard. It was then that he conceded that "the basis of our degrees of belief" was "part of our human outfit" rather than derived from formal logic.[33]

Keynes had already gone a long way down this road in the *Treatise on Money*, where his analysis of "bullishness" and "bearishness" built directly upon the experience of boom and bust on Wall Street. His analysis concentrated on "the fact that *differences* of opinion exist between different sections of the public." No unique objective probabilities here! On the one side there was was an untrammelled "bullishness of sentiment"; on the other, stretching the established sense of a "bear" as one who sold short on the stock exchange, he identified as bears those "persons who prefer to keep their resources in the form of claims on money of a liquid character realisable at short notice."[34] The notion of liquidity preference is clearly glimpsed here – though not yet its significance as the explanation of interest rates.

Further issues arise: not only whether bulls or bears were acting rationally (or entertaining reasonable expectations) but whether such behavior had a self-fulfilling effect. A suggestive passage in the *Treatise on Money* is that in which, with Keynes's practiced ability to find uncanny adumbrations of his current ideas in earlier writers, he turned to 1 Kings 17: 12–16. The parable of the Widow's Cruse was always an unlikely story. Keynes used it to illustrate "one peculiarity of profits (or losses) which we may note in passing." It was that however much of their profits entrepreneurs spent, profits as a whole would not be depleted because the effect would be to increase the profits on consumption goods by the same amount.[35] Alas, it was a fallacy, as he subsequently came to realize in the course of criticism from the so-called Circus in Cambridge, because he had illicitly assumed that only prices and not output would rise. This objection, however, does not have the same force against his parallel example, when entrepreneurs making losses seek to recoup them by curtailing consumption, thus converting the cruse to a Danaid Jar which can never be filled up. These paradoxes intrigued Keynes at the time, as his references to them before the Macmillan Committee indicate. The Widow's Cruse was an example of non-rational behavior which was apparently self-fulfilling in generating economic rewards for those who indulged in it. The Danaid Jar was an example of how individual rationality merely reinforced an adverse outcome for all concerned – through a wholly natural desire to run away from bears.

These paradoxes were resolved by two insights which lay at the heart of Keynes's rapidly evolving theory of effective demand. The first he presented in his university lectures of October 1932. He had now formulated a concept which he termed liquidity preference and which he acknowledged as "somewhat analogous to the state of bearishness." The novelty, however, was not in the language but in the way he put it to work as his explanation of interest rates. It was a notion, as he later claimed, "which became quite clear in my mind the moment I thought of it."[36]

Keynes's other insight was more fundamental, for it broke the chain of rationality between individual decisions and an optimal outcome for the community. "It is natural to suppose that the act of an individual, by which he enriches himself without apparently taking anything from anyone else, must also enrich the community as a whole," the *General Theory* acknowledged; but its message was that the theory applicable to the individual firm did not provide a theory of output *as a whole*.[37] The analysis of the *General Theory* thus shifted the focus away from whether individuals formed reasonable expectations. Instead the problem turned on the psychological forces which governed the state of the market. It was compounded, moreover, by the inability of individuals to buck the trend in a falling market. Even rational individual strategies (going liquid, cutting wages, reducing spending) were collectively self-defeating.

Once seized of this point, Keynes expressed it pithily, variously and frequently, in ways that it would be otiose to document here. The fallacy of composition thus provided a logical reason why individuals, even if they acted rationally to save themselves, might not be able to do so, since competitive strategies could not simultaneously succeed for all. It is tempting to go further. One might say that the *General Theory* disclosed a class of actions about which individuals had no means of determining epistemic probabilities which could warrant the description objective. But this is to forge a more rigorous link between Keynes's evolving ideas about epistemology and economics than is (probably) justifiable. In the absence of specific textual support, it is hazardous to infer what "must have been in his mind" and to look for a tight, formal consistency in the thinking of a man who allowed his intuition free rein to pierce the different problems he tackled. It is safer to rest with the observation that both in his economic analysis, which occupied most of his attention in the early 1930s, and in his fugitive reappraisal of his theory of probability, Keynes now showed a readiness to allow more weight to subjective feelings.[38]

II

In the *Treatise on Money* expectations can be seen as a *deus ex machina*. Their importance was given a new twist in the *General Theory*, where it became an integral part of the analysis. Expectations about demand were problematic in both books. Hence the *Treatise on Money* included as "income" not only the realized receipts of entrepreneurs but also their expected profits (which they actually suffered as windfall losses). The *General Theory* gave a simpler account with its concept of effective demand, comprising actual investment and immediately prospective consumption. The common point is that expectations are always, necessarily, the basis of investment decisions. In the *Treatise on Money*, however, the problem is how expectations are thwarted, producing a position of disequilibrium. In the *General Theory*, conversely, the problem is equilibrium itself – because it may be sub-optimal, with persistent unemployment.

Here Keynes's story no longer depended on expectations not being realized. As he told Harrod in 1937, "the theory of effective demand is substantially the same if we assume that short-period expectations are always fulfilled."[39] Indeed one could argue that expectations are always self-fulfilling via the multiplier, which necessarily increases aggregate income in a determinate way. The catch, of course, is that such an increase in income may not be reflected in an increase in output, but only in prices. To this extent inflation is the escape valve in the model. The elasticity of the supply curve is crucial; Keynes envisaged it responding to increases in effective demand with increasing output until full employment is reached, at which point further pressure on demand would simply produce inflation.

In the *Treatise on Money*, although Keynes had recognized that savings and investment might be in disequilibrium, he had still clung to the theoretical axiom that different forces, acting in opposite directions, had a tendency to bring them back towards equilibrium. In the *General Theory* the self-righting forces had disappeared, and when Keynes generalized further in the 1937 *QJE* article he offered his most comprehensive explanation. Here confidence became the psychological premise of decisions to invest, just as it was of decisions to save. Saving took place in a world permeated by subjective apprehensions. Keynes argued that "partly on reasonable and partly on instinctive grounds, our desire to hold money as a store of wealth is a barometer of our distrust of our own calculations and conventions concerning the future."[40] Hence the inadmissibility of direct extrapolation from barter transactions in devising simple models of how a monetary economy actually worked. The behavior of a monetary economy was unique since it dealt with uncertainty by putting a price upon it, and allowed people to opt for money itself rather than the goods or assets which it could purchase. Keynes's theory of interest, as expressing the liquidity preference of lenders, was founded on this conception. Saving was thus no longer a confident, rational calculation, acting out the virtue of thrift; it was rooted in the precarious psychology of fear and distrust.

Investment, likewise, was not derived from an objective computation of actual yields; instead the *General Theory*'s identification of "animal spirits" stressed the volatility of business confidence. Thus investment, the motor of the economy, "depends on two sets of judgments about the future, neither of which rests on an adequate or secure foundation – on the propensity to hoard and on opinions on the future yield of capital assets." To speak of a *propensity* imports nothing more purposeful than inclination or bias; to speak of *opinions* suggests the disputable and infirm nature of decisions. A dim view of the future would not only stimulate hoarding, and thus depress investment, it would also depress investment by reducing expectations of profit. Since both were expressions of optimism or pessimism, they tended to fluctuate in the *same* direction, as business psychology peaked and drooped. So "the only element of self-righting in the system arises at a much later stage and in an uncertain degree."[41] Keynes concluded: "This that I offer is, therefore, a theory of why output and employment are so liable to fluctuation."[42]

Despite other discrepancies in the secondary literature, there is an impressive measure of agreement over the probabilistic model of behavior which underpins the *General Theory* and was made more explicit in the QJE. Unlike Shackle's reading of Keynes in an irrationalist sense, this stresses Keynes's wish to salvage and identify a modified role for rationalism. O'Donnell makes a persuasive case for seeing this as a "theory of rational behavior under irreducible uncertainty."[43] Fitz-gibbons writes of "the twilight of probability" in which we live, carrying the inference that "it is best to recognize our limitations and act upon them instead of representing to ourselves that our methods of knowl-edge are more powerful than they actually are."[44] Carabelli makes the point that "when stressing the practical cognitive side of uncertainty, Keynes, unlike Shackle, considered it as a condition of knowledge rather than of ignorance (even when the actual knowledge was minimal) . . ."[45] It follows that it is reasonable to rely upon conventions where knowl-edge is insufficient to supply better reasons for acting.[46]

In short, it is not uncertainty as such but *our knowledge of uncertainty* which commands the situation. It is under these conditions that we are persuaded to act, in ways that seem reasonable to us at the time when decisions need to be made. Our current beliefs, opinions and expec-tations are crucial in molding the plastic shape of the future. Moreover, if individuals were impotent to realize their goals in the market, as

Keynes saw it, this was no excuse for fatalism but a demonstration of the need for those decisions which cannot safely be left to the market to be taken within the polity. Although the role of persuasion in achieving this had a directly political element, it was also a question of forming expectations.[47]

The self-sustaining effect of confidence turned economic problems into psychological problems. If effective demand drives the economy, and investment plus expectations of consumption drive effective demand, and confidence drives investment, and expectations drive confidence, then the involuted role of expectations in driving the economy is inescapable. Part of Keynes's project was to conquer public opinion and thereby produce the climate of expectations in which the economy could flourish.

The conquest of public opinion admittedly had a directly political dimension. Keynes obviously wanted to persuade decision-makers to adopt his policies. But his model of opinion-forming surely amounted to more than an elitist or intellectualist fallacy. Though it was rooted in liberal assumptions, it pointed to a coherent conception of social-democratic change – an ongoing process of persuasion at more than one level. It may be that he underestimated not only the difficulties involved in the transmission of ideas but also the perils of misunderstanding along the way. Hume's dictum that reason is the slave of the passions is relevant here, but it was undoubtedly Keynes's hope that the relationship implied between the horse and the rider would permit purposive choice.[48] Keynes was not oblivious of what I would call the ideological problem – the way in which his ideas, in the process of finding the sort of social purchase necessary to make them effective, would necessarily undergo a selective process of simplification and distortion.

In 1934 Keynes advanced a short explanation of why government had not adopted his policies: "Because I have not yet succeeded in convincing either the expert or the ordinary man that I am right." The impediment did not lie, he contended, in the self-interest of the ruling classes but in "the difficulty of knowing for certain where wisdom lies" and in the related difficulty of persuading others. In arguing that it was "not self-interest which makes the democracy difficult to persuade" he provided a snapshot of how he expected public opinion to move.

> In this country henceforward power will normally reside with the Left. The Labour Party will always have a majority, except when something happens to raise a doubt in the minds of reasonable and disinterested persons whether the Labour Party are in the right. If, and when, and in so far as, they are able to persuade reasonable and disinterested persons that they are right, the power of self-interested capitalists to stand in their way is negligible.[49]

A little over a month later Keynes made his better-known claim to Shaw about his hopes to revolutionize economic thinking; and this letter helpfully amplifies the parallel statement at the end of the *General Theory* about ideas ruling the world. For Keynes was concerned with political problems in a far more persistent and fundamental way than has generally been credited, even if he did not succeed in formulating fully adequate solutions, nor purport to do so. He told Shaw: "When my new theory has been duly assimilated and mixed with politics and feelings and passions, I can't predict what the final upshot will be in its effects on action and affairs."[50] His own expectations thus remained bounded by uncertainty; but this did not inhibit him from backing his own judgment about politics and public opinion, as about other, more private concerns. Of course not. This was the same Keynes who said in 1938: "I remain, and always will remain, an immoralist."[51] He still wanted the best of both worlds.

NOTES

1 Donald Moggridge and Austin Robinson, eds, *The Collected Writings of John Maynard Keynes*, 30 vols., London, Macmillan for the Royal Economic Society, 1971–89 (hereafter JMK), vol. 14, p. 124. In exposition this essay has benefited from discussion of my paper at the Harvard symposium and from the criticism of successive drafts by Bradley Bateman, Stefan Collini, John Thompson and Maria Tippett.
2 JMK, vol. 10, p. 173.
3 R.M. O'Donnell, *Keynes: Philosophy, Economics and Politics*, London, Macmillan, 1989; Anna M. Carabelli, *On Keynes's Method*, London, Macmillan, 1988; Bradley W. Bateman, "Keynes's changing conception of probability," *Economics and Philosophy*, vol. 3, 1987, pp. 97–120; idem, "G.E. Moore and J.M. Keynes: a missing chapter in the history of the expected utility model," *American Economic Review*, vol. 78, pp. 1098–106; Athol Fitzgibbons, *Keynes's Vision*, Oxford, Clarendon Press, 1988.
4 R.B. Braithwaite, "Keynes as philosopher," in Milo Keynes, ed., *Essays on John Maynard Keynes*, Cambridge, Cambridge University Press, 1975, pp. 237–46.
5 JMK, vol. 10, p. 436.
6 JMK, vol. 10, p. 448.
7 Robert Skidelsky, *John Maynard Keynes*, vol. 1, London, Macmillan, 1983, pp. 119, 124, 229, 233, 262; cf. pp. 106, 117, 157, 209–10, 245–6, 400–1, cited by O'Donnell, p. 116, making the related point that Skidelsky's Keynes allegedly kept personal ethics in one compartment and relegated public duty to another.
8 JMK, vol. 7, p. 384.
9 A.L. Rowse, *Mr Keynes and the Labour Movement*, London, Macmillan, 1936, p. 61.
10 John Burton, *Keynes's General Theory: Fifty Years On*, London, Institute of Economic Affairs, 1986, p. 15.
11 Roy Harrod, *The Life of John Maynard Keynes*, London, Macmillan, 1951, pp. 192–3.

12 Anne Olivier Bell, ed., *The Diary of Virginia Woolf*, vol. 5, London, Penguin edn, 1985, pp. 168–9.
13 Harrod, *The Life*, p. 80.
14 Skidelsky, p. 143.
15 Leonard Woolf, *Sowing*, London, Hogarth Press, 1970, pp. 144–56, at p. 148.
16 Skidelsky, *Keynes*, p. 146.
17 See Donald Moggridge, *Maynard Keynes*, London, Routledge, 1992, chs 5 and 6, at p. 165.
18 JMK, vol. 14, p. 122.
19 See G.L.S. Shackle, *The Years of High Theory*, Cambridge, Cambridge University Press, 1967, esp. ch. 11.
20 JMK, vol. 14, pp. 113–14.
21 G.E. Moore, *Principia Ethica*, Cambridge University Press, 1903, pp. 162–3, explicated in Bateman, "A missing chapter," pp. 1098–100.
22 O'Donnell, *Keynes*, pp. 149–50. The dating of this paper to 1904, as supplied by O'Donnell and Skidelsky, without further comment on either case, proved troubling to both Carabelli and Bateman, who pointed out that no evidence of date could be found and that references within the paper anticipated the drafts of 1907. (Carabelli, p. 5, n. 5 at p. 152; Bateman, "A missing chapter," p. 1101, n. 5.) Moggridge now proposes to resolve this discrepancy by making a plausible argument for 1907. (Moggridge, *Maynard Keynes*, ch. 5, App. 1.) Bateman meanwhile informs me that he has shifted towards 1904, for good reasons which he should be left to explain in his forthcoming published work. Happily, whichever dating is preferred, there is little dispute over the substance of the case which Keynes outlined and subsequently developed.
23 Bateman, "A missing chapter," pp. 1103–4.
24 Bateman, "Keynes's changing conception," pp. 99–100. A subjectivist position, it should be noted, need not be irrationalist if – as in Ramsey's version, considered below – it still demands that, whatever basis individuals have for adopting their beliefs, these must nonetheless be constrained by consistency and coherence. Betting is thus the favorite analogy here, where the fact that each punter is free to back his favorite is consistent with the fact that a book can be made which sums all the bets. See O'Donnell, *Keynes*, pp. 23–4. O'Donnell's taxonomy cuts the cake in a different way from Bateman's, grouping not only the frequency concept but also the logical concept which Keynes upheld, as two variants of objectivist theories. These stand distinct from subjectivist theories, which are dependent on the confidence with which individuals entertain their beliefs, howsoever generated.
25 Carabelli, *On Keynes's Method*, pp. 16–17, 27.
26 Ibid., pp. 99–100. Indeed, only in Fitzgibbons does a literalist reading of "My Early Beliefs" meet no explicit challenge, and even here its account is implicitly undercut by the author's exposition of Keynes's all-embracing probabilistic vision. Fitzgibbons begins with the principle of indifference, which Keynes regarded as facile because "the world is too complex to be explained by a theory that applies to the tossing of a coin." He relied instead on intuition to grasp a logic of probability that was "the logic of ordinary discourse" and hence applicable to real world decisions. Fitzgibbons, *Keynes's Vision*, pp. 12, 17.
27 Anne Olivier Bell, ed., *The Diary of Virginia Woolf*, vol. 4, London, Penguin edn, 1983, p. 208.
28 JMK, vol. 10, p. 339.
29 Carabelli, *On Keynes's Method*, pp. 96–7.

30 O'Donnell, *Keynes*, pp. 139–48.

31 Bateman, "Keynes's changing conception," p. 107. These interpretations, it should be noted, disagree more sharply about the position from which Keynes began than about that at which he ended, the more so since O'Donnell acknowledges that Ramsey had an indirect influence on Keynes in moving him towards a preference for "weak rationality" rather than the "strong rationality" which had previously underpinned his theories. (O'Donnell, *Keynes*, p. 147.)

32 Thus it is surely misguided to suggest that some of Keynes's ideas anticipate a rational expectationist position, as in Allan H. Meltzer, *Keynes's Monetary Theory: A Different Interpretation*, Cambridge, Cambridge University Press, 1988, pp. 7, 13–14, 68 n. 10, 141, 175; though Meltzer also recognizes the discrepancy at p. 144. For a clarification see Bateman, "Keynes's changing conception," pp. 116–17.

33 JMK, vol. 10, p. 339.

34 JMK, vol. 5, pp. 223–5; cf. pp. 128–31.

35 JMK, vol. 5, p. 125, and Peter Clarke, *The Keynesian Revolution in the Making*, Oxford, Clarendon Press, 1988, pp. 250–1.

36 Clarke, *Keynesian Revolution*, p. 263.

37 JMK, vol. 7, pp. 20, 293.

38 I have had the benefit of reading Bateman's unpublished paper, "Finding confidence," which offers support for a discontinuity thesis while differing in its treatment of the role of expectations as outlined in my next two paragraphs.

39 JMK, vol. 14, p. 181.

40 JMK, vol. 14, p. 116.

41 JMK, vol. 14, p. 118.

42 JMK, vol. 14, p. 121.

43 O'Donnell, *Keynes*, p. 261. Not, as Bateman shows, "rational expectations" in the modern sense, since Keynes's point about how expectations are formed under uncertainty was "that people use epistemic probabilities in decision making and this was still his position at the time he wrote *The General Theory*." (Bateman, "Keynes's changing conception," pp. 116–17.)

44 Fitzgibbons, *Keynes's Vision*, p. 142.

45 Carabelli, *On Keynes's Method*, p. 103.

46 Ibid., pp. 161, 163.

47 As Carabelli puts it, "the analysis of the passivity of *individual* economic behaviour put forward by Keynes did not imply a denial of the possibility of intervention of and on economic agents *as a whole* and of social institutions in an active way in the future" (ibid., p. 228).

48 See Eduardo da Fonseca, *Beliefs in Action*, Cambridge, Cambridge University Press, 1991, pp. 90–2, 184–5, 186, 188–9.

49 JMK, vol. 28, pp. 35–6.

50 JMK, vol. 28, p. 42.

51 JMK, vol. 10, p. 447.

11 John Reith, cartoon by Low.

8

John Reith 1889–1971
Entrepreneur of collectivism
D.L. LeMahieu

He was a Calvinist who helped define the notion of public service broadcasting in Britain; an authoritarian with administrative power over an entire medium of communication; a visionary whose cultural legacy endured deep into this century. Few figures would seem to illustrate better the relationship between private conscience and public duty in twentieth-century Britain than John Reith, the first Director General of the British Broadcasting Corporation. "Reith did not make broadcasting," Asa Briggs later wrote, "but he did make the BBC." *The Times* called him "one of the outstanding personalities of his time" and even his more hostile critics acknowledged the impact of his character and idealism upon a major new institution in Britain.[1] From 1922 to 1938, Reith created a cultural mission for the BBC which later officials could emulate or mock, but not ignore.

Yet to evaluate the relationship between private conscience and public duty in Reith involves a number of problems. First, the early influences which crafted him into such an extraordinary personality necessarily remain a source of controversy. What were the personal origins of his public ambitions? Was Scottish Presbyterianism the central influence on his "private conscience" or were there other crucial experiences which shaped his beliefs? Then too, although Reith provided strong leadership for the early BBC, his success must be evaluated within a specific historical context. How much opposition did he confront in implementing his vision of public service broadcasting? How flexible was his administrative leadership? What role did he play in the rapid expansion and cultural evolution of the BBC during the 1930s? Third, although Reith pursued a productive career after 1938, his work at the BBC remains his major historical contribution. Reith lived for over three decades after his resignation, increasingly bitter and frustrated that he could never regain the power he once commanded. What do these later years reveal about Reith? What clues do they hold for understanding his personality and influence?

I

Commentators invariably tagged Reith as a "son of the manse" to explain his adherence to high moral ideals. Garry Allighan's journalistic biography in 1938 emphasized Reith's religious background, and Andrew Boyle's *Only the Wind Will Listen*, published in 1972, argued that Reith's sense of foredoomed damnation vitiated whatever consolation he garnered from his public achievements.[2] Certainly religion played a central role in shaping his early character. Born in July 1889, John Reith was the seventh and youngest child of George and Adah Reith. A minister in the Free Church of Scotland, George Reith had served the College Church in Glasgow for over twenty years. Both parents taught their children strong Christian values which permeated their later lives. John Reith's intense ambition to achieve "great good," his Sabbatarianism, the Manicheanism of his judgments, his pessimism and characteristic gloom, even the keeping of his extraordinarily detailed personal diary – all might be explained by reference to the Calvinist framework of his youth. Moreover, Reith's later understanding of modern psychology reinforced his Calvinist notion of human moral frailty. Reith believed that an individual's inner life was composed of lower instincts and higher faculties competing for dominance. "The personality is made up of two distinct and often warring elements," he observed in 1922. "We surely want to wipe out as much as we can of the barbarian in case it may get control over us, in a weak moment, with results of a disastrous kind."[3] One theme which united his personal and professional life centered upon his ongoing, often problematic quest for control, over himself and over others around him.

Yet there were at least three other aspects of his youth and early career that contributed enormously to the formation of his character. First, though he was born into a large family, Reith spent his childhood in relative isolation. His nearest sibling was almost ten years older, and throughout his younger years he barely knew most of his brothers and sisters. As Charles Stuart put it in his introduction to Reith's published diaries, "his early life was effectively that of an only child."[4] Reith only became close to his parents well into adulthood; during his crucial early years, his parents devoted their energies to church affairs. "In the corporate sense, there was little or no home life," Reith recalled in his autobiography, "antagonisms and reserves were marked among us. We met perforce at family worship morning and night and at meals; we sought our separate rooms thereafter."[5] Though observations about childhood influences remain necessarily speculative, Reith's instinctive mistrust of other people, difficulty in forming personal relationships, and almost insatiable desire for reassurance, cannot be unrelated to a childhood in which parents and children dwelt in self-enclosed emotional spheres.

A second pivotal element of Reith's early development concerns his education. Though he spent two years at Gresham's School in Norfolk, where he excelled in German and earned a coveted place on the rugby team, he left school at seventeen under mysterious circumstances and became apprenticed as a mechanical engineer to the North British Locomotive Company. From 1906 to 1914, Reith studied and worked as an engineer, first in Glasgow and then for a brief period in London before the outbreak of the First World War. "Eight years of intellectual and social frustration," he later recalled.[6] Throughout his life, Reith deeply regretted never following his schoolmates to Oxford or Cambridge, and his attitude towards university education and higher culture often embodied the exaggerated respect of the outsider.

Yet his technical training in engineering prepared him for a career in mass communication in ways that an Oxbridge education might not. Reith's grasp of technology improved his managerial skills and became one factor, among others, that help explain his life-long preoccupation with "efficiency" as a measure of judgment. "Efficiency implies that a machine does its work to a standard; that a bridge carries its load with a factor of safety; that the value and performance of the product is commensurate with the cost of making it.'"[7] Throughout his career, Reith applied this standard to a long list of subjects, including monarchy, the civil service, British business, democracy and, above all, the use of his own talents. The complaint that he was not "fully stretched" spans virtually his entire public career.

The path to efficiency lay in planning and organization. Here Reith excelled. He loved to reorganize things, whether the rooms in his house, a factory, a government department or an entire new medium of communication. As a factory manager after the War he embraced Taylorism; at the BBC he established chains of command that withstood explosive growth; during the Second World War he helped organize the British supplies for the landings on D-Day. For Reith, however, planning and organization could rarely be collaborative undertakings; genuine efficiency usually depended upon his direction alone. He did not like compromise and he virtually never forgave opponents. Reith's love of efficiency often meshed comfortably with his demands for authority.

The military provided an early outlet for this love of command, as well as his sense of public duty. Reith joined the Glasgow University Officer Training Corps in 1908 and three years later accepted a commission in the 5th Scottish Rifles, a position that ensured his rapid mobilization to the Western Front in 1914. Initially, Reith served as a Transport Officer, a duty he filled enthusiastically, but not always according to military procedure. An acrimonious and self-destructive clash with his superior officers resulted in his transfer to the Royal Engineers. On 7 October 1915, while assigned to inspect damage from night shelling, he flouted all danger by walking upright above the trench line. A sniper rewarded this bravado by shooting him in the face, nearly killing him.[8] The wound healed but left a distinctive jagged scar on his left cheek. Standing six feet six inches tall, with great bushy eyebrows and a baleful stare, Reith was already an astonishing physical presence. Now, for the remainder of his life, anyone who encountered him also gazed upon an emblem of courageous service during the Great War, the defining event of his generation.

The First World War proved a crucial experience for Reith in two other ways. Unlike most of his fellow soldiers, he enjoyed his active participation in combat, and rejected the tragic view of the conflict which dominated the interwar period. In 1930, he wrote a controversial article challenging the "All Quiet School"; and his memoirs of the war, *Wearing Spurs*, so alarmed his friends that Reith postponed publication until 1966. Even at that late date, his eagerness for battle and evident pleasure at its sacrifices took reviewers aback. Reith never suffered the disillusion with nineteenth-century values which characterized so many of his contemporaries. He retained faith in the Victorian ideals of his youth long after others abandoned them as hopelessly tainted by Gallipoli, Passchendaele and the Somme.[9]

The war also provided Reith with managerial experiences crucial to his later appointment to the BBC. After convalescing from his wound, Reith was sent to the United States in 1916 to help organize the manufacture and supply of rifles for the British army. He spent the next eighteen months in Swarthmore, Pennsylvania, where his administrative responsibilities combined with a friendly reception by the Americans contributed enormously to his personal happiness. Reith socialized with the business elite of Philadelphia and became an effective public spokesman for the war effort. His managerial skills and deep moral seriousness impressed a number of influential Americans, who conveyed their high regard for the young officer to British authorities. Reith's talents blossomed in America.[10]

He returned to England late in 1917, and completed his active service working as an engineer on a major project for the Admiralty. In 1918 he met Muriel Odhams, the daughter of a wealthy publisher and, after a long engagement, they married and eventually had two children. In 1920, Reith agreed to administer a factory in Coatbridge that manufactured a variety of goods, including oil engines and rotary pumps. Reith quickly improved organization and sought to raise morale. In his dealings with labor, he proved to be a classic paternalist, eager to upgrade working conditions but only on terms dictated by management. Despite his efforts, however, the factory at Coatbridge eventually closed and by

1922 he was again looking for suitable employment. Though ambiguous in his political allegiances, he worked briefly for Sir William Bull, a Conservative politician who probably arranged for Reith to have an interview with the British Broadcasting Company, a new consortium of wireless manufacturers eager to enter broadcasting. "I think they had more or less made up their minds that I was the man before they saw me," he confided in his diary.[11] In December 1922, Reith became the first general manager of the BBC. He had found a position almost perfectly suited for his temperament, ideals, skills and ambitions.

II

On 30 December 1922, John Reith came to offices that lay empty in order to manage a business only recently formed.

> As the liftman bore me upwards he looked at me curiously; conducted me to a labelled door; opened it ceremoniously. I entered; the door was shut; footsteps echoing in the corridor; clang of iron gate. Utterly alone. . . . Having discovered what broadcasting was, reflected, given rein to imagination, I realized to some extent at least what had been committed to me. For to me it was committed. I had thought that the chairman or Sir William Noble might be around a good deal, and when Noble came to see me . . . I asked him about this. "Oh no," he replied, "we're leaving it all to you. . . ." *Leaving it all to me.*[12]

Reith believed strongly that individuals shaped institutions, that, as he put it in 1960, "the success of a business depends on one man."[13] His autobiography stressed the powerful social and political forces that opposed his ideas of public service and unified control. In his own eyes, he overcame tremendous obstacles from government and commercial interests to lead the BBC into the uplands of moral greatness. When he assumed control of the BBC, it was a tiny company of limited resources and no fixed identity. When he left it sixteen years later, it was a major British cultural institution with an international reputation for quality.

While not without foundation, this version of events needs to be qualified. Reith and the BBC confronted remarkably little opposition when they sought to create a monopoly over an entire medium, a feat difficult to imagine for any other major source of information and entertainment. Despite the often heroic self-portrayal of his early struggles at the BBC, Reith pushed against an open door when he leveled arguments against competition. Neither the government nor the producers of commercial culture objected to a service whose organization, financing and programming often unintentionally served their own agendas. The wireless manufacturers who initially formed the BBC welcomed an opportunity to choke off foreign competition and share an expanding market for their goods. The music and entertainment industry acquiesced to the Reithian ethos because they feared that radio would shorten the life of songs, undermine the quality of performers through poor reception, and discourage attendance at live concerts. Ironically, Reith needed to persuade commercial entertainers to perform on the early BBC. The popular press regarded radio as a potential rival for news but soon learned that it was easier to deal with a regulated monopoly that encouraged their support, rather than a competitive system which might have ignored it. The press embraced a broadcast system which prohibited advertising, a major source of their own revenue. The Newspaper Proprietors' Association, the Newspaper Society and the Scottish Newspaper Society all accepted the essential arguments for unified control.[14]

Among government officials and politicians, arguments for monopoly control involved both ideology and convenience. The essentially private monopoly controlled by manufacturers which the Sykes Committee approved in 1923 and the Crawford Committee transformed into a public corporation in 1926, simplified the bureaucratic tasks of the Post Office, which oversaw broadcasting under the Wireless Telegraphy Act of 1904. The BBC proved to be a lucrative source of income for the Post Office.[15] Politicians, on the other hand, supported the monopoly for diverse ideological reasons. The Left quite naturally welcomed an experiment in public control. Indeed, Ramsay MacDonald strongly endorsed Reith's cultural elitism. On the Right, the paternalist tradition, repeated assurances of the monopoly's political neutrality, and the BBC's skillful cultivation of social respectability muted any reservations that back-benchers might have harbored about unified control. Only a handful of politicians, drawing upon a divided and virtually exhausted Liberal tradition, offered serious reservations. The BBC proved an experiment in public ownership and control which drew support across the political spectrum.[16]

If in later life Reith tended to exaggerate the opposition to his ideals, his early tenure as Director General was not without difficulty. During the General Strike in 1926, he withstood the efforts of Conservative politicians, most notably Winston Churchill, to commandeer broadcasting. Still, the BBC proved anything but impartial during that difficult period in May. "There could be no question about our supporting the Government in general," Reith informed his subordinates, "particularly since the General Strike has been declared illegal in the High Court." Although news bulletins sometimes quoted trade union officials, no Labour politician was allowed to speak. As Briggs puts it, "there is little doubt that BBC news assisted the government against the strikers."[17] Reith prided himself on the restraint of his institution during the crisis, and firmly believed that broadcasting soothed public opinion. "If there had been broadcasting at the time of the French Revolution," he often boasted, "there might have been no French Revolution."[18]

Within the BBC, Reith's authoritarian manner suffered few challenges, with one significant exception. When the BBC first began functioning as a public corporation in 1927, it was not clear how the new Board of Governors would exercise the considerable powers granted to them under the Charter. Not surprisingly, Reith believed that the Governors ought to play a fundamentally passive role, not unlike some boards in private corporations. The first chairman, Lord Clarendon, and one governor, Ethel Snowden, sought more active participation. From 1927 to 1930, Reith faced constant aggravation from a Board two of whose members he could not respect. Clarendon he found "incredibly stupid"; Snowden he labeled "The Red Woman," "a truly terrible creature."[19] For their part, Clarendon and Snowden considered Reith too dictatorial for his own good; more than once he was called "Mussolini." As in the First World War, Reith once again confronted superiors who refused to accept his authority unconditionally. "What a curse it is to have outstanding comprehensive ability and intelligence, combined with a desire to use them to maximum purpose," he confessed to his diary in 1927. "I am much burdened with a sense of my own ability, and this is not conceit," he wrote two years later after an annoying Board meeting.[20]

Reith defined his notion of public service in testimony before the Sykes Committee, which granted the BBC its first charter in 1923, and in scores of subsequent articles, speeches and, most comprehensively, in the book *Broadcast Over Britain* published in 1924. Reaffirming Victorian traditions of rational recreation, Reith viewed culture as a form of self-improvement, a means of personal and social discipline. "Enjoyment may be sought, not with a view to returning refreshed to the day's work, but as a mere means of passing the time, and therefore of wasting it," he wrote in his book. "On the other hand, it may be part of a systematic and sustained endeavour to re-create, to build up knowledge, experience and character...."[21] Reith's "high moral standard" involved an intense suspicion of amusements which served no didactic purpose. He shared with the Victorian middle classes a public distrust of the frivolous and the sensual. Reith would not have understood the feelings of ecstasy which absorbed some figures within the Bloomsbury circle whenever they encountered works of genius. Like Thomas Arnold and other Victorians, Reith placed culture within the context of moral character.[22]

Perhaps the most characteristic feature of Reith's vision of public service, however, lay not in its Victorian morality, but its self-assured paternalism. Here he clearly separated himself from the frequent boast of commercial culture that it fulfilled public demands. As he once put it bluntly in a speech at Cambridge University, "The best way to give the public what it wants is to reject the express policy of giving the public what it wants."[23] This startling paradox meant that the BBC demanded and received not only unity but centrality of control, an institutional arrangement that paved the way for the benign rule by experts which Reith advocated so forcefully. Drawing its adherents from both sides of the political spectrum, Reith's middle-class paternalism reversed the classical liberal orientation of some Victorians by arguing that centralized power proved more, not less, efficient than competing authorities. As Briggs notes, Reith never saw a contradiction between individualism and certain forms of collectivism, as long as public servants acted from pure motives. "The broadcasting system of a nation is a mirror of that nation's conscience," he observed in 1931, "there are no loopholes to duty, and no compromise is possible with what one considers to be right." The BBC, like other experiments in public ownership such as the Central Electricity Board and the London Passenger Transport Board, buttressed the conviction of planners that the future belonged to them.[24]

Reith argued in *Broadcast Over Britain* that high culture need only be made available for most people to embrace it. Despite private moments of profound disillusion, he retained in public the rationalist faith in the liberating potential of great ideas. Supply would create demand. Hostility could usually be explained by ignorance, and ignorance, in turn, might be banished by repeated exposure to "everything that is best in every department of human knowledge, endeavour and achievement."[25] He presumed, but rarely made explicit, the notion that the working class lacked a legitimate culture of its own. Reith conceived of the BBC, in part, as a vital institution of public education, and to him this mission necessarily excluded the notion of popular choice. "A man may be as good a democrat as another," he proclaimed in a speech at Manchester University, "and yet reject, in the light of philosophy, history, or experience, democratic process to accomplish democratic ends." Reith believed that democracy meant equal access, not equal choice. Broadcasting allowed every social group to hear the same programs at the same time. "The same music rings as sweetly in mansion as in cottage."[26] To Reith, the vulgarities and inefficiencies of democracy could be eliminated once individuals parted with the shibboleth that they best understood their own self-interest.

To implement Reith's ideals, BBC programmers in the 1920s constructed a schedule that reflected the biases and treasured aspirations of their social class. Though committed formally to providing balance within their broadcast schedule, programmers defined "music" to mean only such things as symphony, opera and chamber concerts. Though it occupied less than a third of the total broadcast hours, such music was usually scheduled from between eight and ten o'clock on weekday evenings, prime listening hours. After 1927, the BBC provided alternative programs, but even these occasionally "balanced" such things as symphonic music with, say, the reading of poetry.[27]

Even in the 1920s, Reith became famous for his commitment to religious broadcasting. "The Christianity which is broadcast is unassociated with any particular creed or denomination," he assured his readers in *Broadcast Over Britain*. "It is a thoroughgoing, optimistic and manly religion." The BBC's religious policy mirrored the Sabbatarian discipline of the Victorian middle classes, long since eroded by declining church attendance and other social changes.[28] Reith deplored what he called "the surrender of the principles of Sunday observance" and made sure the BBC honored the Christian sabbath strictly. Church services alternated with serious music or extended periods of silence. By 1929, the amount of religious broadcasting increased to include a daily service and weekly evensong.[29] Yet, though some clerical figures grasped early the possibilities of radio, Reith felt the churches never really seized the opportunity he presented them. "If they had," he wrote late in life, "there might have been a national revival. . . ."[30]

The Reithian ethos allowed the BBC to portray itself as the embodiment of British culture and tradition. Such a stance brilliantly foreclosed most criticism not only of radio as a new and therefore suspect technology of communication, but also the BBC as a monopolistic institution. To argue against the programming policies of the BBC often amounted to an embarrassing admission of one's own philistine tastes. To be sure, some criticized Reith and the Corporation for failing to be even more refined and culturally uplifting in its programming. In a somewhat ironic bow to democratic argument, the BBC replied that it needed to serve the entire nation, not simply a small minority. By the early 1930s, the BBC compared itself favorably with other established institutions in Britain, such as the Bank of England, *The Times* and the Royal Academy. "Under its aegis," the *Listener* proclaimed in 1930, "it has been possible to build up in a very few years a tradition of commercial and political disinterestedness, and of service to national culture such as usually requires generations to establish."[31]

Reith became a prominent national figure. Though he sought to keep his name out of the newspapers, the Director General of a major new diversion in British life could not remain anonymous. The popular press ran features on him and *The Times* covered his major speeches. Prime Ministers sought his advice on how to make known their policies; lesser politicians scrambled to get themselves heard on a medium covering an entire nation. The Royal Family counted him as a valuable, reliable acquaintance. Artists, writers and celebrities courted his good favor. When he traveled, he consulted with major foreign dignitaries. His visit to the United States in 1933 became a triumphal return to a country whose people he enjoyed but whose broadcasting he loathed.[32]

Reith's notion of public service broadcasting, easy to enforce within a small organization during the 1920s, confronted different challenges during the 1930s. Between 1929 and 1933 the number of license holders doubled, and by 1935, ninety-eight per cent of the population had some access to programs.[33] As its audience expanded, the BBC grew in size and complexity. In the early 1930s, Reith presided over both a move to new headquarters in Portland Square, and a major reorganization of the internal bureaucracy. In 1932, the BBC launched its broadcasts to the Empire and a few years later initiated a television service. Though Reith still played an active managerial role during these years, he gradually began to detach himself from the organization's routine operations. The chain of command became more complex and impersonal. The size of the staff increased from 773 in 1926 to over 5,000 by the end of the 1930s. Subordinates exercised more authority. "I have, it seems, organized myself out of work ..." he recorded in his diary in 1935.[34]

Expansion contributed to pressures that challenged the Reithian ethos. The popular press, still committed to the notion of monopoly, hired radio critics who often deplored the BBC's cultural elitism. Continental stations, such as Radio Luxembourg and Radio Normandie, beamed a steady stream of popular programming that for many listeners provided an attractive alternative to the BBC's often sober fare, especially on Sunday. BBC functionaries began to modify the assumptions and attitudes that buttressed Reith's cultural mission.[35]

The BBC responded to these pressures in the 1930s with greater flexibility than might be imagined. The number of variety and related programs increased dramatically, and light entertainment prospered. Dance music filled more prime listening hours and even jazz found a place on the broadcast schedule. In 1933, the Corporation finally created a separate Variety Department, with more money, staff and time for broadcasts than ever possible under earlier arrangements. Even religious broadcasting, in some ways the cornerstone of the Reithian ethos, adjusted to new realities. In 1934, Reith told his staff that "Sunday programmes were too highbrow."[36] The Corporation began to abandon gradually its Sabbatarianism and respond to competition from Radio Luxembourg. During key listening hours on Sunday, virtually all "silent periods" became filled with alternative programming, including popular music. The BBC also accepted the notion of systematic listener research and hired an expert from advertising to discover what the public wanted. In a statement of policy in 1939, the *BBC Handbook* reported that "no one whose business it is to supply things to people – least of all those who supply entertainment – can afford to be ignorant about what people want." This statement, virtually inconceivable ten years

198

before, illustrated how far the Corporation had traveled during the decade.[37]

Yet it was not simply pragmatism and the inevitable compromises of rapid institutional expansion that explain the BBC's accommodation to change. Already in the late 1920s, Reith had become restless in his job and sought greater opportunities to become "fully stretched." "I ought to go to some much bigger job," he recorded in his diary in 1927. "What on earth can I go to?" By the mid-1930s, these feelings of frustration and discontent became more insistent. "Very disgusted with everything and feeling that I simply cannot stand things longer in the BBC," he wrote in 1936.[38] Discreetly, Reith canvassed his friends and political contacts for new positions of responsibility. Only one solid offer presented itself: the leadership of Imperial Airways, another relatively new technology in need of strong guidance. Because he retained mixed feelings about leaving the BBC, Reith sought a direct order from the Prime Minister to take the job. Though a bewildered Chamberlain refused to be quite so authoritative, Reith accepted the position in June 1938. His last days at the BBC proved awkward and wounding. He was not retained on the Board of Governors, which chose his successor without consulting him. Though letters of gratitude poured into his office and the press hailed his tenure, he felt uneasy and betrayed. For a number of years, he severed all connections with the BBC, refusing even to listen to its programs.[39]

When Reith joined the BBC in 1922, his timing had proven unexpectedly propitious. With virtually unchallenged authority, he directed a rapidly expanding medium that, like the cinema, helped define an entire era. Now in 1938 his timing proved unexpectedly disastrous. He left the BBC precisely at the moment when, with war impending, the Corporation once again demanded firm leadership. He took on a position which, despite its later potential, possessed only a limited immediate future. Reith always believed that leaving the BBC was the most calamitous decision of his entire life. Never again would he occupy an office of such power, prestige and access. Although, as many have pointed out, his subsequent positions in government and commerce would have satisfied most individuals, Reith believed his great managerial skills atrophied after 1938. In his heart, he longed to become Prime Minister, especially during a period of grave national peril. Instead, he occupied a series of lesser posts, always responsible to authorities above him, that embittered his spirit and poisoned his legacy.

III

In his autobiography, Reith drew an ironic parallel between his first day at Imperial Airways in 1938, and his inauspicious beginnings at the BBC.

On Monday morning, July 4, as fifteen and a half years earlier, but
under very different circumstances, I had to find my new office. . . .
I was brought to the door of an old furniture depository behind
Victoria Station. It was Imperial Airways; a plate on the wall said
so. Inside were some counters, luggage on the floor, a few
people. . . . From Broadcasting House to this. And the first decision
demanded of me was indication of what had happened to me
otherwise. Would I approve the expenditure of 238 pounds on
passengers' lavatories at Croydon?. . . It seemed I was to work in
very low gear.[40]

In less than two years, Reith reorganized the airline, transforming a
mismanaged organization into the British Overseas Airways Corporation, with routes planned or operating throughout the world. Once
again, he made a mark on the development of a major twentieth-century
technology. Unlike his work at the BBC, however, the task of building
commercial air travel would be disrupted, and his achievement all but
forgotten.[41] Reith never liked his work at Imperial Airways and almost
immediately made known his desire for political office.

He got his wish in January 1940, when Chamberlain appointed him
Minister of Information. One month later, he was found a safe seat in
the House of Commons as a National MP for Southampton. Reith
became Minister of Transport in May, and Minister of Works in October,
a position he occupied for less than eighteen months, when Churchill
dismissed him early in 1942. Despite his life-long ambition to be a high
government official, Reith floundered as a politician. "I think I enjoy
being an MP," he wrote in his diary, "as long as I don't need to bother
with a constituency."[42] As a minister, he found cooperation and compromise difficult to accept personally and "inefficient" administratively.
Because his self-absorption frequently blinded him from other points of
view, seasoned politicians easily maneuvered around him, or manipu-
lated him in ways he failed to perceive. Halifax once told him half-
jokingly that to be a successful minister, Reith needed to spend much
more time in the lobby and smoking-room of the House of Commons.
For weeks, Reith left his office each afternoon to patrol those areas, much
to the relief of his subordinates in the ministry. Cecil King recorded in
his diary in 1940 that Reith would "get around to a lot of the right
answers – but long after everyone else."[43]

Reith also wounded himself with his indiscreet, almost pathological
hatred of Churchill. "I expressed myself with some freedom about
Churchill and his rotten gang," he wrote in 1942. "He is the greatest
menace we have ever had – country and Empire sacrificed to his megalo-
mania, to his monstrous obstinacy and wrong-headedness."[44] Reith's
problems with the Prime Minister began during the General Strike and

throughout the 1930s Churchill felt that the BBC prohibited him from broadcasting his controversial views on India. At one point, he even offered the Corporation money in exchange for broadcast time, a proposal that shocked and disgusted Reith.[45] When Churchill assumed power, Reith tried to make peace with the new prime minister, but all efforts failed. "He never shows any friendliness to me," Reith complained in 1940, "and therefore I dislike him intensely, which is a pity – especially as he reminds one so much of myself in his methods."[46]

Reith joined the Navy in 1942 and, for the duration of the war, served in a number of administrative capacities. He assisted in the reorganization of Coastal Forces, and helped organize supplies for the D-Day invasion, an immensely time-consuming task that often shielded him from frustration about his blocked political career. He hoped in vain that he would be summoned to assume a position of high leadership worthy of his talents. "For hardly an hour had passed since I joined the navy," he wrote in his autobiography "but I was listening for a call that never came; a call from Churchill." After VE Day and the election of Labour into office in 1945, Reith wrote Churchill an extraordinary letter, admonishing him that "you could have used me in a way and to an extent you never realized." Churchill replied that whenever he considered him for a post, "I always encountered considerable opposition from one quarter or another on the ground that you were difficult to work with."[47]

Reith's dismissal from office in 1942 contributed to a recurring depression that hounded him the remainder of his life.

2 January 1943 Having a tremendous struggle with myself not to be in absolute despair. . . .
23 August 1943 I have made such a mess of everything and I wish I had never been born.
14 May 1944 I am utterly alone. No one to help me; no one to talk to. All the swarming people that push against me in trains and tubes – they are all more or less happy. . . . I really feel I could contemplate killing myself.
20 May 1944 I suppose I am and I always have been almost completely self-centered. . . . I have no ordinary human kindliness or tolerance. . . . I am obsessed by my own fate and by a desire for revenge for my treatment; by a sense of injury. . . . And now I am querulous and embittered and small and shrunken . . . submerged by the pettiness of my own preoccupations.[48]

Virtually nothing said against Reith by his enemies was not said by himself, to himself. He tortured himself with his own limitations. Only a few activities, especially furious work for a higher cause, provided relief from self-loathing, veneered over by fantasies of self-aggrandizement.

Yet, no amount of external reward and reassurance could possibly extinguish the resentment smoldering within his personality.

Reith entitled his autobiography, published in 1949, *Into the Wind*, emblematic of both the ephemerality of a radio signal and his own achievements. He dedicated his memoirs to his children, who "may be interested in them; but that is incidental." He said the book would be "more biography than autobiography; written about someone the writer used to know." Based upon his diaries, the book began the process of public confession and open self-laceration that provides at least one theme of his final years. In his years at the BBC, Reith's aloofness and personal reserve masked the raw feelings of his diary. He justified himself publicly through his good works and became a major national figure. After he left the BBC and, from his point of view, descended into obscurity and oblivion, Reith began to draw attention to himself, in print and with his friends, through the open and painful exposure of his inner struggles. It was as if he now justified himself to others through intense personal suffering. "Much that I was brought up to pursue and prize now seems of small account," he wrote in the conclusion of *Into the Wind*. "What purpose or direction now?"[49]

Despite this sense of drift, Reith continued to acquire new responsibilities, usually related to mass communication and often well paid. He joined the board of Cable and Wireless in 1943, and by the late 1940s found himself chairman of the New Towns Committee, the Commonwealth Telecommunications Board, the Hemel Hempstead Development Corporation and the National Film Finance Corporation. From 1950 to 1959, he led the Colonial Development Corporation. Once again, others handed him an institution in need of strong leadership. Deep in debt and overstaffed, the CDC had floundered in its responsibilities to provide assistance to a rapidly diminishing empire. Reith took control with his usual vigor. Within five years, the CDC balanced its budget, in part by Reith's merciless trimming of its staff. To fulfill his various duties, he traveled throughout the world on tours of inspection, a task filled with sufficient novelty and adventure to enliven his diary with vivid reflections and observations. Yet, at the CDC the old patterns of behavior once again emerged. Reith proved an effective manager, but a rebellious subordinate. Inevitably, he quarreled with his superiors in the Colonial Office, who made allowances for the Great Man, but failed to renew his chairmanship in 1959. As Stuart observes, "He left CDC, as he had left the BBC more than twenty years before, in bitterness and misunderstanding."[50]

Reith was seventy years old when he left the CDC, and a man of many honors. He had been elevated to a peerage in 1942, awarded honorary degrees by many universities, including Oxford, and showered with praise. In the years 1967–8, he served as Lord High Commissioner of the General Assembly of the Church of Scotland, a position whose elaborate ceremonial duties much pleased him. Yet, the 1960s would not prove a serene retirement for Lord Reith. His children, long since grown, resented his intrusions into their private lives. He could not find activity to occupy his time meaningfully, an old complaint worsened by age. His depressions deepened; he underwent shock treatments; and in 1971, after a short illness, he died.[51]

For many observers, including Reith himself, the decades after the BBC represented a tragic anti-climax to a remarkably successful early career. The posthumous publication of the diaries in 1975 confirmed in painful detail the price of frustrated ambitions and often destructive self-absorption. Yet these later years, for all their psychic drama, merely accentuated an essential element within Reith's complex personality. To an exaggerated degree, Reith believed in his own personal autonomy. He was convinced that individuals shaped their own character and destiny; that success in life depended upon intense effort for a lofty goal. This view, which flourished within the tangled bank of Victorian liberalism, stemmed from a variety of influences in Reith's background: an isolated childhood in a Calvinist home, a technical education that detoured his ambition onto precisely the right road, an unconventionally positive experience of a devastating war. Reith's astonishing rise from an engineer's apprentice to the inner corridors of the British Establishment strengthened immeasurably his conviction that history rested upon personal agency.

To the biographer, who must constantly balance claims for individual achievement against the larger historical forces which shape personal destiny, Reith's career reveals both the efficacy and innocence of such a philosophy. His convictions and managerial skills guided the BBC as it grew from a struggling private business monopoly with no clear mandate into a major public institution of enormous cultural significance. Yet the success of the early BBC also proved very much the complex product of a particular conjuncture in British cultural history. Reith's concept of public service broadcasting met little active resistance; the risks he undertook were almost always respectable; his authoritarian leadership proved more flexible than his public posture might indicate, especially during the 1930s. After 1938, Reith never recaptured the triumph of his early career: his successes at Imperial Airways faded into obscurity; the art of politics during wartime defeated him; the opportunities for public service after 1945 never approached what was handed him in 1922. Characteristically, this entrepreneur of collectivism searched his private conscience for the source of his thwarted public ambition. To the end, he remained innocent of factors outside himself which molded his extraordinary career and which, taken to heart, might have graced his later years with self-forgiveness.

D.L. LEMAHIEU

NOTES

1 Asa Briggs, *The History of Broadcasting in the United Kingdom. Volume One: The Birth of Broadcasting*, London, Oxford University Press, 1961, p. 4; "Lord Reith" in Frank N. Roberts, ed., *Obituaries from The Times, 1971–75*, London, Meckler Books, 1978, p. 438.
2 Garry Allighan, *Sir John Reith*, London, Stanley Paul, 1938; Andrew Boyle, *Only the Wind Will Listen*, London, Hutchinson, 1972, p. 23. (Ian McIntyre, *The Expense of Glory: A Life of John Reith*, London, HarperCollins, 1993 appeared too late to be consulted for this chapter.)
3 Quoted in Allighan, *Sir John Reith*, p. 113.
4 Charles Stuart, ed., *The Reith Diaries*, London, Collins, 1975, p. 18.
5 J.C.W. Reith, *Into the Wind*, London, Hodder and Stoughton, 1949, p. 9.
6 Ibid., p. 12.
7 Ibid., p. 20.
8 Ibid., pp. 56–9; John Reith, *Wearing Spurs*, London, Hutchinson, 1966, pp. 219–22.
9 J.C.W. Reith, "Why Libel the Soldier?", *John O'London's Weekly*, 15 March 1930, n.p.; Raymond Fletcher, "Nuisance Value," review of *Wearing Spurs* by John Reith, *New Statesman*, 16 September 1966, p. 400; Alan Thomas, "Subaltern Year," review of *Wearing Spurs* by John Reith, *The Listener*, 8 September 1966, p. 359. On the war and later disillusion, see Samuel Lynn Hynes, *A War Imagined: The First World War and English Culture*, London, Bodley Head, 1990.
10 Reith, *Wind*, pp. 60–9; Stuart, ed., *Reith Diaries*, pp. 30–4.
11 Stuart, ed., *Reith Diaries*, p. 128. For differing views on how he obtained the post, see Briggs, *Birth of Broadcasting*, pp. 135–42; Boyle, *Only the Wind*, pp. 118–23; Stuart, ed., *Reith Diaries*, pp. 126–8. See also Reith to Sir William Noble, 13 October 1922, BBC Written Archives Centre.
12 Reith, *Wind*, pp. 87–8.
13 "Lord Reith on his Life and Work," *The Listener*, 10 September 1960, p. 829.
14 D.L. LeMahieu, *A Culture for Democracy: Mass Communication and the Cultivated Mind in Britain Between the Wars*, Oxford, Clarendon Press, pp. 148–50; Briggs, *Birth*, pp. 91–142; R.H. Coase, *British Broadcasting: A Study in Monopoly*, London, Longman, Green, 1950, pp. 12–15; Testimony Before the Crawford Committee, Minute 15796/26, File 7, General Post Office Archives, London; Asa Briggs, *The History of Broadcasting in the United Kingdom. Volume Two. The Golden Age of Wireless*, London, Oxford University Press, 1965, pp. 76–9.
15 Briggs, *Birth*, pp. 190–7, 229–30.
16 LeMahieu, *A Culture*, pp. 150–1. For an example of the Liberal view, see E.A. Harney, speech to the House of Commons, 15 November 1926, 199 *H.C. Debates*, 5th ser., col. 1611. For Liberal ideology during this period, see among others, Michael Freeden, *Liberalism Divided: A Study in British Political Thought, 1914–1939*, Oxford, Clarendon Press, 1986.
17 Reith quoted in Briggs, *Birth*, p. 365; ibid., p. 373.
18 Reith, *Wind*, p. 109. Among many assessments of Reith and the General Strike, see John Reith, "Forsan," *Parliamentary Affairs*, vol. 17, no. 1, 1963–4, pp. 23–30; and Charles Curran, "Reith and the General Strike," *The Listener*, 13 May 1976, pp. 597–8.
19 Stuart, ed., *Reith Diaries*, pp. 143, 147.
20 Ibid., pp. 142, 147; Briggs, *Golden Age*, pp. 424–35; Colin Cross, *Philip Snowden*, London, Barrie and Rockliff, 1966, pp. 230–1. In 1930, Clarendon resigned to assume another position; Mrs Snowden, however, remained.

21 J.C.W. Reith, *Broadcast Over Britain*, London, Hodder and Stoughton, n.d. (1924), p. 18.
22 For the nineteenth-century background, see Peter Bailey, *Leisure and Class in Victorian England: Rational Recreation and the Contest for Control, 1830–1885*, London, Methuen, 1978, 1987.
23 Quoted in *The Times*, 29 July 1930, p. 12. See also John Reith, "Broadcasting," *Quarterly Review*, vol. 242, 1924, pp. 398–414; and J.C.W. Reith, "Ten Years of Broadcasting," *John O'London's Weekly*, 28 May 1932, pp. 285–6.
24 Briggs, *Golden Age*, pp. 414–15; Paddy Scannell and David Cardiff, "Serving the Nation: Public Service Broadcasting Before the War," in Bernard Waites, Tony Bennett and Graham Martin, eds, *Popular Culture: Past and Present*, London, Croom Helm, 1982, pp. 165–7; William A. Robson, ed., *Public Enterprise: Developments in Social Ownership and Control in Great Britain*, London, George Allen and Unwin, 1937, pp. 73–104; Lincoln Gordon, *The Public Corporation in Great Britain*, London, Oxford University Press, 1938, pp. 156–244. See also Janet Minihan, *The Nationalization of Culture: The Development of State Subsidies for the Arts in Great Britain*, New York, New York University Press, 1977.
25 Reith, *Broadcast Over Britain*, p. 34; John Reith, "What's in the Air," *Radio Times*, 29 February 1924, p. 361; John Reith, "Memorandum of Information on the Scope and Conduct of the Broadcasting Service Submitted as Evidence to the Broadcasting Committee, 1925," Minute 15796/26, General Post Office Archives, London; John Reith, "Broadcasting and a Better World," *The Spectator*, 22 November 1930.
26 John Reith, typescript of speech to Manchester University, 17 May 1933, BBC Written Archives Centre; Reith, *Broadcast Over Britain*, pp. 217–18. See also C.A. Lewis, *Broadcasting From Within*, London, George Newnes, n.d., p. 47; and Walter T. Rault, "Masts for the Millions," *Radio Times*, 4 January 1929, p. 11.
27 LeMahieu, *A Culture*, pp. 184–5.
28 Reith, *Broadcast Over Britain*, p. 194. On Sabbatarianism, see John Wigley, *The Rise and Fall of the Victorian Sunday*, Manchester, Manchester University Press, 1980. On the decline of religion, see, among others, Jeffrey Cox, *The English Churches in a Secular Society: Lambeth, 1870–1930*, New York, Oxford University Press, 1982.
29 Reith, *Broadcast Over Britain*, p. 195; Kenneth Wolfe, *The Churches and the British Broadcasting Corporation, 1922–1956: The Politics of Broadcast Religion*, London, SCM Press, p. 13.
30 John Reith, "Forword," to Melville Dinwiddie, *Religion By Radio: Its Place in British Broadcasting*, London, George Allen and Unwin, 1968, p. 9.
31 "What the Public Wants," *The Listener*, 5 February 1930, p. 232; LeMahieu, *A Culture*, pp. 188–90.
32 On Reith's visit to the United States, see J.C.W. Reith, "Visit to Canada and the United States" (typescript report to Board of Governors), 25 November 1933, BBC Written Archives Centre.
33 Briggs, *Golden Age*, p. 253.
34 Stuart, ed., *Reith Diaries*, p. 168; Briggs, *Golden Age*, pp. 449–51.
35 LeMahieu, *A Culture*, pp. 274–81. On Continental stations, see Igor Vinogradoff, "History of English Advertising Programmes Broadcast to the United Kingdom From Foreign Stations Down to the Outbreak of War" (1945), BBC Written Archives Centre; and Donald R. Browne, "Radio Normandie and the

IBC Challenge to the BBC Monopoly," *Historical Journal of Film, Radio and Television*, vol. 5, no. 1, 1985, pp. 3–18.

36 Reith quoted in Minutes, Director General's Meeting, 23 January 1934, BBC Written Archives Centre.

37 "Listener Research in 1938," in *BBC Handbook, 1939*, London, British Broadcasting Corporation, 1939, p. 55; LeMahieu, *A Culture*, pp. 285–90; Paddy Scannell and David Cardiff, *A Social History of British Broadcasting. Volume One, 1922–1939. Serving the Nation*, Oxford, Basil Blackwell, 1991, pp. 181–273.

38 Stuart, ed., *Reith Diaries*, pp. 143, 171.

39 Briggs, *Golden Age*, pp. 632–6.

40 Reith, *Wind*, p. 327.

41 On the development of Imperial Airways, see R.E.G. Davies, *A History of the World's Airlines*, London, Oxford University Press, 1964, pp. 111–12, 170–86. See also R. Higham, *Britain's Imperial Air Routes, 1918–39*, London, G.T. Foulis, 1960, and John Stroud, *Annals of British and Commonwealth Air Transport, 1919–60*, London, Putnam, 1960.

42 Stuart, ed., *Reith Diaries*, p. 241.

43 Kenneth Young, ed., *The Diaries of Sir Robert Bruce Lockhart. Volume Two. 1939–1965*, London, Macmillan, 1980, p. 49; William Armstrong, ed., *With Malice Toward None: A War Diary by Cecil H. King*, Madison, N.J., Fairleigh Dickinson University Press, 1971, p. 32.

44 Stuart, ed., *Reith Diaries*, p. 297.

45 Martin Gilbert, *Winston S. Churchill. Volume Five. 1922–39*, London, Heinemann, 1976, pp. 358–9.

46 Stuart, ed., *Reith Diaries*, p. 268.

47 Reith, *Wind*, pp. 462, 526–7.

48 Stuart, ed., *Reith Diaries*, pp. 299, 308, 321–2.

49 Reith, *Wind*, pp. 1, 530–1.

50 Stuart, ed., *Reith Diaries* pp. 374–5, 379, 391, 410–11.

51 On Reith in the 1960s, see especially Boyle, pp. 15–27, 338–51. See also, "Lord Reith in Conversation with Malcolm Muggeridge," *The Listener*, 7 December 1967, p. 746, and 14 December 1967, pp. 776–8.

12 J.B. Priestley

9

J.B. Priestley 1894–1984
Englishness and the politics of nostalgia
Chris Waters

In their attempt to map the contours of the national culture, Robert Colls and Philip Dodd argue that we are still living in the shadow of the significant changes that took place between 1880 and 1920. It was in these years, they suggest, that the idioms of national identity we now take for granted were first constituted in a recognizably modern form, that Englishness as we understand it was first articulated. This was the period, according to Dodd, when "the conviction that English culture was to be found in the past was stabilised," when the "people of these islands were invited to take their place, and become spectators of a culture already complete and represented for them by its trustees."[1]

Despite the importance of such claims, the notion that Englishness was more or less "complete" by 1920 needs to be revised given that components of the national culture have been contested and reworked throughout the twentieth century. Indeed, as the editors of the present volume suggest, significant elements of the national culture were extensively reconfigured between the wars by intellectuals who were disillusioned by politics and who sought in that culture the vital glue that might stick the nation back together. Some stressed the importance of the "country turn," developing those conservative strands of Englishness that emphasized the healing nature of rural nostalgia – as had Raymond Unwin, according to Standish Meacham in this volume, earlier in the century. Others romanticized elements of urban, working-class culture, a culture they represented, perhaps for the first time, as central to the nation's heritage. In short, the Depression, along with the Second World War, witnessed extensive attempts to remake the symbols of national identity. Moreover, many activists in these years worked to develop new idioms of Englishness that could be harnessed – as turn-of-the-century Englishness could not – to a democratic and populist politics of the Left.

Born in 1894, J.B. Priestley contributed extensively to this transformation of the idioms of national identity. In his plays and his novels, through his journalism and his broadcasting, Priestley never tired of offering his audience a sense of themselves as vital participants in an elaborate, richly-textured national story. If the story he told was only a national fiction, it nevertheless consisted of a series of interconnected myths that resonated deeply with many people, particularly in the 1930s and 1940s.[2] The older he grew, the more obsessed Priestley became with fine-tuning the tale he was so fond of telling the English about themselves. On the eve of his eightieth birthday, for example, he devoted an entire book to a discussion of what he termed "the essential Englishness of the English."[3] It was here that he offered an analysis of what he believed to be unique in the national character, focusing in particular on the common sense, humor and stoic fortitude of the English people. These themes had always been central to Priestley's definition of Englishness: eager to recycle his old stories in new packages, he had made the same point about the English, in virtually the same words, as early as 1929.[4] Nevertheless, by the 1970s Priestley was less sanguine than he had once been about the future of the national culture: "Englishness," he wrote in despair, "is not as strong as it was.... It needs to be nourished."[5] Throughout his life, Priestley saw it as his task not only to define "essential Englishness," but to put himself forward as its moral guardian. An activist in the cultural sphere, he worked to develop an inclusive vocabulary of belonging that he hoped might serve as a bulwark for the nation in a period of unsettling change.

I

"In a bakelite house the dishes may not break, but the heart can"[6]

Between the wars, Priestley's constructions of Englishness emerged both out of his engagement with a present he very much disliked and out of the memory of his own past. Priestley's autobiographical story was thus crucial to the story he told the nation about itself; more specifically, his remembered past provided him with incidents, characters and values that he could weave together into a seamless narrative of Englishness, a morality play about a nation in peril of losing its identity. His search for Englishness in this period began, as it did for others, in a panic about the present, especially about the ways in which the advent of mass culture seemed to imperil everything he cherished. The most elaborate articulation of that panic appeared in the pages of his *English Journey*, the work that established his credentials as a social critic. First published in 1934, the book not only recounted Priestley's search for "essential Englishness," but also contributed to a far-reaching reconstitution of the components of the national heritage and catapulted Priestley to the center of cultural debate.

Priestley was alarmed by what he perceived as the growing American-

210

ization of English culture. In the South, the starting point for his trip around the country, Priestley encountered elements of a new way of life that he found profoundly unsettling. Commenting on the road from Southampton to Bristol, for example, he wrote, "they only differ in a few minor details from a few thousand such roads in the United States, where the same tooth-pastes and soaps and gramophone records are being sold, the very same films are being shown."[7] Later, Priestley journeyed to the industrialized Midlands and the North, hoping to discover an "enduring England." But even Blackpool seemed "machine made and not really English."[8] "Essential Englishness," Priestley concluded, was rooted in the nation's natural heritage: "The beauty of the Cotswolds," he wrote, "belongs to England and England should see that she keeps it."[9]

On this level, Priestley's rural nostalgia was similar to that of many of his contemporaries. Both F.R. Leavis and Stanley Baldwin had similarly stressed the importance of the rural components of Englishness, holding them up as a bulwark against the changes that appeared to be undermining a more settled way of life.[10] But Priestley's notions of Englishness moved beyond the theme of rural nostalgia in significant ways, and at the end of his book he reflected on the existence of three, distinct Englands. His first "England" was "Old Merrie England," a pre-industrial world that he desired to see preserved, especially in places like the Cotswolds. Priestley's second "England" was the product of an industrial revolution that "had found a green and pleasant land and had left a wilderness of dirty bricks."[11] Then there was a third "England," largely imported from the United States, an England of congested roads, factories that looked like exhibition halls, cinemas, Woolworths and cocktail bars. Priestley detested these phenomena, but this forced him to reconsider his second, industrial, "England." At least the old factories, he argued – those that looked like factories and not like exhibition halls – had "solid lumps of character in them."[12]

Priestley's dislike of imported mass culture was intense, and while it dominated much of his *English Journey* it was also present in a good deal of his writing between the wars and earlier. Even as a teenager, writing in the socialist *Bradford Pioneer*, Priestley attacked American films for their sensationalism, noting the way in which they tended to distance their viewers from the rich associational life of the local community through fantasies that undermined the stability of Englishness.[13] Moreover, his first encounter in a Leeds music hall with the "syncopated frenzy" of American ragtime offered him a metaphor for the changes he feared, a metaphor he would deploy repeatedly throughout the next seven decades:

It was as if we had been still living in the nineteenth century and then suddenly found the twentieth glaring and screaming at us. We were yanked into our own age, fascinating, jungle-haunted, monstrous. . . . Out of those twenty noisy minutes in a music-hall . . . came fragmentary but prophetic outlines of the situation in which we find ourselves now, . . . the domination of America . . . the end of confidence and any feeling of security, the nervous excitement, the underlying despair of our own century.[14]

Although Priestley developed these themes in many of his essays in the 1920s, it was in the 1930s that he began quite specifically to define the essence of Englishness against imported forms of mass culture from the United States: "Let's be British," he pleaded, "I like the British to be British."[15] He particularly liked them to be British after witnessing American culture first-hand on his extended visits to the United States in the 1930s. There, in a convocation address at the University of Colorado, Priestley argued against what he termed "passive-minded, robot-like people, with no real initiative, no genuine appetites, no free intelligence." The future, he suggested, offered a vision of a consumer paradise, full of bakelite houses and synthetic rubber highways. But for Priestley the vision was really a nightmare: as alluring as bakelite and synthetic rubber might be, he argued, we "cannot seek grace through gadgets."[16] It was thus against the promise of the New World that he defined the enduring characteristics of Englishness: against the world of Hollywood, where "not a thing looked solidly real,"[17] Priestley juxtaposed the nineteenth-century English factory, full of its "solid lumps of character."

Two of Priestley's lesser novels of the 1930s, *Wonder Hero* (1933) and *They Walk in the City* (1936), developed these themes further, both suggesting that the "essential Englishness of the English" was being undermined by processes similar to those at work in the United States. *Wonder Hero*, in particular, operates around a series of binary oppositions between working-class innocence and the corrupting effects of mass culture: the working class of Priestley's imagination was at once both noble and threatened (indeed, noble because it was threatened), in need of protection and guidance. But as Simon Frith has suggested, commenting on those who, like Priestley, praised the working class, although "mass culture was resisted in the name of working-class 'community,'" that community was largely "the product of a decidedly middle-class nostalgia."[18] In short, Priestley's working-class culture – as imagined in his fiction and to some extent fictionalized in his social criticism – was little more than a nostalgic fabrication, juxtaposed against insidious forms of mass culture.

Priestley's working-class culture was also a decidedly masculine affair. Throughout the 1930s he extolled the virtues of imagined working-class communities but constantly denigrated the role of women in them; without failure he positioned women as the conduit through which mass culture infected the very communities he wished to see preserved. If, for Priestley, the United States was filled with "tough blonds throwing their legs about,"[19] Britain was in danger of succumbing to similar influences. As Sally Alexander has suggested, while the image of the cloth cap and spare frame of the unemployed working man often elicited pity in the 1930s, the image of the lipsticked, silk-stockinged young woman was viewed with contempt.[20] Priestley was thus not alone in suggesting that a heroic working-class culture was slowly being feminized by the wireless, movie-star worship, silk stockings and hire purchase.

Throughout the 1930s, Priestley contrasted the "people" with the "masses," praising the former and wishing to encourage their creativity, largely because he feared their degeneration under American influences. In so doing, he sought actively to reshape the way in which people comprehended the national heritage, creating new spaces in that heritage in which the character and lifestyle of the English "common *man*" at his best could be inserted. But it must be emphasized that Priestley never wished to extol the virtues of working-class life as it was actually experienced by most workers: he was not in favor, he claimed, of "a policy of giving us great slabs of English working-class life, miles of celluloid showing us factories ... folks sitting down to endless meat teas, and a dreary round of housework, machine-minding, football matches and whist drives."[21] Rather, it was a selective tradition of working-class customs and practices that Priestley attempted to articulate as a central idiom of national identity, a tradition that cannot be understood without reference to his own turn-of-the-century childhood.

II

"Part of me is still in Bradford"[22]

Priestley liked to contrast the present with images from his Bradford childhood and his memories thus served as a benchmark against which he could measure subsequent loss, offering him material he could use in constructing his ideal working class. Priestley's search for a usable past led him to sift through his memories, organizing them in an elaborate and coherent narrative of the self – and through the self of the nation. Just as Henrietta Barnett refashioned her own past in the biography she wrote of her husband, according to Seth Koven in this volume, so Priestley refashioned his own past in order to make it usable in the story he told the English about themselves. The narrative he recounted of his origins was often refined, reaching its apogee in his third volume of autobiography, *Margin Released* (1962), and in his lavishly illustrated popular history, *The Edwardians* (1970). In these works, Priestley sought to make his private memories central to a new, public discourse of Englishness. Hence the past he recounted was always related to his desire to reshape national identity. His past was, in short, a product of the present, for as David Lowenthal reminds us, "memories are not ready-made reflections of the past, but eclectic, selective reconstructions based on subsequent actions and perceptions and on everchanging codes by which we delineate, symbolize, and classify the world around us."[23]

Priestley's identity was anchored in the late Victorian and Edwardian past: "I was born in the nineteenth century," he wrote, "and my most impressionable years were those just before World War I."[24] Early twentieth-century Bradford gave Priestley his bearings in life, bearings he tried in vain to hold on to: "Part of me is still in Bradford," he lamented in the 1960s, "though when I return there now I wander about half-lost, a melancholy stranger."[25] In the 1930s and 1940s, before his nostalgia for Edwardian Bradford became incapacitating, Priestley consciously deployed his remembered experience of those years in an attempt to validate his social criticism, despite the fact that his past "experience" was always a construct of the present. "I know from my own experience,"[26] he was fond of saying, always contrasting his own practical wisdom with the more abstract knowledge of others. He believed, for example, that his "experience" permitted him to speak with "authentic" knowledge of the working class. As he wrote on the eve of the Second World War, "I did not discover 'the proletariat' in late night talks in some tutor's rooms at Oxford. I grew up with proletarians ... and indeed their blood is mine."[27]

While Priestley's constant reference to his own experience became an important rhetorical device in his efforts to gain credibility as a social critic, it was slightly disingenuous of him to say that he "grew up with proletarians." Although his mother's family had been mill workers, Priestley grew up in one of Bradford's more salubrious suburbs, raised by a father who was a teacher and later a headmaster at a large elementary school. In one of his more candid moments Priestley admitted that he was brought up as a member of the Edwardian lower middle class.[28] Despite the contradictions in Priestley's accounts of his background, it is clear that he inhabited a world dominated by the values of self-help, self-culture, thrift and moral sobriety, values that had been so central to Victorian autodidact culture. His father was an ethical socialist, a Sabbatarian and a Sunday School teacher, and while Priestley came to reject his father's puritanism in favor of Robert Blatchford's cakes-and-ale variety of English socialism, he devoted much of his life to extolling the virtues of his father's values against the "machine-made values" of his own world.

In the 1930s and 1940s Priestley judged the present against the world of his remembered childhood and found it wanting. Specifically, he lamented the loss of "a kind of regional self-sufficiency" that he recalled existing in his youth.[29] In towns like Bradford, he argued, local choral societies, arts clubs, theaters, music halls, subscription concerts and an independent press all flourished, offering residents the opportunity to light up "some of the dreariest towns in the world by an evening's enthusiasm."[30] Priestley looked for such institutions in working-class communities on his English journey in the 1930s; when he discovered them he positioned them as central to those idioms of Englishness that needed to be identified, defended and encouraged before they vanished forever.

Priestley's nostalgia went beyond the rich, associational culture he fondly recalled to the people who inhabited that vanished paradise of memory – to the "solid lumps of character" he wrote about in *English Journey*. He often praised those sturdy English workers, who, he believed, were to be found in abundance in pre-1914 Bradford, strategically positioning them against the new "mass man" of the 1930s. Nevertheless, not all workers were included in Priestley's dense iconography of Englishness. As early as 1913 he wrote: "Bradfordians can be divided into two classes, those who go to Morecambe every year and those who don't. The latter is a small group; I don't go to Morecambe."[31] Later he argued that "with the exceptions among the nonconformists in the industrial North, the Edwardian working class tended to be . . . shallow and silly, the women particularly."[32] But among the skilled craftsmen of Edwardian Bradford Priestley retrospectively identified an immense repository of hope for the future of the English, a group of men who would keep alive English traditions in the face of cheap American imports between the wars and who, in the Second World War, with their deeply-entrenched memories of clog-dancing and choral singing, would become the backbone of the struggle to defend native customs against the menace of Hitler.

These remembered aspects of his youth in Bradford became for Priestley the filter through which he perceived English society in the 1930s and 1940s. Moreover, other critics in those decades drew on their Edwardian backgrounds in similar ways. A major determinant in George Orwell's attitude towards the working class was, for example, his own "emotional commitment to what he considered to be 'decent' and 'honest' in Edwardian England."[33] Unlike Orwell, however, Priestley not only made his remembered past central to his critique of the present, but also wrote and extensively rewrote that past as an argument against, and as an antidote to, the present. By the time his faith in the future of the English had largely evaporated, Priestley had manufactured an elaborate narrative about pre-1914 Bradford which not only served as a metaphor for an Englishness that increasingly seemed to be waning, but also offered him a psychologically comforting world into which he could escape.

III

"My politics are based almost entirely on compassion"[34]

Priestley's politics in the 1930s drew extensively on the Utopian imagery of nineteenth-century forms of socialism that were the product, as he termed it, of middle-class compassion rather than proletarian resentment.[35] He disliked Marxist intellectuals, refusing to accord them a place in his populist vision of Englishness: they had a "central European and not an English air about them."[36] With his English distrust of theory, Priestley was indebted more to the performances of Charlie Chaplin than to the tracts of Karl Marx: "twenty Marxian treatises about the proletariat," he argued, "would not make you feel a tenth of the compassion for the dispossessed urban masses as ... [a] bit of pantomime does. That is the genius of Chaplin."[37]

Throughout the 1930s Priestley railed against the "masses." But, distrusting Marxists, he also refused to adopt the language of class. Against the masses and the classes he posited the existence of the English common people, and it was out of his notion of, and compassion for, "the people" that his politics emerged. A twentieth-century populist, Priestley might best be understood as one of the last major contributors to the populist discourse that, according to Patrick Joyce, was pervasive in the nineteenth century.[38] But this won him few friends on the Left and most socialists found his constant appeal to "the people" vacuous and rather tiresome. Even Priestley had difficulty defining what he meant by the term: "And who are the people? We are all the people so long as we are willing to consider ourselves the people."[39] Despite his vagueness, Priestley's conception of "the people" was a specific construct, rooted in his memories of the Edwardian working class. It was the robustness of the remembered past, a robustness that Priestley found on the music-hall stage, that Priestley mapped onto "the people" in the 1930s. Richard Hoggart's observation that Orwell never lost the habit of "seeing the working-class through the cosy fug of an Edwardian music hall" is as applicable to Priestley as it is to Orwell.[40] Unlike Orwell, however, Priestley went one step further, strategically positioning his imagined "people" against the masses and the classes. Specifically, it was the tenacity of "the people" in the face of adversity that

Priestley remembered from the past and viewed as crucial once again in the struggles of the 1930s.

Much of Priestley's literary production in the late 1920s and 1930s offered a particular image of "the people," derived from the past and yet put forward as an alternative to the politics of class and mass in the present. It was his third novel, *The Good Companions*, published in the summer of 1929, that both catapulted Priestley to fame – it was soon selling 3,000 copies a day – and drew most explicitly on his memories of the world of popular culture in pre-1914 Bradford. The story of various individuals dissatisfied with their lot and brought together to form a touring theater company, it charts their heroic struggle to survive in a world increasingly dominated by the alien forces of big business. It portrayed the England that Priestley both loved and wished to see preserved, an England in which "the people" were keenly aware of the need to defend their heritage and way of life. Similar themes pervade the novel he wrote a decade later, *Let the People Sing*, commissioned by the BBC to be read on the air. Once again Priestley portrayed "the people" as the backbone of England; once again "the people" consisted of resurrected "types" from his childhood; and once again their virtues were conferred on them by the very struggles they were engaged in. Moreover, in both novels Priestley infused life into his imaginary "people" by drawing heavily on character types in the works of Dickens, an author he greatly admired. This made him immensely popular, largely because many of his readers, like Priestley himself, had been taught to see the world through the eyes of Dickens.[41]

If, in his early novels, Priestley defined the essential Englishness he wished to encourage by mapping its attributes onto particular kinds of people, mostly resurrected from his Bradford childhood and presented in familiar Dickensian terms, he attempted a similar feat in the two screenplays he wrote for Gracie Fields in the 1930s, *Sing as We Go* (1934) and *Look Up and Laugh* (1935). Although he regularly attacked Hollywood films, Priestley also saw in film an opportunity to contribute to the myth of Englishness he was eager to promote.[42] In his screenplays he thus made Gracie Fields a vehicle for the dissemination of that myth. In the process, "Our Gracie" helped open up a space in the national culture for the inclusion of representations of working-class life: as Jeffrey Richards has suggested, she played an important role in bringing a particular version of industrial Britain into the midst of discourses of national identity.[43] Priestley himself recognized not only that Fields stood for all that he liked in northern music-hall culture, but also that she could appeal to her audience as one of them, as one of "the people":

The secret of Gracie Fields' vast popularity is that not only does she know ... how to entertain people, but she knows, too, how to represent the people. In a country in which privilege is still the rule and snobbery is the most characteristic weakness, the people do not get much of a chance to express themselves. But in Gracie Fields for once they are expressing themselves. . . . [44]

Despite his enthusiasm, Priestley orchestrated Fields's representations of the people in specific ways. In *Sing as We Go*, in which Gracie leads unemployed workers through the streets of Blackpool in song until, miraculously, they get their jobs back, and in *Look Up and Laugh*, in which she rallies small shopkeepers against the threat posed by a modern department store, Dickensian sympathy and comic effect triumph over more politicized forms of understanding. As in his novels, Priestley was eager in these films to resurrect elements of the world of his remembered youth. But he was less eager to show how "the people" might realistically defend their culture against the threats posed to it.

Writing at the end of the Second World War, the Marxist literary critic and novelist, Jack Lindsay, praised Priestley's work and suggested that it contributed "something essential to our national culture," that it heralded "the first basic movement towards revivifying our tradition" and gathered the "forces that lead into our democratic future."[45] While it was true that Priestley managed to incorporate "the people" in discourses of national identity in the 1930s, it was unclear whether or not his compassion for "the people" had any radical political edge to it. As Alick West once noted, Priestley reduced "the power of the collective people to the comparative powerlessness of individuals."[46] Certainly this was the case in most of the novels and screenplays he wrote before the war. While Priestley attempted to attach memories of his own past to public idioms of national identity, "the people" in his works often remained little more than appealing Dickensian caricatures.

IV

"All of us ordinary people"[47]

The Second World War brought into sharp focus the meanings of Englishness and led to the production of a vast number of works that attempted to identify and codify those essential characteristics of the nation that its people were being ask to defend. Priestley played a major role in many of the representational struggles over Englishness during the war, further elaborating his imagery of the nation and its people.

Priestley often portrayed the heritage in danger as a rural heritage, as he had in the 1930s.[48] In his famous "Postscripts," broadcast on the BBC on Sunday evenings following the nine o'clock news, he drew heavily from the repository of rural nostalgia, discovering England's "real truth" in its countryside. In his broadcast of 9 June 1940, for example, he commented on the bucolic English village and its local volunteer forces, claiming that such scenes

> made me feel sometimes that I'd wandered into one of those rich chapters of Thomas Hardy's fiction in which his rustics meet in the gathering darkness of some Wessex hillside. . . . There we were, ploughman and parson, shepherd and clerk, turning out at night, as our forefathers had often done before us, to keep watch and ward over the sleeping English hills and fields and homesteads.[49]

Three weeks later, he praised the "massive yeoman figure of Mr Bevin," clearly legitimating such figures by linking their "deep kindness" and "natural goodness" to the nation's pastoral inheritance. In short, the war encouraged Priestley to rediscover Englishness in the "Deep England" of the countryside, and he played an important role in revitalizing rural nostalgia as a major component of the war effort.

Despite his tributes to the rural elements of Englishness, Priestley was never entirely comfortable inhabiting the realm of rural nostalgia. Thus, while he strategically deployed rural metaphors during the war, they were always subordinated to his emphasis on the Englishness of the English common people, an Englishness which – as in his description of Bevin – transcended rural nostalgia in significant ways. The "real Englishmen" Priestley invoked in the war, the "ordinary folk" of his imagined community, may have kept alive the sturdy independence of the countryside, but they were now more likely to be found in the pub or the music hall: "There you will find the English much as they were in Shakespeare's time."[50]

During the war, Priestley called on those people not only to defend the nation against the external enemy, but to reclaim their birthright from their aristocratic and plutocratic enemies at home as well. If, in the 1930s, Gracie Fields became the vehicle through which Priestley depicted "the people" cheerfully struggling against the forces of a new, impersonal world, then in the 1940s the entire country was invited to join her struggle. As Angus Calder has argued, the language of pre-existing mythologies was easily adapted to the necessities of wartime "with remarkable naturalness and fluency."[51] Those mythologies were centrally deployed in Priestley's wartime "Postscripts": taken together, they played a crucial role in generating national unity by inviting their listeners to feel part of a great national tradition, an all-encompassing Englishness of the heart and soul. By speaking personally to his audience and including himself as one of them – by referring to "you and I," to "all of us ordinary people"[52] – Priestley made his listeners complicit in his construction of Englishness to a far greater extent than he had in the 1930s.

In his "Postscripts," Priestley was particularly adept at defining the struggle against Germany by invoking his recollections of the lost world of popular culture from his Yorkshire past. In his discussion of Dunkirk, for example, he focused on the pleasure steamers (including the "Gracie Fields") that sailed across the channel to bring "the people" "home," and he conjured up images of the holiday steamers from his own remembered past, of boats packed with people "full of high spirits and bottled beer, the ladies eating pork pies, the children sticky with peppermint rock." There was, he wrote, "always something old-fashioned, a Dickens touch, a mid-Victorian air about them."[53] Likewise, a deserted Margate allowed Priestley to recall other images from his past – "children shouting and laughing, bands playing, concert parties singing, men selling ice-cream, whelks and peppermint rock."[54] This was the world of pre-1914 popular holiday-making, as remembered in *The Good Companions* and reinvented by Gracie Fields, but now harnessed to the war effort.

Many of "the people" on whom Priestley focused in his "Postscripts" bore striking resemblance to those recognizable "types" from the pre-1914 music-hall stage he had so often invoked. For example, he began his broadcast on 15 September 1940 with a passage from Dickens' *Pickwick Papers* in order to suggest that the old cockney of his memory had not become "soft," had not perished in the face of mass culture, but was again displaying his true spirit of "independence, ironic humour, cheek and charm" in the battle against the Nazis.[55] Originally a symbol of Englishness in the face of American culture, the cockney had become the "unlikely embodiment of the spirit of national defence."[56] In fact, all around him Priestley found characters from a past he had once believed lost to be alive and well after all. This gave Priestley faith in the future of England and the English and encouraged him to articulate what might be termed a forward-looking nostalgia, to borrow from the remembered past in an attempt to imagine a different future. The battle, he argued, was "not merely to recover what has been lost," but to march forward "to something better than we've ever known before."[57] The image of a transformed future, populated by recognizable characters from the past, made Priestley's broadcasts appealing to his wartime audience, although it worried those less concerned with the future and more concerned with the war at hand.

Priestley further developed these themes in articles and pamphlets he wrote for the 1941 Committee, a Leftist brain trust. He argued, for example, that "the people" in England were unique, distinct from Hitler's "masses." And he also looked beyond the war to the future, claiming, "If I thought for a moment that the people were ... fighting the war only to get back to the drivel [of the tabloids] and dog-racing ... I would not be writing these pages."[58] Following the cancellation of the "Postscripts," and after a brief period of infatuation with Richard

Acland's Forward March movement, Priestley continued to campaign tirelessly for a postwar Britain that would be genuinely democratic, where planning would triumph and a national minimum be guaranteed, where industry would be subordinated to the needs of the people, and where a vital popular culture would again flourish. In the polemical tracts he wrote during the later part of the war,[59] in plays like *They Come to a City* (1942), and in his demobilization novel, *Three Men in New Suits* (1945), Priestley imagined a bold new order where all the virtues he had identified with "the people" at war would flourish, where Englishness would, at last, be safe.

Despite his general optimism, Priestley was not without his anxieties about the future, and on several occasions his old worries about the United States resurfaced. On the eve of victory, for example, he warned a returning serviceman to "be a real citizen, not a hermit in a bungalow": "Refuse with scorn the great dope-dreams of the economic emperors and their sorcerers and Hollywood siren. Don't allow them to inject you with Glamour, Sport, Sensational News, and all the other De-luxe nonsense, as if they were filling you with an anaesthetic."[60] Despite the fact that individuals in the armed forces were presumably part of "the people" whose virtues he extolled during the war, Priestley was not at all sure they would, in peacetime, be able to preserve the Englishness of the English nation at war. Priestley's fears won him few friends, and a "returning serviceman," irritated by Priestley, wrote back to him: "Your tone in addressing me is one of patronising but 'matey' vulgarity. You assume that my chief objects in life are slippers and bungalows and tunes on the wireless."[61] After the war Priestley assumed just that and came to feel that "the people" were not living up to his expectations of them.

V

"I often have a nightmare vision"[62]

Looking back on 1945 from the vantage point of the 1960s, Priestley argued that at the end of the war "the people" demanded a whole new way of life but their hopes soon faded and a "general English togetherness seemed to vanish." Society, he lamented, became "a slobbering mess of irresponsibility, mean devices, and self-deception."[63] As early as 1946, Priestley had already carved out a new role for himself, not as the spokesperson for a triumphant Englishness, but as the bitter, disillusioned critic of the postwar settlement, of a world in which "the people" were offered "an extra tin or two of spam and a new overcoat" while being denied the tools and the inspiration required to generate a much-needed spiritual renewal.[64] In 1947, in a mood of despair, Priestley again trekked around the nation, writing a series of articles, "Crisis Journey." His conclusions bore a resemblance to those of *English Journey*: textile workers in Lancashire needed a reminder that romance did not begin in Beverly Hills, while Liverpudlian picture-goers "looked a bit doped." By contrast, in South Wales, argued Priestley, one could still find "a good crop of fruity characters."[65] Amidst the gloom, one of the few rays of hope Priestley seemed to encounter was at a Butlin's holiday camp: the whole phenomenon, he claimed, was very English, and the festivities illustrated the people's desire for some color and fun in the drab, postwar world. "Does Butlin know better than Bevin?," Priestley asked pensively, tacitly suggesting that the bureaucracy of the welfare state had robbed "the people" of their birthright.[66]

By 1949 Priestley was complaining loudly that the space available for the kind of good-humored cultural self-sufficiency that he remembered from his Bradford youth and identified with the nation at its best seemed to be fast disappearing.[67] While he had uttered similar warnings before, Priestley made few friends with these outbursts. Individuals on the Left who placed their faith in Bevin, rather than Butlin, began to tire of his cynicism. Michael Foot, for example, claimed that Priestley had become the new High Priest of a defeatist cult, a nihilist who no longer deigned "to join the strivings of the common people."[68]

Priestley still believed he was on the side of "the people." Nevertheless, his image of "the people" remained rooted in the jolly band of characters he had conjured up in *The Good Companions*, in the Dickensian caricatures of a remembered childhood. Thus, in 1951, when the Festival of Britain promised temporarily to lift the gloom of postwar austerity, Priestley became one of its most enthusiastic supporters, largely because it permitted him to imagine an England full of those convivial gatherings that were central to his fictitious constructs of the nation in the 1930s.[69] Fired by enthusiasm, Priestley contributed *Festival at Farbridge* (1951) to the celebrations, a comic novel that chronicled the attempts of a provincial town to stage its own festival. While the Bradford-born novelist and admirer of Priestley, John Braine, praised the work and viewed the Festival as "the last gasp of what we had begun to hope for during the war,"[70] Priestley was deeply disappointed that his novel was received so unfavorably. While the imagined community of his Bradford childhood seemed alluring during the Depression, and while it could be deployed in the consolidation of national identity during the war, it appeared curiously anachronistic in the postwar world.

VI

"Is some of my work haunted by a certain feeling of nostalgia?"[71]

Following the Festival, Priestley became more and more disillusioned

222

and retreated into nostalgia for his own remembered past. His Bradford childhood, once the most important source for his definition of the essential characteristics of the nation in the 1930s and 1940s, had become little more than a safe retreat from a hostile world, a hazy memory that gave rise to sudden bursts of longing for a ground already lost. If late Victorian and Edwardian Bradford had once given Priestley hope of direction – if it had offered him a cognitive map on which he could chart the Englishness of the English common people – direction no longer seemed possible. Priestley's remembered past came to offer him consolation rather than inspiration, a past yearned for simply for its own sake: "At least that is how it is with me," he wrote in 1962, "a tune from a forgotten operetta, an old music-hall ditty, is my equivalent of Proust's madeleine."[72] His memories of the pre-1914 music-hall stage became a particularly important element in Priestley's nostalgia. Although the halls had once provided him material he could deploy in his own "essential Englishness," in his novel of the Edwardian halls, *Lost Empires* (1965), they were merely part of a forgotten world into which he could escape. After "the people" grew weary of his exhortations, all Priestley was left with was his own bittersweet nostalgia for an earlier golden age.

Other individuals examined in this volume shared many of Priestley's anxieties about the twentieth century, although they did not attempt to negotiate them in the same way. In the terminal note he wrote in 1960 to his pre-1914 gay novel, *Maurice*, E.M. Forster lamented that two world wars had left the nation with forms of regimentation that had destroyed an England in which he felt at home.[73] Priestley, like Forster, lamented the loss. Unlike Forster, however, Priestley fought back, drawing from his own remembered past in order to propagate idioms of national identity that he believed could serve as valuable weapons in the present. As successful as such images may have appeared in the 1930s and 1940s, twentieth-century Britons could not be compelled to see themselves in terms of a nostalgically-invoked, pre-1914, music-hall tradition. Ultimately, Priestley's attempt to make his remembered past the basis of a new public discourse of national identity failed. "Perhaps," he wrote in 1949, "for all my pretence of being up to the minute, I was not even living in the right age; and when I looked for my own enduring delight, I became an anachronism."[74]

NOTES

1 Philip Dodd, "Englishness and the National Culture," in Robert Colls and Philip Dodd, eds, *Englishness: Politics and Culture 1880–1920*, London, Croom Helm, 1986, p. 22.
2 My attempt to conceive of Englishness as an invented tradition is indebted

CHRIS WATERS

to Eric Hobsbawm and Terence Ranger, eds, *The Invention of Tradition*, Cambridge, Cambridge University Press, 1983. The term "national fiction" is borrowed from Geoff Hurd, ed., *National Fictions: World War Two in British Films and Television*, London, BFI, 1984.

3 J.B. Priestley, *The English*, London, Heinemann, 1973, p. 11.

4 J.B. Priestley, "The English Character," in Priestley, *English Humour*, London, Longman, Green, 1929.

5 Priestley, *The English*, p. 243.

6 J.B. Priestley, *Midnight on the Desert: A Chapter of Autobiography*, London, Heinemann, 1937, p. 236.

7 J.B. Priestley, *English Journey*, 1934, rpt Harmondsworth, Penguin, 1977, p. 26.

8 Ibid., p. 252.

9 Ibid., p. 67.

10 See F.R. Leavis, *Mass Civilisation and Minority Culture*, Cambridge, Minority Press, 1930; Stanley Baldwin, *On England*, 1926, rpt Harmondsworth, Penguin, 1937. On rural nostalgia between the wars, see Bill Schwarz, "The Language of Constitutionalism: Baldwinite Conservatism," in *Formations of Nation and People*, London, Routledge and Kegan Paul, 1984, pp. 1–18; Patrick Wright, *On Living in an Old Country: The National Past in Contemporary Britain*, London, Verso, 1985, chs 1–3; Martin J. Wiener, *English Culture and the Decline of the Industrial Spirit 1850–1980*, Cambridge, Cambridge University Press, 1981, pp. 72–80, 98–118; Malcolm Chase, "This is no Claptrap: This is Our Heritage," in Christopher Shaw and Malcolm Chase, eds, *The Imagined Past: History and Nostalgia*, Manchester, Manchester University Press, 1989, pp. 128–46.

11 Priestley, *English Journey*, p. 374.

12 Ibid., p. 378.

13 *Bradford Pioneer*, 28 February 1913, p. 6; 29 August 1913, p. 6.

14 J.B. Priestley, *Margin Released: A Writer's Reminiscences and Reflections*, 1962, rpt, London, Mercury Books, 1966, pp. 66–7.

15 J.B. Priestley, "Why Does Britain Stand It?," *Sunday Chronicle*, 10 December 1933, p. 9.

16 Priestley, *Midnight on the Desert*, pp. 234–6.

17 J.B. Priestley, "The Strange Country Shows Us Our Future," *Sunday Chronicle*, 24 March 1935, p. 6.

18 Simon Frith, "The Pleasures of the Hearth: The Making of BBC Light Entertainment," in Frith, *Music For Pleasure: Essays in the Sociology of Pop*, London, Polity Press, 1988, p. 25.

19 J.B. Priestley, "American Journey," *Sunday Chronicle*, 17 March 1935, p. 9. See also "In Praise of the Normal Woman," in Priestley, *I For One*, London, John Lane, 1923, pp. 85–92.

20 Sally Alexander, "Becoming a Woman in London in the 1920s and 1930s," in David Feldman and Gareth Stedman Jones, eds, *Metropolis – London: Histories and Representations*, London, Routledge, 1989, pp. 245–6.

21 J.B. Priestley, "English Films and English People," *World Film News and Television Progress*, vol. 1, November 1936, p. 3.

22 Priestley, *Margin Released*, p. 32.

23 David Lowenthal, *The Past is a Foreign Country*, Cambridge, Cambridge University Press, 1985, p. 210.

24 J.B. Priestley, "Making Writing Simple," in Priestley, *Delight*, London, Heinemann, 1949, p. 71.

25 Priestley, *Margin Released*, p. 32.

224

26 Priestley, *The English*, p. 68. For a critique of "experience" as a category of analysis, see Joan W. Scott, "The Evidence of Experience," *Critical Inquiry*, vol. 17, Summer 1991, pp. 773–97.

27 J.B. Priestley, *Rain Upon Godshill: A Further Chapter of Autobiography*, London, Heinemann, 1939, p. 253.

28 J.B. Priestley, *The Edwardians*, London, Heinemann, 1970, p. 104.

29 Priestley, *Margin Released*, p. 30. See also his preface to Fenner Brockway, *Socialism Over Sixty Years: The Life of Jowett of Bradford (1864–1944)*, London, George Allen and Unwin, 1945, and "Born and Bred in Bradford," *The Listener*, 27 December 1945, pp. 753–4.

30 Priestley, *Edwardians*, p. 108.

31 *Bradford Pioneer*, 21 March 1913, p. 6.

32 Priestley, *Edwardians*, p. 84.

33 Chris Pawling, "George Orwell and the Documentary in the Thirties," *Literature and History*, vol. 4, Autumn 1976, p. 82.

34 J.B. Priestley, *Instead of the Trees: A Final Chapter of Autobiography*, London, Heinemann, 1977, p. 87.

35 Priestley, *Rain Upon Godshill*, p. 260.

36 J.B. Priestley, "Thunder on the Left," *News Chronicle*, 14 January 1937, p. 6.

37 Priestley, *Midnight on the Desert*, pp. 195–6. On his nostalgia for pantomime and the music hall, see: "Variety," in *Apes and Angels: A Book of Essays*, London, Methuen, 1928, pp. 155–62; "Good Honest Vulgarity," *Sunday Chronicle*, 12 November 1933, p. 9; *The Moments and Other Pieces*, London, Heinemann, 1966, pp. 62–8; *The Edwardians*, pp. 172–6; *Particular Pleasures*, London, Heinemann, 1975, pp. 166–8, 177–9, 185–7, 189–90.

38 Patrick Joyce, *Visions of the People: Industrial England and the Question of Class, 1840–1914*, Cambridge, Cambridge University Press, 1991.

39 "Priestley Tells Britain," *Life*, 19 May 1941, p. 86.

40 Richard Hoggart, *The Uses of Literacy*, 1957, New York, Oxford University Press, 1970, p. 17.

41 See Jonathan Raban, "Priestley and Bainbridge in England," in Raban, *For Love and Money*, London, Pan, 1987, p. 292.

42 See R.B. Marriott, "Priestley on British Films," *The Era*, 6 July 1939, p. 1. See also J.B. Priestley, "They've Slighted Britain," *Sunday Chronicle*, 8 October 1933, p. 9; J.B. Priestley, "An Idea for British Films," *News Chronicle*, 3 July 1939, p. 8; Priestley, *Rain Upon Godshill*, pp. 78–84. For Priestley and the mass media, see D.L. LeMahieu, *A Culture for Democracy: Mass Communication and the Cultivated Mind in Britain Between the Wars*, Oxford, Clarendon Press, 1988, pp. 318–26. For his work in film, see Peter Stead, *Film and the Working Class: The Feature Film in British and American Society*, London, Routledge, 1989, pp. 100–8.

43 Jeffrey Richards, *The Age of the Dream Palace: Cinema and Society in Britain 1930–1939*, London, Routledge and Kegan Paul, 1984, pp. 172–7.

44 *Sunday Chronicle*, 18 June 1939, p. 7. See also the suggestions made by Joanna Macfadyen, "Gracie's Artistry Reflects the Psychology of the Masses," *World Film News and Television Progress*, vol. 1, June 1936, p. 5.

45 Jack Lindsay, "J.B. Priestley," in Val Denys Baker, ed., *Writers of To-Day*, London, Sidgwick and Jackson, 1946, pp. 72–3.

46 Alick West, *The Mountain in the Sunlight: Studies in Conflict and Unity*, London, Lawrence and Wishart, 1958, p. 169.

47 J.B. Priestley, *Postscripts*, London, Heinemann, 1940, p. 19.

48 See, for example, J.B. Priestley, "The Beauty of Britain," in Charles Bradley

Ford, ed., *The Beauty of Britain*, London, Batsford, 1935, pp. 1–10; J.B. Priestley, ed., *Our Nation's Heritage*, London, J.M. Dent and Sons, 1939.

49 Priestley, *Postscripts*, see esp. pp. 5–6, 9, 12.

50 J.B. Priestley, "Misconception: The Real Englishman," *Lilliput*, vol. 7, September 1940, p. 179.

51 Angus Calder, "The Myth of the Blitz," *The Guardian*, 19 August 1991, p. 30.

52 Priestley, *Postscripts*, p. 19. On the "Postscripts," see Priestley, *Margin Released*, pp. 220–2; Vincent Brome, *J.B. Priestley*, London, Hamish Hamilton, 1988, pp. 241–61; Asa Briggs, *The History of Broadcasting in the United Kingdom*, Oxford, Oxford University Press, 1970, vol. 3, pp. 206, 210–11; James Curran and Jean Seaton, *Power Without Responsibility: The Press and Broadcasting in Britain*, London, Fontana, 1981, pp. 174–7; Paul Addison, *The Road to 1945: British Politics and the Second World War*, London, Quartet, 1977, pp. 118–19, 144–5; Alistair Thomson, "Out of the People: J.B. Priestley as Wartime Populist," *Journal of the Scottish Labour History Society*, no. 21, 1986, pp. 4–13.

53 Priestley, *Postscripts*, p. 3.

54 Ibid., pp. 30–1.

55 Ibid., pp. 71–2.

56 Gareth Stedman Jones, "The 'Cockney' and the Nation, 1780–1988," in Feldman and Stedman Jones, *Metropolis*, p. 278.

57 Priestley, *Postscripts*, p. 32.

58 J.B. Priestley, *Out of the People*, New York, Harper Brothers, 1941, p. 42.

59 Especially J.B. Priestley, *Here Are Your Answers*, London, Common Wealth Popular Library, no. 1, 1944; J.B. Priestley, *The New Citizen*, London, Council for Education in World Citizenship, 1944.

60 J.B. Priestley, *Letter to a Returning Serviceman*, London, Home and Van Thal, 1945, p. 31.

61 E.O. Siepmann, "Letter to Mr Priestley from 'A Returning Serviceman,'" *Nineteenth Century and After*, vol. 138, December 1945, p. 255.

62 J.B. Priestley, *Thoughts in the Wilderness*, London, Heinemann, 1957, p. 127.

63 J.B. Priestley, "Fifty Years of the English," in *The Moments*, pp. 213–16.

64 J.B. Priestley, *The Secret Dream: An Essay on Britain, America and Russia*, London, Turnstile Press, 1946, pp. 10–13. See also the transcripts of his 1947 radio broadcasts, "Hard Times", in *The Listener*, 23 October 1947, pp. 711–12; 30 October, pp. 755–6; 6 November, pp. 804–5.

65 J.B. Priestley, "Crisis Journey," *Daily Herald*, 22 September 1947, p. 2; 20 October, p. 2; 9 October, p. 2.

66 Ibid., 15 September 1947, p. 2. For his views on culture and the welfare state, see J.B. Priestley, *The Arts Under Socialism*, London, Turnstile Press, 1947.

67 J.B. Priestley, "The Truth about Democracy," *Sunday Pictorial*, 23 January 1949, p. 6.

68 "The Futility of Mr Priestley," *Tribune*, 28 January 1949, pp. 1–2. For his response, see "J.B. Priestley Replies to His Critics," *Sunday Pictorial*, 6 February 1949, p. 46.

69 J.B. Priestley, "On With the Festivals," *The Listener*, 10 May 1951, p. 740.

70 John Braine, *J.B. Priestley*, London, Weidenfeld and Nicolson, 1978, pp. 130–1.

71 Priestley, *Instead of the Trees*, p. 61.

72 Priestley, *Margin Released*, p. 60.

73 E.M. Forster, *Maurice*, New York, New American Library, 1971, p. 254.

74 Priestley, "The Delight That Never Was," in *Delight*, p. 262.

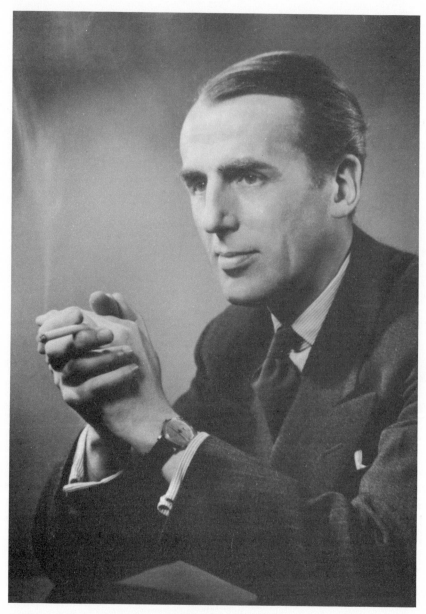

13 John Summerson

10

John Summerson 1904–1992
The architectural critic and the quest for the Modern

Peter Mandler

"Architecture is the Cinderella of the Arts": this complaint, repeatedly raised in Britain by the architecturally-minded in the first half of the twentieth century, not only voiced distress with a temporary lull in architectural creativity over a generation or two, but also tendered a broader, longer-term indictment of modern British culture. At least for the preceding century, both among the middle classes and public opinion more generally, buildings had been considered in a utilitarian light as private property, and rarely as works of art. Even among aesthetes, reared in the literary culture of the public schools, the three-dimensional image was overshadowed by the flat and figurative image and both were held decidedly second-best to the word. While France and Italy were learning to cherish their historic architecture, and Holland, Scandinavia and Germany were inventing the modern, Britain before the Second World War was getting only the architecture it deserved – the slapdash, the derivative, the all-too-easily ignored – and it was rapidly losing by casual vandalism and deliberate re-development the treasures of its pre-Victorian Golden Age.

Then, suddenly, briefly – from the mid-1930s to the mid-1950s, we could say – the lamp of architecture flared up and helped illumine the world of general culture itself enjoying something of a renaissance during and after the Second World War. A distinguished cohort of critics of whom any nation would be proud flourished on the airwaves and in the papers as well as between hardcovers: both professionals like Nikolaus Pevsner, J.M. Richards and John Summerson, and amateurs such as Osbert Lancaster, Sacheverell Sitwell and John Betjeman. All spread the gospel of historic architecture to an ever-growing audience, but the professionals – feeling more responsibility to the present vitality of their craft – strove also to advertise (to a degree, even to invent) the British modern. This latter enterprise proved a failure. Today's architectural consciousness, greatly heightened from prewar levels, is historic but not modern. Modern architecture did not tread the path urged upon it by the critics, and the path it did take diverged so far from the public's needs and tastes that it seems now to have wandered into oblivion.

With this failure, this divergence, architectural criticism has lost the ability to treat of its art as a living tradition. It seems now worth trying to recall how one critic in particular briefly brought together that living tradition and the widest possible audience, and how and why these things slipped from his grasp. In the process, we may learn something about the failure of modern architecture – indeed, of modern art – in Britain, and something more generally about the weakening position of the cultural critic in the years that followed the false dawn of the Festival of Britain.

PROBLEMS (TO 1933)

John Summerson was born in 1904 in Darlington, the birthplace of the railway. His father was the dreamy, bookish scion of a manufacturing family, who perhaps characteristically married a vicar's daughter from a down-at-heel Anglo-Irish gentry family. Sam Summerson died when John was still an infant, leaving him a sizeable chunk of the family business in trust, and mother and child led a prosperously vagrant existence for some years in English seaside towns and shabby Continental watering-spots. It is just a bit too neat to attribute the young Summerson's classical side to his mother – disciplined, traditional, public-school (for she paid the fees for Harrow) – and his romantic side to his father – who left a legacy of books as well as cash, instilling an unrespectable fascination with the Gothic and the half-ruined. It is too neat because when in 1922 Summerson leant to his romantic side, gave up the place at Cambridge coveted for him by his mother and quixotically enrolled at the Bartlett School of Architecture at University College London, his mother took this project, too, in hand and set up housekeeping for the two of them in a cramped flat off Harley Street.

The architectural world into which this unhappily dependent young man entered in the early 1920s was in a doldrums of its own; together, the apprentice and his profession stumbled along uncertainly for over a decade. As Summerson later deciphered them, the problems were these. Despite its low social status, the architectural profession had been stimulated aesthetically in the eighteenth and early nineteenth centuries by a set of patrons with strong functional and ideological motives for building: landowners who wanted country houses to impress and urban developments for profit, churchmen who wanted buildings to attract and uplift, even some quasi-public authorities ambitious to plan entire towns. The Victorians abandoned many of these ambitions, whether out of philistinism, too-rapid expansion or speculative greed. Their greatest architectural achievements were viewed as engineering, not architecture. Otherwise there were only fragments of the old patronage-structure for which architects continued to scramble. Few large country houses were built any longer, though those few could still inspire a Lutyens. Smaller town and country houses for the upper-middle class temporarily offered an alternative outlet for talent, allowing Norman Shaw and the Arts and Crafts to thrive, but this proved too narrow a base upon which to launch either a stylistic or a professional recovery. Even that market had collapsed in the deepening slump of the 1920s. Speculative housing, in contrast, required little or no architecture – at best, pallid retrievals of once-living styles, catering at the same time to suburban snobbery and cheap-jack building methods. Government commissions and retail and office developers offered more work but had little reason to swim against the aesthetic stream; they were content with the large-scale adaptations of country-house styles offered by the prestige architectural firms: thus Bankers' Georgian at worst, a slightly cleaner Scandinavian neo-classicism at best. After the raising of hopes before the First World War by the Arts and Crafts movement, the reversion to a crude and clumsy historicism was deeply depressing to would-be reformers. And on top of this psychological depression came the real thing, in the form of a deep construction-industry slump in the early 1930s.[1]

Such an aesthetic and material shambles was unlikely to attract talent and imagination into the profession, and the system of apprenticeship then prevalent only aggravated things, holding the younger generation in thrall to the old and safe. Summerson found at the Bartlett a decent and dutiful "lower-middle" cohort laboring to get into a private country-house practice if they were lucky or better-connected, slipping into bland public departments if not. Though physically located in the same world, the Bartlett, the Architectural Association and the RIBA had few overlaps with the literary and artistic avant-garde of Bloomsbury and Fitzrovia. Summerson recalls his amazement and excitement at finding a genteelly dandified Old Etonian, Peter Fleetwood-Hesketh, standing aloof among the grammar-school boys at the Bartlett, but equally, Hesketh found Summerson a welcome relief from his usual Bright-Young-Thing round, where architecture was decidedly *outré*: "When people asked me what I was interested in and I said 'architecture,' they'd back away."[2]

Hesketh had the wealth and connections to strike out on his own. He could practice his idiosyncratic scholarly Georgian on the family estates and on commissions from friends; he could even buy (with his elder brother Roger) his own magazine, *The Master Builder*, to propagandize for his rather elevated views. Summerson had no such choices. He drifted miserably through a succession of prestigious but unfulfilling apprenticeships, a teaching post at the Edinburgh College of Art, and finally back to London – still living with his mother – into some money-spinning architectural journalism, including for Hesketh's *Master Builder* and some collaborative work with the neo-Georgian architect Clough Williams-Ellis. At some kind of nadir in 1933, Summerson's early brushes with journalism yet brought him into contact with circles who were striving to make something more original and more attractive of architecture. Within a few years, Summerson's career and the vitality of the art were together to be dramatically turned around by the emergence of two distinct but related intellectual movements. These were the Modern Movement, finally arrived from the Continent, and – a current with more ambiguous national origins – the rise of architectural history.

SOLUTIONS (1933–51)

As had been the case with modernist painting a generation earlier, modern architecture's advent in Britain was late, halting and, at first, painfully narrow and abstruse. Le Corbusier's *Vers Une Architecture* was translated by Frederick Etchells in 1927, and Etchells' tentative realization of Corbusian principles, his office building for Crawford's which went up on High Holborn in London in 1930, is usually accepted as the first modern public building in Britain. A few cosmopolitans took up this gospel because it was Continental and because it promised to shock the Establishment; this in turn caused some intellectual elements hitherto uninterested in architecture to give it a look over for surprises. Something was stirring.

In the leading architectural schools, students received the news with delight, exaggerating Le Corbusier to make him everything their teachers, bosses and clients were not. Out went the old architecture: a snobby craft indebted to rich private patrons, hierarchical, history-ridden, stagnant. In came the new: architecture as science, a business of appraising the community's social and economic needs and realizing them in the most advanced materials, collective, above history, animated by social usefulness and a new connection to the other socially-conscious branches of modern art. The reaction was extreme, aggravated by its coincidence in the early 1930s with the general consciousness of social crisis among the intellectual or aesthetic young.

But this reaction was at the same time rather attenuated and effete. It hardly went beyond a certain stratum at the chief architectural schools in London and Liverpool, and was luckily reinforced by a trickle of architectural refugees from the Continent after 1933. In that year a Modern Architectural Research Group – the MARS Group – was founded to act as a propaganda and "research" focus for the new movement in Britain, but it never attracted more than sixty or seventy members, of whom only about a dozen were consistently active, and it did far more propaganda than "research."[3] That there was a wider, younger audience for modernism is evident in the *Architectural Review*'s commercial decision to give the movement a more favorable airing from around 1935, yet the real stability of architecture's material base is betrayed by the *Review*'s advertising pages, where the neo-Georgian and the neo-Renaissance and – at its most daring – the Jazz Deco continued to predominate. Few modern buildings were actually built. Those few were mainly private commissions by wealthy professionals who did now at least recognize architecture as part of the avant-garde.[4]

For John Summerson, there were opportunities here, personal, aesthetic and economic. Architectural writers, so recently the obscurest of the obscure, were increasingly welcome in real Bloomsbury circles. Summerson finally decamped from his mother's flat and took up residence in a collective house in Taviton Street. He was taken under the wing of Geoffrey Grigson, who introduced him to a wider circle, including the novelist Antonia White, the sculptress Barbara Hepworth and her actress sister Elizabeth. These connections opened up Summerson's world considerably, and led also to his marriage to Elizabeth Hepworth in 1938. The assistant editor's job he had accepted desultorily in 1934 at the *Architect & Building News* provided a ready pulpit, much as the equivalent job at the *Architectural Review* did for J.M. Richards. By the outbreak of war, he was broadcasting regularly for the BBC and writing frequently for a wide audience in *The Listener*, beginning to adumbrate an interpretation of architecture's future.

This interpretation was both more cautious and more optimistic than the Corbusian effusions of the practicing modernists.[5] He welcomed enthusiastically the new currents in architecture striving to re-connect art to society. The old patronage structure was clearly collapsing. The flagging demand for labor-intensive private homes and churches simply could not sustain the profession in the 1930s and beyond. This collapse manifested itself directly in the etiolation of style: the clingy reliance on old materials and old variations on old traditions which Summerson once labeled "architectural Toryism." But a new architecture could not wish itself into existence out of abstractions, or out of the Continent, either. It had to become "*effective* in English life." This required two transformations. One was a transformation in English society already underway, but not fully realized in slump – much less in wartime – conditions. A new patron had to emerge, and this would inevitably be a public patron, seeking not country houses and cathedrals but blocks of flats, schools, libraries, hospitals and offices. The pent-up demand for these public buildings was bound to lead to a building boom – this became clearer still once the bombs began to fall in 1940 – but high demand was no guarantee of quality supply. For this the architectural profession required a shake-up as well. The old private practice, seeking private commissions and large-scale "monumental" work for public authorities, was yielding in importance to the public department which served as executive for the new patron: the public itself.[6]

Summerson felt that the Modern Movement, unlike the architectural Tories, had at least recognized the reality of these transformations, but that it had not by the early 1940s gone very far towards responding to them. Modernists had embraced the new materials, the new building methods and the new building programs, but they did not really know what to do with them. Here Summerson wished to reinsert the importance of architecture – the artistic interpretation of the patron's program – into the modernists' social theory. Architectural success had always combined an appropriate response to the program with a stylistic interpretation that spoke aesthetically to the patron and preferably to a wider audience still; what was needed was something novel and useful, suited to "our contemporary way of living," but at the same time expressive and even romantic.[7] The modernists' dislike for the traditionalists' tinkering with the styles – "art nonsense" – had led them to imagine, delusively, that the program could be realized without a style – a representation of pure function, what Summerson called "machine nonsense." A closer reading of the patron's program, he believed, would demonstrate that the public needed the architect to remain an artist, to offset the greater homogeneity of modern life with greater individuality in the home and workplace, bringing "a sense of dignity, refinement, subtlety, gaiety, to all the places where we live and work." This could only emerge if modern architects ceased worrying about "filling in the history form correctly" and started offering from the drawing-board their individual analyses of modern requirements.[8] If the public's demand for this kind of creativity was not yet fully in evidence, Summerson's own demand that his craft aspire to the high standards set by the other modern arts certainly was.[9]

He had reached these conclusions about the dual role of the architect as social interpreter and artist partly as a journalist appraising modern architecture, but partly also by another route. Odd as it may seem today, when these roles are perfectly polarized, Summerson's career as a modern art critic unfolded contemporaneously with a career as an architectural historian. Accident undoubtedly played a part. In the summer of 1933, browsing in the bargain bins outside a Bloomsbury bookshop, Summerson had stumbled across and carted away for a few shillings a bundle of early nineteenth-century architectural drawings. These proved on examination to be a set of drawings from the *atelier* of John Nash, architect to George IV and the man who laid out and designed the skeleton of the West End of London. What began as a piece of antiquarian research then blossomed into a full-scale study of Nash, published in 1935, a series of highly-regarded essays on other architectural innovators of the seventeenth and eighteenth centuries (Wren, Soane, Wyatt), and finally research on the making of the modern metropolis that appeared in book form after the war as *Georgian London*, Summerson's most influential work.[10]

Accidental the discovery of the Nash designs might have been, but Summerson's architectural history was of a piece with his architectural criticism. His analyses of historic buildings were precisely designed to reveal the interplay of individual artistic interpretation and the demands of the functional program. Nash fitted this bill neatly because he was not a genius, or even much of an innovator, but rather a skillful adapter of existing stylistic traditions to new programs. In his biography, and even more so in *Georgian London*, Summerson showed that it was possible to write an architectural history that was not only about Great Men, but also about society and economy. Such a demonstration might have the dual effect of showing how architects might re-connect with their own societies, without abandoning either existing aesthetic loyalties or the urge to innovate, and of awakening the public to the presence of an Art already imbedded in their daily lives. Again, he was here proposing for architecture only what the other arts had already begun to achieve, and his architectural history was directly inspired by the new German art history that had fortuitously arrived (with the Warburg Institute) on English shores in 1933.[11] It was also, of course, influenced by the light, humanistic Marxism blowing through the British avant-garde of the 1930s, and Summerson has some claim to be a forerunner of the "British Marxist historians" who prospered in the field of social history a generation later.

Summerson was not precisely alone, among modernists, in this attachment to historic buildings. His friend J.M. Richards of the *Architectural Review* held many of the same views; so did another German émigré, Nikolaus Pevsner, who arrived in 1933 and whose *Pioneers of Modern Design* published a few years later controversially suggested a British pedigree for the Modern Movement in industrial design and the Arts and Crafts movement. In their different ways all three saw older buildings as better exemplifying architecture as living art than anything in the contemporary ragbag: Pevsner championing the Arts and Crafts, Richards and Summerson favoring Georgian town planning and playing a leading role in the first activist preservation society, the Georgian Group, founded in 1937. But it is fair to say that, in the late 1930s, this cluster of "moderns" who were simultaneously "ancients" sat rather uneasily between the majority of history-denying modernists on the one hand and the majority of anti-modern nostalgics on the other. Neither group made much of a dent on the consciousness of either the governing or the chattering classes.

At this point – we have reached the early years of the war by now –

235

it might be reasonable to ask what importance we can justifiably attach to the writings of John Summerson (and Richards and Pevsner), if they remained so distant from most architects (whether modern or traditionalist) and most of the still indifferent public as well. The answer is that they did not remain so distant. The war changed a good deal. Many of Summerson's hopes and predictions, articulated a little sketchily between the mid-1930s and the early 1940s, began to be realized. Of course, we all know about the boost given by the war to general culture as well as to public-sector initiatives. What is often missed is the enhanced role that architecture played in both. German bombs ensured that postwar "reconstruction" would entail a new physical as well as social and economic order. At the same time the "Baedeker" raids aimed specifically at historic buildings generated an attachment to the architectural heritage that no amount of history lectures could match. Richards and Summerson moved quickly to meet this new interest with a book, *The Bombed Buildings of Britain*, which sold out on publication in 1942 and continued to sell well after the war. It was only one of a large number of popular publications, exhibitions, lectures and debates over what would be the appropriate design and style for the New (postwar) Britain.[12]

Government responded to and stimulated this physical planning debate in much the same way as it interacted with the more familiar welfare state debate. The Beveridge Report had its analogues in the Barlow, Scott and Uthwatt Reports on land use and planning. A Ministry of Town and Country Planning was set up, initially under Lord Reith, in 1943. Government began to take more seriously its role as patron. Among the early, small victories was the extraction of a grant from the Treasury by Summerson and others for the systematic photographing of historic buildings endangered by bombing – an enterprise which, institutionalized as the National Buildings Record, incidentally provided Summerson with official war work. Although the wartime coalition was more tentative about commitments in physical reconstruction than in welfare provision, the postwar Labour government was more bold. At least on paper, the planning legislation of 1947–9 equipped the local authorities and their architectural departments with all the powers they needed to take on fully the work of patronizing design within a national planning system that Summerson had cited as one of the prerequisites for the flourishing of a modern architecture.

Initially the profession looked like rising to the occasion. Summerson's call for a British modernism – functionalism and formal experimentation, but in modes suited to British means, tastes and traditions, such that the experiments could speak to a newly-aroused public – was answered in a variety of pleasing and surprising ways. Center-city redevelopments in places like Plymouth, Exeter, Bristol, Coventry and

Hull made use of modern notions of traffic and pedestrian management, while retaining the medium densities of the traditional English "street-picture" and traditional materials (brick, tile, Portland stone) wherever relevant. The low-density, semi-detached suburb was preserved in the modern form of the New Town, where a kind of mélange of modernism with the Arts and Crafts was adopted. Public departments employed new materials and modular construction in creative ways to produce schools and houses that were "heightened expressions of their function and not merely crisp statements of it": we might call this functionalism-plus.[13] And there was still room for fine new work in genres largely extinct, where the program was incapable of analysis and a sense of orthodoxy, symbolism and pure decoration was necessary, as in Basil Spence's Coventry Cathedral.[14]

In all this, Summerson saw a kind of unity emerging.[15] Just as he had prescribed before the war, modern architects in Britain were getting on with the business of interpreting the new programs, and, without worrying too much about "filling in the history form correctly," were creating "a real school of modern design in Great Britain."[16] For him as for so many contemporaries, this British school of design was on happiest display on the South Bank in 1951, when government fulfilled its patronal responsibilities in the Festival of Britain. Here, Summerson felt, was a modern understanding of style – urban, "life-enhancing," useful and whimsical, new and familiar, "light and informal" – worlds away from the crippling heritage of "the styles," the "old, preserved architecture" that was all London had had previously to offer.[17]

These peak years of the British modern were Summerson's peak years, as well. Upon leaving the National Buildings Record at the end of the war, he was offered the curatorship of Sir John Soane's Museum, that curious cubby-hole in Lincoln's Inn Fields which was then (and is now) Britain's sole architectural museum. This haven, now properly funded by the architecturally-alert public patron, allowed him to redouble his critical activities. For some years he darted about the country, lecturing around London, in Bristol, Hull, Leicester and Liverpool, broadcasting incessantly, writing regularly now not only for *The Listener* but also for the *New Statesman* and the usual array of professional journals, serving on no fewer than sixteen central and local government committees, and, from 1947, regularly chairing the Critics' Panel on the Third Programme, where, often, he was partnered by Richards. Adding (perhaps excessively) to the efforts now coming to fruition, Elizabeth Summerson – hitherto childless – gave birth in 1946 to triplets: "the Georgian Group," Osbert Lancaster called them. Richards and Pevsner enjoyed a similar productivity: Richards as editor of the *Architectural Review* at its peak of circulation and influence, and from 1947 the first regular

14 "A real school of modern design in Great Britain"? (a) South Bank
Exhibition, Festival of Britain (top); (b) Market Square, Harlow New Town
(bottom)

architectural correspondent for a daily newspaper (*The Times*); Pevsner's great volumes on *The Buildings of England* began to appear in 1951.

I dwell on these immediate postwar years, as a brief renaissance, because I want to suggest – against much recent architectural history – that it was only thereafter, from the mid-1950s onwards, that modern architecture took a profoundly different course, one which Summerson and his cohort neither predicted nor approved. It is on the reasons for this divergence, and Summerson's withdrawal from the practice of architectural criticism, that I want to conclude – and from which I will draw my moral.

DISILLUSION (FROM 1951)

The deeper we get into the 1950s, the deeper became the disillusionment of John Summerson (and, roughly, of the general public) with the course of modern architecture. Away went the British school of modern design and back came the ultra-Corbusian "machine nonsense" that Summerson had decried in the mid-1930s. Pure form – perhaps interpreted as pure function – pushed ornament back into the closet. Traditional materials were replaced with glass and concrete; the traditional "street-picture" was replaced with the inhuman densities of the slab and tower block. Already by 1955 the epithet, "New Brutalism," had been coined, by Reyner Banham in the *Architectural Review*. It was, argued Banham, a conscious rebellion *against* the distinctively English modern style championed by Summerson and the *Review*.

Why did this happen? Recent architectural history, still painfully inward-looking and polemical, sees the New Brutalism as the inevitable unfolding of modernism's fatal flaws: its abstraction, its totalitarianism, its erasure of tradition. In his 1950s criticism, Summerson shared some of this analysis. He recognized, for example, that modern art involved peculiar dilemmas not faced by earlier generations. The formal rather than pictorial or stylistic experimentation in which it indulged was predicated on an understanding of the art *history* that warranted such a breach: "this feeling for art as a 'problem' . . . ties so much of modern art to art of the remoter past and detaches it at the same time from the currency of modern life." Modern art was thus dangerously susceptible to losing touch with the "modern life" that supposedly gave it birth.[18]

Now, modern architecture bid for exemption from this general rule by claiming that its formal experiments derived directly from the patron's program, specifications which are part of the fabric of modern life. The more modern architects thought or worried about their relationship to society, the more they fell back upon this escape-clause: the program, argued Summerson, was the source of unity for modern architecture that had formerly been supplied by some stylistic language, particularly the classical language. This retreat to the program, he felt, had caused architects to abdicate their responsibility to communicate by means of style or some other language, and handed everything over to the engineer or the planner for whom the program really did supply all things necessary. As a result, modern *architecture* – as opposed to mere construction – had remained an idea, a schematic, at best an intellectual rather than an imaginative experience.[19]

The modernists with whom Summerson was arguing here had their responses ready, of course. Architectural forms could not possibly emanate straight from the program, they pointed out, and they had any number of explanations for the forms they did produce, from the new ideals of proportionality championed by Le Corbusier to the related topological arguments of Banham and the New Brutalism.[20] But the aridity of these analyses does tend to support Summerson's more basic worry about the status of modern art, and it certainly points to another, rather simple explanation for modernism's sad 1950s trajectory: that is, the yawning generation gap between men of Summerson's age (by now over fifty) and the younger active practitioners. The fact is that Summerson's generation, while it produced fine critics, never had the chance to produce many working architects: first came the slump, then the war, then postwar austerity. The Festival of Britain was for them not the first swallow of spring, but the last leaves of autumn. By the mid-1950s, when professional blood was beginning to circulate again, the leading lights – the Smithsons, Stirling, Banham – were already defining themselves *against* what they saw as "picturesque English-Festival-style compromise" and for something starker, harder, more ruthless.[21]

Yet to blame this descent only on the architects – to adopt the analysis of most recent architectural history[22] – is to tell only part of the story, the "horizontal" or formal part, and to miss out the "vertical" or social narrative. The fact is that the patronage and professional structures which Summerson saw forming in the 1940s, and on which he pinned the future of modern architecture, were dissolving in the 1950s. The public did not become the ideal patron of Summerson's imagining; on the contrary. The public sector was overwhelmed by the actual building demands of the 1950s, fueled by unforeseen baby and traffic booms and political pressures for housing and commercial development. Few public architects' departments of the 1950s were able to follow the sterling examples set by London and Plymouth and Coventry and a few others in the controlled environment of the late 1940s. Nor were they much encouraged by their local authorities, which in the 1950s colluded with developers to boost densities and rateable values to ever-higher levels. Increasingly, the actual work both of planning and design was put out to consultants, themselves linked to developers, and public architects' offices became administrative rather than aesthetic bodies. If architects were abdicating to engineers, it was hardly by their own choosing. Can there be any doubt that the New Brutalism blossomed because it matched the requirements of these public and private patrons so neatly – that, in short, it derived its unity from the ghastly program of its day? Certainly by 1960, the New Brutalism was no longer one intellectual response among many to the dilemmas Summerson was concerned to point out: it had become the modern style of choice for developers and local authorities alike, from Centre Point in London to the slab blocks of Roehampton to the monumental Park Hill estate which looms over Sheffield.

Summerson's response to this degeneration was to beat an abrupt retreat from criticism, into the refuge of the Soane Museum and the consolations of his alternative career as an historian. Here he prospered, and, perversely, found his historical work enjoying renewed commercial success from the mid-1960s as the anti-modern backlash raised consciousness about historic architecture. As the anti-modern current continues to swell today, most of this work is still in print – indeed, it reappears regularly in new editions with careful updating by the author – while the criticism (to which the history was initially so closely linked) languishes in a shadow that I have tried here to dispel slightly.

Because he offered no real explanation for his abandonment of criticism,[23] and because (in an increasingly polarized climate) his historical work was taken as implying anti-modernism, Summerson was occasionally cited as an apostate whose disillusionment with the Modern Movement was one more proof of its malignancy (a fate shared by Richards and, with more justice, Pevsner).[24] But on the rare occasions when he broke his silence, Summerson tried to demonstrate that it was not so. From the 1960s into the 1980s, he spoke out sporadically against the indiscriminate preservation of what he saw as sub-standard Georgian buildings, and promoted what he saw as possibly fruitful modernist departures, including the notorious proposal to plant a Mies van der Rohe tower in the heart of the City of London. These interventions puzzled and frustrated both sides of the widening modern/anti-modern divide; they were usually written off as simply "perverse."[25] But it seems clear enough that Summerson continued to believe in a modern architecture, while on the whole distancing himself from the modern architecture of his time. His generation had failed, both as architects and as patrons; it behooved him to recognize this failure by withholding further comment, especially since the exaggerated self-consciousness of modern artists – undoubtedly stimulated by modern art critics – had formed part of the problem. But this failure did not invalidate Summerson's general views on the delicate relationship between art and society, and it would have been perverse indeed had Summerson *not* hailed the occasions when architects working in a new environment seemed to have successfully negotiated that relationship.

How does Summerson's story – and the fate of modern architecture – fit into a broader cultural history of mid-twentieth-century Britain? One possible moral would be to recall Michael Frayn's conclusion about the Festival of Britain: it was the last fling of the Herbivores – the *bien-pensant* liberal and radical middle classes – before the Carnivores resumed their inheritance. But this focus on a "domestic split in the privileged classes" would merely reproduce, though inversely, the internalist tale of a struggle for the English soul between evil modernists and wholesome traditionalists. Much more is involved. Above all we need to look more closely at the Herbivores' interaction with the democracy they were trying to shape. They were most successful in social policy enterprises where intellectual and popular energies both ran strong and roughly in parallel, and where a satisfactory division of labor between providers and clients could emerge. Politically more marginal enterprises, where a public had first to be created, were bound to remain half-baked and unsatisfying. The nationalization of culture remained, after all, a political side-show throughout the 1940s and 1950s, and architecture was still the Cinderella of the Arts. Public engagement and political mobilization were *more* important for architectural propagandists than for other cultural missionaries. Yet modern architects, Summerson pointed out, placed heavy demands on the public and offered too little in return; they insisted so sternly on the iron link between art and society that they took it for granted, and neglected to forge one.

But in the meantime, while the conversation between architects and the public was suspended, a great rebuilding of Britain took place over which other forces necessarily presided. A massive apparatus of architectural patronage clanked into action, dominated by developers, borough councillors, civil servants at the Ministry of Housing and Local Government, Treasury officials, housing speculators. Next to these leviathans the *Architectural Review*, the Royal Fine Arts Commission, journalists and broadcasters look puny indeed. The big battalions constructed an architecture of their own on political and economic criteria which simply steamrollered the tentative connections forged between critics and public from the 1930s to the 1950s.

In his last years, Summerson claimed to see a glimmer of hope in the passing of his generation: whether or not the Modern Movement is actually dead, he wrote, the *idea* of its death is "liberating. It means that there may be, once again, some point in discussing architectural language ... and entering into the whole question of architecture as a vehicle of social meaning."[26] Perhaps, by the same token, the discrediting of the whole planning and development apparatus of the 1950s and

242

1960s will be liberating, too, clearing the site for a more successful encounter between the public's program and the architect's imagination.

NOTES

My principal debt is to Sir John Summerson, who shared his memories and manuscripts with great liberality. Sir James Richards was equally hospitable. Both men commented critically and usefully on earlier drafts of this essay, the former within a few months, the latter within a week of his death. I also have to thank the BBC Written Archives Centre for permission to consult their treasure-house of files and scripts.

1 The interwar years remain obscure in architectural history; they are usually tackled only in order to trace the origins of the Modern. An excellent survey, despite this bias, is David Dean, *The Thirties: Recalling the English Architectural Scene*, London, Trefoil, 1983. See also Lionel Esher, *A Broken Wave: The Rebuilding of England 1940–1980*, London, Allen Lane, 1981, pp. 15–30, and, for John Summerson's (hereafter JS) early diagnosis, "Forty Years of British Architecture," *The Listener*, 13 January 1937, pp. 60–2.

2 Quoted by Bevis Hillier, *Young Betjeman*, London, John Murray, 1988, pp. 362–3.

3 J.M. Richards, *Memoirs of an Unjust Fella*, London, Weidenfeld & Nicolson, 1980, pp. 125–6, 130–1; see also Dean, *The Thirties*, pp. 112–15.

4 Ibid., esp. pp. 14–36.

5 Not that JS was entirely innocent of these effusions. He was an active member of the MARS Group and the author of the catalogue for its single public exhibition, at the New Burlington Gallery in 1938: much later he was to regret its "starry-eyed idealism" as slightly "nauseating." See the extract from his Gold Medal speech in the *RIBA Journal*, December 1976, pp. 494–5.

6 "Building Boom – I and II," *The Listener*, 29 December 1937, pp. 1418–20, 5 January 1938, pp. 20–2; "The Fate of Modern Architecture," *Horizon*, October 1942, pp. 233–43.

7 For admiring comments on the "romantic and irrational" qualities of the best Modern Movement work, see "Romance and Realities," *Country Life*, 13 February 1937, Country House and Flat Equipment Supplement, pp. ii–iii.

8 "Architecture," in Geoffrey Grigson, ed., *The Arts To-Day*, London, John Lane, 1935, pp. 253–88; "The Mischievous Analogy," originally a talk to the Architectural Association in 1941, revised version published in JS's collection *Heavenly Mansions*, London, Pleiades, 1949, pp. 195–218.

9 For some interestingly ambivalent comments about the connection between public demand and modern art supply, see "The Villa Vernacular," *The Listener*, 27 July 1939, pp. 188–90.

10 JS's first report on the Nash drawings appeared as "A Repton Portfolio," *RIBA Journal*, 25 February 1933, pp. 313–24; this led to a paper for the RIBA, "John Nash," ibid., 22 December 1934, pp. 225–36, and to *John Nash: Architect to King George IV*, London, Allen and Unwin, 1935. There followed "James Wyatt," in B. Dobrée, ed., *From Anne to Victoria*, London, Cassell, 1937; "Sir John Soane," *The Times*, 20 January 1937; and the RIBA Silver Medal-winning essay on Wren, "The Tyranny of Intellect," *RIBA Journal*, 20 February 1937, pp. 373–90. See also "The Great Landowner's Contribution to Architecture,"

ibid., 6 March 1939, pp. 432–49, the germ of *Georgian London*, London, Pleiades, 1945 (actually appeared early 1946).

11 For the influence of the Warburg Institute, and especially of Rudolf Wittkower, see the Gold Medal speech in *RIBA Journal*, December 1976, pp. 494–5. Surprisingly, this connection is not made by David Watkin, *The Rise of Architectural History*, London, Architectural Press, 1980, which has much to say about Wittkower and Summerson separately. Partly for this reason, I believe, Watkin fails to read the messages in Summerson's "detached" approach to Nash.

12 See JS's introduction to *Fifty Years of the National Buildings Record, 1941–1991*, London, Royal Commission on the Historical Monuments of England, 1991, pp. 2–10.

13 Summerson, "Mischievous Analogy," pp. 200–1.

14 "Coventry Cathedral," *New Statesman*, 8 September 1951, pp. 253–4.

15 He did not go so far as the *Architectural Review*, which talked up the new style as Picturesque Modernism: "a rationalization of the traditional vernacular English way of looking at the world ... the tendency to take the functional approach to build up the human background in those visual terms the layman calls picturesque." [H. de C. Hastings], "The English Planning Tradition and the City," *Architectural Review*, June 1945, p. 170. Appended to this article is a mild criticism by JS under the pseudonym of "John Coolmore."

16 For this and for JS's overall assessment of postwar architecture, see his introduction to Trevor Dannatt, *Modern Architecture in Britain*, London, Batsford, 1959. A similarly optimistic survey, for a wider audience, is J.M. Richards, *An Introduction to Modern Architecture*, Harmondsworth, Penguin, 1956, esp. ch. 7. Though under much pressure from anti-modernists in later life, JS did not recant his high opinion of early 1950s "British Modern." See, as an example, "Records and Recollections 1930–1960," lecture to the Thirties Society, 13 December 1983, photocopy in author's possession.

17 JS, introduction to Dannatt, *Modern Architecture*, pp. 19–20; "South Bank Architecture," *New Statesman*, 12 May 1951, pp. 529–30; "South Bank Postscript," *New Statesman*, 6 October 1951, pp. 363–4.

18 "New Patterns in Art and Society," *The Listener*, 15 March 1951, pp. 417–18, and "A Question of Taste," *The Listener*, 31 January 1952, pp. 175–6; these were originally both Home Service (not Third Programme) broadcasts; *What is a Professor of Modern Art?*, Hull, University of Hull Publications, 1960, esp. pp. 16–18.

19 "The Case for a Theory of Modern Architecture," *RIBA Journal*, June 1957, pp. 307–10. This celebrated lecture to the RIBA – which was also partly broadcast on the Third Programme – was JS's last major critical statement; it stirred up considerable irritation among modernist architects, though on the whole JS did not participate in the subsequent discussion. But see note 20 and his Third Programme review of Banham, "Architecture, the Machine and the Prophets," 27 August 1960, script in BBC Written Archives Centre.

20 See, for example, the comment by Peter Smithson in *RIBA Journal*, June 1957, p. 312, and Reyner Banham, "Vitruvius Go Home!," *A.A. Journal*, March 1960, pp. 146–50, with reply by JS, pp. 151–2.

21 See Reyner Banham, "Revenge of the Picturesque: English Architectural Polemics, 1945–1965," in JS, ed., *Concerning Architecture*, London, Allen Lane, 1968, pp. 265–73. Uncannily, Summerson had warned already in the late 1940s that his generation would have only a few postwar years to stake

their claim, "to remember how to build at all," before the inevitable generational revolt – which would come, he guessed, around 1957, the precise year in which he announced his virtual abandonment of criticism. Summerson, "Mischievous Analogy," p. 218.

22 For example, J. Mordaunt Crook, *The Dilemma of Style*, London, John Murray, 1987, ch. 8, and Kenneth Frampton, *Modern Architecture: A Critical History*, London, Thames and Hudson, 1985, pp. 262–9, to cite two relatively nonpolemical (but still fairly internalist) surveys, or a more opinionated version, Charles Jencks, *Modern Movements in Architecture*, 2nd edn, Harmondsworth, Penguin, 1985, pp. 242–70. Esher, *Broken Wave*, ch. 2, is again by far the best contextual analysis, although even here the "consensus of the 1940s" and the "consensus of the 1960s" are rather bizarrely elided together.

23 Wearied, perhaps, by the storm over his 1957 RIBA lecture, Summerson flatly refused to give reasons for his disengagement when prompted by a friendly BBC producer. JS to Leonie Cohn, 4 August 1960, BBC Written Archives Centre, Talks-JS-File 2. He was still refusing when talking to me thirty years later.

24 For a modernist criticism, see Banham, "Revenge of the Picturesque"; for a preservationist criticism, see Hillier, *Young Betjeman*, pp. 276–9. Richards defended himself against the charge of apostasy in *Memoirs*, pp. 263–4.

25 For intelligent but ultimately unresolved approaches to the Summerson "puzzle," see (on the preservationist side) [Gavin Stamp], "Sir John Summerson: The Last Whig," *Spectator*, 6 April 1985, pp. 12–13, and (on the modernist side) Martin Pawley, "John Summerson, Defender of Modernism?," *Modern Painters*, Spring 1991, pp. 96–7.

26 From new material added to the second edition of *The Classical Language of Architecture*, London, Thames and Hudson, 1980, p. 114. The same spirit is evident in JS's revaluation of the modernist James Stirling, "Vitruvius Ludens," *Architectural Review*, March 1983, pp. 19–21.

15 John Clive

11

John Clive 1924–1990
TBM and John
Simon Schama

You always remember where it was that you first read the books that changed your life.

I first read *Macaulay: The Shaping of the Historian* in September 1976 in rocky, medusa-infested coves on the Aegean islands of Hydra and Spetsai. While Macaulay was storming the Whig citadel of Holland House, Mavrocordatos and his fellow pan-Hellenes were launching armed fishing boats from those thyme-scented bays against the Turkish fleet. But such was the spell cast by John Clive's book that my imagination did not drift towards Missolonghi or Navarino. It was quite elsewhere, in virtuous Clapham, industrious Leeds and pullulating Calcutta. Later, John would give me a respectable cloth-bound signed edition of his book. But it is the dog-eared, suntan-oil-stained paperback hauled around the islands, that I truly cherish. For it was in its pages that I first began to comprehend the deep wells that produced the glorious gush of Macaulay's famous *vehemence*. And it was in its pages that I first encountered John Clive.

It is the mark of a truly powerful biography to leave the reader vexed with the author for ending it, robbing him of a companion with whom he has become easily familiar. And by the time I reached "In more ways than one, Zachary had cast a long shadow"[1] I was all the more sorry to have Macaulay abruptly removed after a mere five hundred pages of close acquaintance, especially since I longed to dog his footsteps through Italy; eavesdrop on his Cabinet gossip in 1840; commiserate with his electoral defeat in Edinburgh; sample his rich satisfaction at the record sales of the *History*; listen as he recited his rhymes to his niece Baba Trevelyan and marched the children past the giraffes of Regents Park, the waxworks of Madame Tussauds or (to little George Otto Trevelyan's bored dismay) the masterpieces of Eastlake's National Gallery.

I consoled myself with the knowledge that before too long I would meet the famous National Book Award-winning author whom I supposed I already knew pretty well. The jacket carried no photograph, but from the elegant, penetrating prose, the controlled sympathy shown towards Macaulay, the rigorous analysis of his intellectual formation, the shrewd delineation of his life as a political and social animal, I assumed that John Clive would turn out to be an elegantly understated, impeccably turned-out Harvard Professor. His sense of humor, I thought, would be gentle and loftily Jamesian; someone who carried his colonial name with an air of Brahminical Bostonian *savoir-faire*. The biographer's relationship with his subject whose public mask he had removed to expose the conflicted, passionate and often troubled man beneath, had to be, I supposed, that of a sympathetic doctor who would calmly listen and offer spoonfuls of cool understanding to his distracted patient.

So much for my powers of literary deduction. Two months later, John knocked (or rather pounded) on the doors of my rooms in Brasenose, tripped over the door-sill and fell spread-eagled on my couch. After we had exchanged flustered apologies it took about five minutes and a cup of tea (which John drank as if it were a famous vintage, inquiring after brand, store of origin, length of brew) for me to see how spectacularly wrong I had been. The name "Clive" remained mysterious (as it did for many years), but it didn't take a genius to see that my rumpled guest who was enjoying his tea and cake so visibly was hardly a representative of the Boston class famous for its cool detachment and sensuous self-denial. By the end of an hour I was in a state of delighted amazement that the historian whose extraordinary work I had so admired had also become an immediate friend. After John departed (without further hazard) I ran through the character description which now replaced my hopelessly misjudged extrapolation from his prose style. The historian I had met was warm-hearted, affectionate, voluble; mischievously hilarious, gossipy; clumsy, and self-indulgent. His speech moved from embarrassed stammering to flights of eloquence; the sentences broken with puns and rhymes and even snatches of song performed with exaggerated operatic trills. In the moldy dimness of the Oxford room his large eyes sparkled with pleasure at a well-taken idea or a well-turned phrase and at the delicious prospect of routing a common enemy, he would smack a fist into his palm with boyish exultation.

But I had run through this anatomy of a personality before, hadn't I? It was John's account of Macaulay.

The best thing I know on the problems of biography is Richard Holmes's *Footsteps*.[2] Its premise is the inescapable *glissade* between biography and autobiography. Are there any biographers who never ask themselves why they have chosen their subjects; whether indeed their subjects have not in some disconcerting sense chosen *them*? Why indeed, you might